Entertainment WEEKLY.

1996 year book

"WHAT-EVER"

**—ALICIA SILVERSTONE
IN "CLUELESS"**

Entertainment WEEKLY

1996 YEARBOOK

THE YEAR IN ENTERTAINMENT

Who accomplished what, said it when, and was seen where in '95: George Clooney clowns on the *ER* set, politicians frown from D.C., Jim Mullen gives a yearful of Hot Sheet, and more.

ENTERTAINERS OF THE YEAR

From the ever-expanding Blowfish to the god of *Apollo 13*, they made us smile, sing, search for the supernatural, and understand *CBC, chem 7, stat !* Also: the year's most notable rookies.

THE BEST OF
ENTERTAINMENT
WEEKLY

The highlights in feature reporting from the past year, covering Hugh Grant's fall (and rise), the coming of Alicia Silverstone, Jerry Garcia's passing, and nine other important stories.

THE YEAR
IN REVIEWS

Our critics choose the best and worst: *Nixon* wins again, Joan Osborne *Relishes* success, *Friends* is in high places, and more—including what we learned from entertainment in 1995.

ALMANAC

The year's biggest hits in film, TV, video, music, books, and multimedia, plus fabulous facts, award winners, best-sellers, TV shows with the most websites...and other must-know info.

1996 YEARBOOK

THE YEAR 1995 *was notable for*
ENTERTAINMENT WEEKLY. *We marked*
our fifth year of publication, we put out
our 300th issue, our circulation reached
an all-time peak of 1.2 million (or nearly
8 million readers every week), and, as if
in celebration of all that, we took home
the National Magazine Award for General
Excellence (above) among U.S. magazines
with circulations of more than one million.
Now we are publishing our first annual
ENTERTAINMENT WEEKLY *Yearbook, a*
compendium of the high points, as well as
some of the intriguing low ones, of the year
as recorded in our pages. We hope you enjoy
looking back over the memorable, exciting,
and occasionally goofy year that has just
ended as much as we have enjoyed
observing and preserving it for you.

—*The staff of* ENTERTAINMENT WEEKLY

The

ea

in

a i nmer t

JUST TRY GETTING A FIX on—let alone building a yearbook around—a year in which one of the best shows on television had the simplest, least controversial idea imag-

inable behind it, friendship (*Friends*); NC-17–rated sex bombed at

the movies (*Showgirls*) but was a smash in Congress (so many protests against sleazy TV talk

shows, rude rap music, and cyberporn); the Grateful Dead broke up in the wake of Jerry Garcia's

death, but rock proved its vitality by yielding a bumper crop of new stars, like Joan Osborne and

Alanis Morissette; two of the best films were about a

President we can't get out of our heads (Oliver Stone's *Nixon*)

and a '60s underground cartoonist whose early work sold in

head shops (*Crumb*). ◆ Well, to us at ENTERTAINMENT

WEEKLY, it is not just our job but our mission to slap the

unruly year that was 1995 into manageable shape. Thus, our

first yearbook, chockful of facts and opinions, business

analysis and fashion frippery, triumphs and scandals, politics

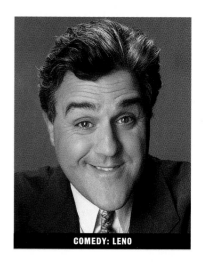

COMEDY: LENO

and literature (virtuous William Bennett, meet virtuous Elizabeth Bennet, one of the many Jane

Austen heroines to be adapted for TV and the movies this year). ◆ It is now clear that

entertainment means all things to all people. Even a terrible real-life murder turned into a grim

diversion, as everything from Court TV to *The Tonight Show With Jay Leno* used the O.J.

Simpson trial as popular programming material. (Indeed, Leno's inelegant Dancing Itos bit helped him surge past David Letterman in the ratings). Entertainment is not just stuff people use to fill spare time; it's material central to nearly everyone's life. ◆ That's why we've reported on the big corporate takeovers (the Walt Disney Co.'s gobbling up Cap Cities/ABC, Time Warner's merger with Turner Broadcasting System) in entertainment. That's why we devoted an entire issue to examining the influence of gay talent and taste in showbiz. That's also why many trends are given careful consideration—whether it's the popularity of a cult TV show like *The X-Files* or the rise and use of the Internet to make entertainment of every sort an interactive event. ◆ Of course, what would a yearbook be if it didn't include lists? Herein you'll find our critics' lists of the best and worst in movies, TV, music, books, video, and multimedia. Reading all this, you'll laugh, you'll argue, you'll nod your head in sage agreement; you'll use this book as a reference tool, you'll use it to settle bar bets. What makes us so sure? Because the one thing that distinguished 1995 from years past was not just the pop culture it produced, but the wide-ranging discussion of

TRAGEDY: LETTERMAN

that culture; what we put into our minds is very much on our minds. Debate rages over whether hostile music inspires hostile actions. Will the increase in movies with refined pedigrees promote educational betterment? Is wanting to know about the embarrassing kafuffle that Hugh Grant was involved in a matter of harmless curiosity or an invasion of privacy that dumbs down America? ◆ These sorts of disagreements are healthy, air-clearing ones. When EW started up six years ago, we had a lighthearted motto: "Kick Back, Chill Out, Hang Loose, Have Fun." We've outgrown slogans, but if we had to pick a motto now, as the century draws nearer to a close, it would be something like "Dig In, Heat Up, Get Involved, Have Fun." That's why this yearbook may well remind you of the kind you used to see in high school—it's got winners and losers, parties and memorials, finely tempered nostalgia and bold predictions. It's got life in it.

ictures
of the Year

GEORGE CLOONEY got catty with a prop from an *ER* episode in which a little boy has put his head where it doesn't belong. But Clooney, who's also nurturing a film career, says the Emmy-winning medical series is exactly where he belongs. "I've fought my whole life to get on a show like this. I'm not going anywhere."

PHOTOGRAPH BY
David Strick / Onyx

LAUREN HOLLY said she "kicked herself" for turning down a role opposite Jim Carrey in his 1994 breakout, *Ace Ventura: Pet Detective.* So when the *Picket Fences* co-star got a second chance with Carrey's *Dumb and Dumber,* she wised up, scoring a $126.4 million hit and its leading man's heart.

PHOTOGRAPH BY
Jeffrey Thurnher/Outline

JIM CARREY has few intellectual pretensions. "A lot of my stuff is dumb. I've been dubbed responsible for the dumbing of America." But with his *Ace Ventura* sequel, *When Nature Calls,* a solid hit and $20 million to star in the upcoming *Cable Guy,* the comic is clearly no monkey's uncle.

PHOTOGRAPH BY
Dan Winters

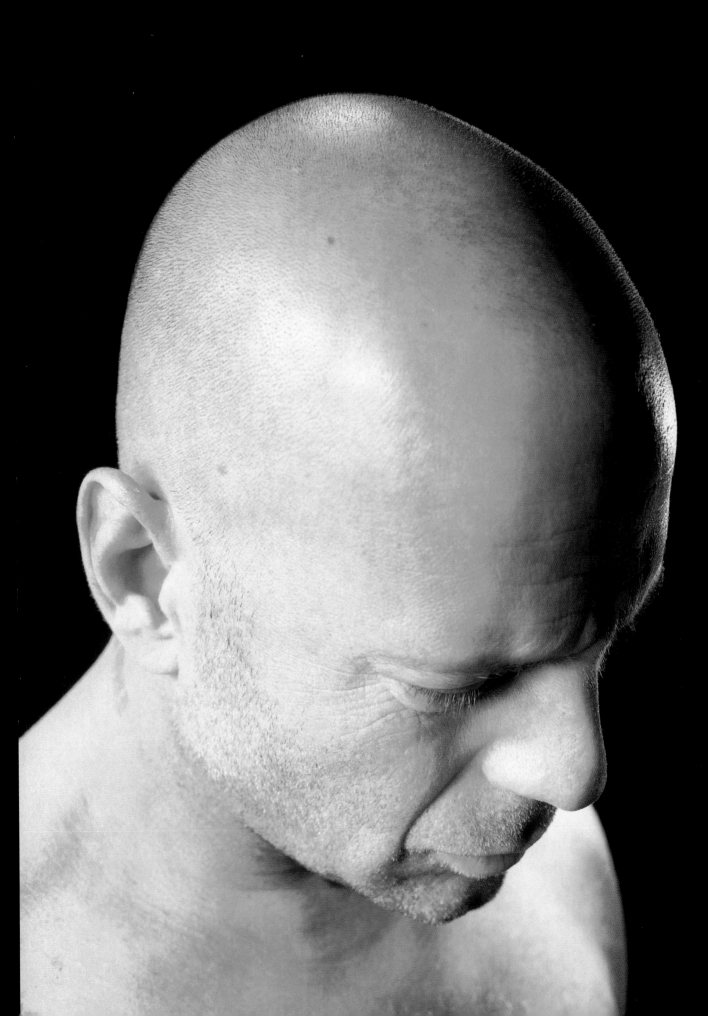

NICOLE KIDMAN laid to rest what she calls "the Mrs. Tom Cruise thing" with *Batman Forever* and a wicked turn in *To Die For*. "[Tom and I] were naive. We thought, Do tons of work, and nobody will judge you." The verdict was favorable.
PHOTOGRAPH BY
Stephanie Pfriender

ISAAC HAYES, best known for the 1971 "Theme From *Shaft*," found that success a tough act to follow. But with two new CDs in '95, Hayes discovered a new appreciation for his early hit. "Removed from it now, I can finally enjoy *Shaft*."
PHOTOGRAPH BY
Jesse Frohman

BRUCE WILLIS (left) proved he's an action *Die Hard* when world grosses for his third outing as John McClane hit $350 million. But, he said, superstardom is a media perception. "No big superstar I know behaves like a superstar."
PHOTOGRAPH BY
George Holz/Onyx

ANTONIO BANDERAS has made 43 films. In 1995, the Spanish hunk (and Melanie Griffith flame) starred in four more, keeping up both his pace and perspective. At the height of his *Desperado*'s $25 million success, he said, "You can be at the top, and the next week, because you've got a failure, you go down again. The hottest thing in Hollywood right now is probably me and a pig named Baby."

PHOTOGRAPH BY
Stephanie Pfriender

JULIANA HATFIELD (right), whose highly anticipated *Only Everything* turned out to be only *another* drop in the alterna-rock bucket, wondered about her teen fans. "It kind of scares me sometimes. It makes me wonder if I'm really retarded in my emotional growth."

PHOTOGRAPH BY
Dan Borris/Outline

MELISSA ETHERIDGE played with her idol Springsteen on MTV and saw her *Yes I Am* album go triple platinum. "I worked *hard* for this."

PHOTOGRAPH BY
Jeffrey Thurnher/Outline

ELLEN DEGENERES snagged a re-ported $2 million for her movie *Mr. Wrong*, more than $1 million to write a book, and a new lease on life. "My career [was] based on wanting people to like me. After a while, it's like, I'm exhausted. I can't please everyone."

PHOTOGRAPH BY
Stephanie Pfriender

RICHARD PRYOR penned a memoir, *Pryor Convictions and Other Life Sentences,* about his fight with drugs, violence—in himself and on the tough streets where he grew up—and MS. "This s--- is not funny to me," says Pryor of his 10-year illness. "This is God's sense of humor? I don't get it."

PHOTOGRAPHS BY
Eric Tucker

PAUL NEWMAN won a Best Actor nomination for *Nobody's Fool,* as a misanthropic construction worker named Sully who's coming to terms with the son he abandoned. Newman, who lost his only son to an accidental drug overdose, confessed, "Sully is a lot closer to me than I would care to admit."

PHOTOGRAPH BY
Mary Ellen Mark

LISA LOEB released her debut, *Tails*, a year after her No. 1 single, "Stay." "We have an audience for a song," she said. But enough for an album?

PHOTOGRAPH BY
Gentl & Hyers/Outline

ELIZABETH BERKLEY, the fallen star of Joe Eszterhas and Paul Verhoeven's much-hyped-and-vilified *Showgirls,* was stripped of her inhibitions: "I just had to accept the fact that I was going to be completely naked in front of hundreds of crew members. It wasn't a big deal."

PHOTOGRAPH BY
Mary Ellen Mark

VAL KILMER, shrink-wrapped in a 40-pound latex-based suit, saved Gotham and Warner Bros.' *Batman* franchise. "I've done an absurdly commercial cartoon and now I'm more likely to get hired [than] I was before, because I hadn't done enough movies," he said. There *is* more than one way to skin a bat.

PHOTOGRAPH BY
Ruven Afanador

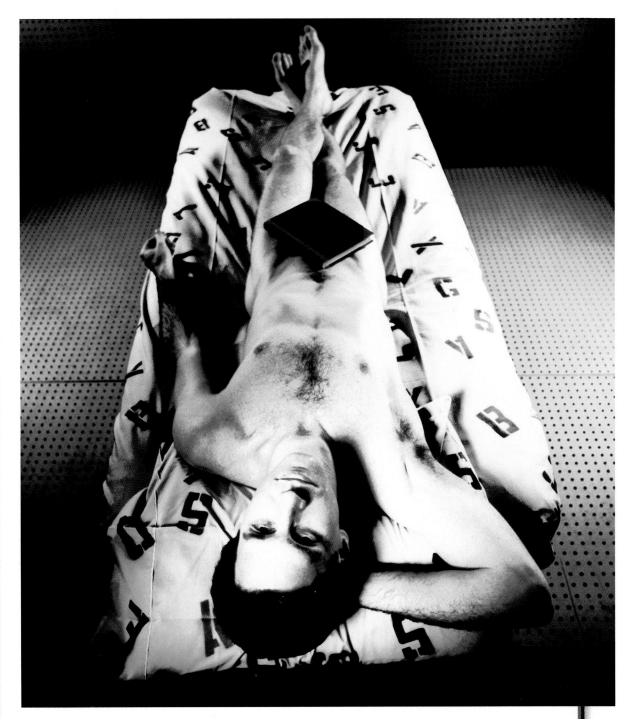

DOUG SAVANT braves his parents' angst at his playing the gay Matt on *Melrose Place* and some critics' ire for really being straight: "If only gay actors play gay roles, then you have to preclude gay actors from taking straight roles."

PHOTOGRAPH BY
Jon Ragel/Onyx

PHILIP WEISS, *New York Observer* columnist, wrote a political satire, *Cock-a-doodle-doo*, that played off his onetime romance with Sen. Pat Moynihan's daughter. "It's about an individual separating himself from orthodoxies," he revealed.

PHOTOGRAPH BY
Silvia Otte/Outline

SARAH JESSICA PARKER guest-VJ'd MTV's *Top 20 Video Countdown* but confessed she knew only about three of the tunes and doesn't watch MTV: "Once I moved out on my own, my social skills were retarded, as well as my knowledge of music, and so I didn't bother to watch."

PHOTOGRAPH BY
Chris Buck

GARY OLDMAN began the year playing Beethoven in the modest *Immortal Beloved* and ended it as a lovestruck Reverend Dimmesdale in Demi Moore's characteristically immodest misfire *The Scarlet Letter.* "I don't think Hollywood knows what to do with me," says Oldman. Or, perhaps, he with it.

PHOTOGRAPH BY
Ruven Afanador

flashes

ILLUSTRATIONS BY
David Cowles

Hugh **Grant**
SEPTEMBER 8

On his Oscar night:
"I saw Clint East-
wood, and the only
thing I thought of
saying was 'Hey,
are you presenting
an award?' It was
my biggest show
business blunder to
date." He wishes.

Tom **Hanks**
MARCH 31

On the likelihood of a *Forrest Gump*
sequel: "I'll be saying 'box of
chocolates' again about the same
time that Sean Connery says 'I'm
Bond, James Bond.'"

John
Travolta
`OCTOBER 20`

"I'd be happy to dance," said Travolta, after his *Get Shorty* costar Rene Russo reported that the former disco king refused to cut a rug for her. But, Travolta stipulated, on only one condition: "We'd have to choose an empty club."

Brett
Butler
`JULY 21`

Vowing her upcoming memoir would prove she's "no demonic outtake from a Tennessee Williams play," the *Grace Under Fire* star says she gave the book the working title *Myth Dixie* so folks like Jay Leno would be "forced to lisp as they announce me on talk shows."

Jeanne
Tripplehorn
`OCTOBER 20`

The *Waterworld* costar said no to a nude scene but insisted on vetting the backside of her stand-in. As the finalists entered her trailer, Tripplehorn recalled, "I said, 'Ladies, drop the robes!' We were all laughing so hard because the situation was so bizarre!"

Garry **Shandling**

APRIL 28

Simon & Schuster was "hassling" Shandling over the "fictional autobiography" he's currently penning for his *Larry Sanders* alter superego. At issue was the title he had in mind: "I wanted to call it *Far From an A--hole*."

Tom **Snyder**

JANUARY 20

On his philosophy for *The Late Late Show With Tom Snyder*: "I want people to have a good time. I don't think folks want to see guests suffering on TV, especially not at 1 a.m. Our competition isn't another talk show, it's Mr. Sandman."

Sharon **Stone**

FEBRUARY 10

"Aren't you relieved you don't have to watch me in a sex scene? I know I am," said Stone after *The Quick and the Dead* director Sam Raimi cut her love scene with costar Russell Crowe.

RuPaul

MARCH 10

The M.A.C. cosmetics rep liked sporting the natural look as a regular guy in the USA Network's *A Mother's Prayer*. "I got to concentrate on acting, instead of worrying if my face is cracking."

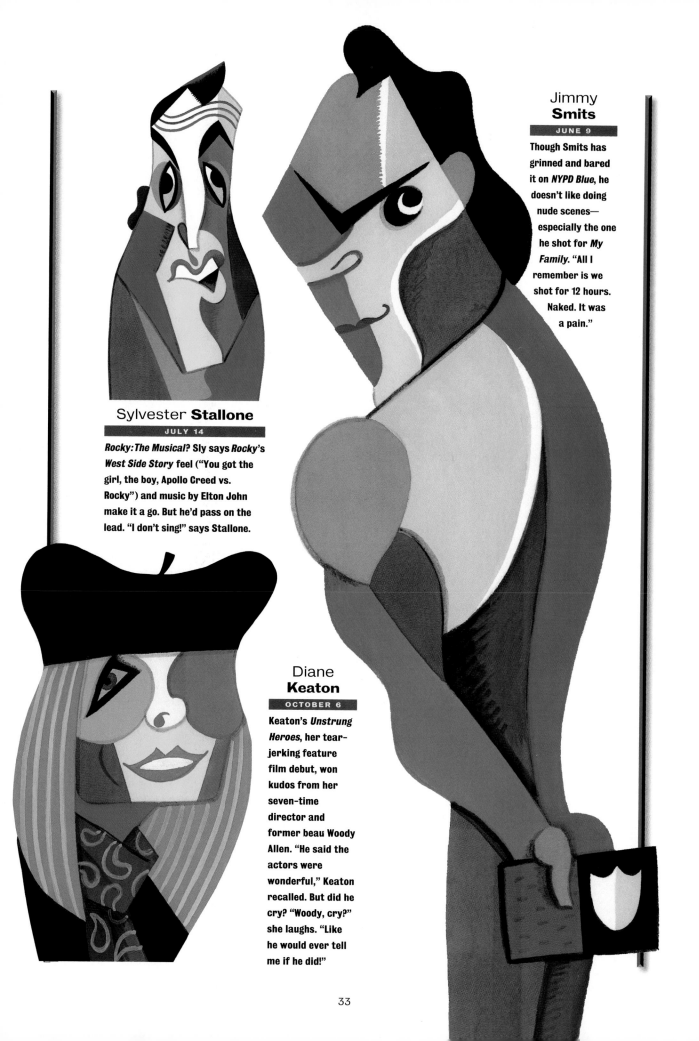

Jimmy **Smits**

JUNE 9

Though Smits has grinned and bared it on *NYPD Blue*, he doesn't like doing nude scenes—especially the one he shot for *My Family*. "All I remember is we shot for 12 hours. Naked. It was a pain."

Sylvester **Stallone**

JULY 14

Rocky: The Musical? Sly says *Rocky*'s *West Side Story* feel ("You got the girl, the boy, Apollo Creed vs. Rocky") and music by Elton John make it a go. But he'd pass on the lead. "I don't sing!" says Stallone.

Diane **Keaton**

OCTOBER 6

Keaton's *Unstrung Heroes*, her tearjerking feature film debut, won kudos from her seven-time director and former beau Woody Allen. "He said the actors were wonderful," Keaton recalled. But did he cry? "Woody, cry?" she laughs. "Like he would ever tell me if he did!"

JANUARY 5

After assuring Kathleen Gingrich that her whispered "She's a bitch" would remain between the two of them, Connie Chung airs son Newt's opinion of Hillary Clinton.

JANUARY 12

Keanu Reeves sells out his 24-day run as Hamlet in Winnipeg despite one critic's likening his speech to a driver "falling on the accelerator."

JANUARY 9-22

At an auction in New York, an electric guitar autographed by Kurt Cobain ($17,000) and John Lennon's sink ($450) go to the highest bidder.

JANUARY 24

With opening statements by the prosecution, O.J. Simpson's murder trial begins.

WHO'S ANY COMMONER to tell **Michael Jackson** that "King of Pop" shouldn't be a title for life? Recent evidence might suggest he abdicate, but self-appointed monarchs rarely ask for referendums. Still, Jackson's 1995 was the kind of humbling year that might make lesser lords go lighter on the self-congratulation: ◆ Despite the most expensive promotional launch in music-biz history—$30 million, by most accounts—his double-disc

HIStory exited the top 10 five weeks after its June debut and by Thanksgiving had dropped to No. 83. ◆ When Jackson opened the MTV Video Music Awards telecast in September with the 15-minute hits medley that was supposed to jump-start his stalled sales, the main buzz was that the emperor had no live mike. To complement his lip-synch, Jackson brought along a pumped-up applause track and a hired army of audience plants.

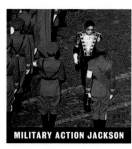

MILITARY ACTION JACKSON

◆ Although 60 million or so tuned in to survey the damage on *Prime-Time Live*, **Diane Sawyer**'s reputation was sullied as she pitched Jackson puffballs about the molestation investigation, snootily attributing the icky consummation question to tacky civilians. At least Lisa ("Eat it!") Marie earned good reviews for her nouveau biker-chick demeanor. ◆ An anti-Semitic slur in the song "They Don't Care About Us" raised suspicions that Jackson was trying to score points in the hardcore hip-

LOVE AMONG THE RUINS

hop community. But he disclaimed any notion that "Jew me" might be offensive. (Never mind that "sue me" was the rhyme or that the attorney who represented the boy making child molestation claims was Jewish.) His infamous "Some of my best business associates are Jewish" defense *did* win Jackson points for chutzpah, but one of his friends, **Steven Spielberg** (who'd penned *HIStory*'s liner notes), excused himself from the king's court.

ON THE BIG "SCREAM"

◆ By year's end, his PR was so bad that when he collapsed in New York while rehearsing for an imminent HBO broadcast, Internet speculation ran rampant that it was all a publicity stunt.

The backlash of '95 might give anyone a persecution complex, but Jackson came into the year laboring under a hefty dose of paranoia. If the breezy hits disc that made up half of *HIStory* climaxed with "Heal the World," the theme of the disc of new stuff was "Screw the world." "Stop f---in' with me," he hissed in "Scream." "They wanna get my ass," he protested in "D.S.," a thinly veiled snipe at Santa Barbara D.A. Thomas Sneddon Jr., who investigated the molestation charges (and whose name is strikingly similar to the "Dom Sheldon" of the song's chorus). Radio wasn't buying. "He's just pissed off [in the song]," said Tracy Austin, music director at L.A.'s KIIS, on why so many Top 40 stations like hers dropped "Scream" from playlists after a few weeks. "It's like, get it out of your system and make fun music again!"

Missing from the newlywed's 15 new tracks was any sign of affection, except for "You Are Not Alone," a love song written and produced by R&B star **R. Kelly**—and a hit, not incidentally. Though divided over whether Jackson was predator or prey in the molestation investigation (now dormant), the public would forgive almost anything of an entertainer with the gift of great escapism.

*PRIMETIME'*S LITE GRILLING

Assuming that the success of "Not Alone" meant that character was not an issue, was it *HIStory*'s persecution-complex theme that turned kids off? Was it the hype, including a multimillion-dollar ad, on TV and in movie theaters, featuring soldiers goose-stepping behind a uniformed Michael to the unveiling of his own statue—all scored by a "hallelujah" chorus? Or was it the irreconcilability of playing both demagogue and underdog? Jackson himself seemed not to notice the gulf between "Have you seen my childhood?" and *Look at me, I'm the Statue of Liberty.*

Bright spots did appear: The jolting, space-age "Scream" video became hot on MTV, proving that with the right director (Mark Romanek) and costar (sister **Janet**), Jackson can still occupy the video vanguard. Some new *HIStory* tracks, most notably "Stranger in Moscow," hinted that he remains capable of melodic and thematic sophistication. But the

STATUE OF INTIMIDATION

real reason Jackson should be cruising into '96 had nothing to do with *his* music. In November he made a deal to merge his ATV Music group (which controls most of the Beatles' early tunes) with Sony Music, his record label's publishing arm (which owns many of **Lisa Marie**'s dad's hits, such as "Heartbreak Hotel"). The merger was said to be worth $95 million to Jackson, who, despite his well-cultivated naïveté, is one tough entrepreneur.

And it's in the boardroom that the mini-mogul can still be on the upswing. More than a decade after *Thriller*, traipsing uneasily into his late 30s in an environment that is called "youth culture" for a reason, the Man Who Would Be Pan can never again seriously hope he's still growing as a pop icon. But there's no biological clock ticking in acquisitions. The erstwhile sovereign of pop has all the time in the world to work on becoming King of Business. —*Chris Willman*

FEBRUARY 6

Beach Boy Brian Wilson weds a car saleswoman. Formerly estranged daughters Carnie and Wendy serenade them with Dad's "God Only Knows."

FEBRUARY 12

O.J.'s jailhouse opus *I Want to Tell You* debuts at No. 1 on the *New York Times* bestseller list.

FEBRUARY 14

Two months pregnant, Roseanne weds hubby No. 3, ex-bodyguard Ben Thomas, at Caesars Tahoe in Nevada.

FEBRUARY 14

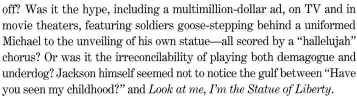

Harlequin romance novels begin testing in China, where books will be edited to conform with local sensibilities.

FEBRUARY 15

One day after *Hoop Dreams* fails to receive an Oscar bid, the Academy of Motion Picture Arts and Sciences announces it will reexamine its documentary nomination process.

CONTINUED ON NEXT PAGE

po| at a

THIS WAS THE YEAR that Washington and Hollywood sparred for the souls of Americans—and both of them lost. You *could* trace the battle's first blow back to Dan Quayle's 1992 attack on single mom Murphy Brown. But this year, as the Capitol's morals monitor, Bob Dole, journeyed to David Let-

Sidebar

FEBRUARY 15

Madonna's "Take a Bow" tops *Billboard*'s pop chart, giving her the record for the most No. 1 hits—11!—by a solo female artist.

FEBRUARY 19

Wearing a white bikini, *Baywatch*'s Pamela Anderson marries Heather Locklear's ex, tattooed Mötley Crüe drummer Tommy Lee, on a Cancún beach.

FEBRUARY 28

The Lion King roars into stores, quickly becoming the best-selling video ever.

MARCH 2

Pearl Jam denies lending its name to a campaign to end frog dissections in school labs after PETA claims to have the group's endorsement.

MARCH 21

New Jersey Gov. Christine Todd Whitman renames a rest stop on

POLITICS

HIGHS

FEBRUARY: Sucking up to the family-values set, BILL CLINTON asks Hollywood, in his State of the Union speech, "to understand the damage that comes from incessant, mindless violence."

MAY: DOLE reviews films he has not seen, thumbing down "nightmares of depravity" *True Romance, Natural Born Killers.* Thumbs up: "family flicks" *The Lion King, True Lies, Forrest Gump.*

LOWS

JANUARY: A foe of public-TV funding, House Speaker NEWT GINGRICH says he'd personally kick in $2,000 a year to "adopt" Barney to help keep the PBS dino on the air.

APRIL: Perhaps taking a cue from Ross Perot's 1992 campaign gambit on *Larry King Live,* BOB DOLE announces his candidacy for the Oval Office on Letterman's *Late Show.*

THE MEDIA

HIGHS

MARCH: ABC's SAM DONALDSON is the target of muckraking attacks for accepting $97,000 in government subsidies for his New Mexico sheep ranches. Donaldson later cries foul.

MAY: Holier-than-thou tabloids pillory Republican senator and presidential hopeful PHIL GRAMM for his 1973 investment of $7,500 in an abandoned low-budget skin flick, *Beauty Queens.*

LOWS

JANUARY: Not everyone on Capitol Hill's a square. Sony Bono, the formerly groovy, shorter half of Sonny and Cher, gets sworn in to the House of Representatives (R-Calif.).

FEBRUARY: Lefty activist BARBRA STREISAND ably defends the National Endowment for the Arts while speaking at Harvard's John F. Kennedy School of Government.

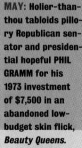

oks as Usual

terman's sector of the liberal establishment to announce he was running for President on *Late Show*, events took a decided turn for the weird. What could be more bizarre than that? We found a few things, as this chart of the year's attention-grabbing highs and heavy-handed lows reveals. —*Chris Nashawaty*

MAY: C. DELORES TUCKER and **WILLIAM BENNETT** urge Time Warner to stop releasing gangsta rap with objectionable lyrics. In September, TW sells its stake in rap-heavy Interscope Records.

JUNE: ELIZABETH DOLE piously announces she will sell more than $15,000 in Walt Disney stock to protest subsidiary studio Miramax's *Priest*, a drama about a gay clergyman. Heaven forbid!

JULY: GINGRICH ducks the "boxers vs. briefs" question on MTV's *Newt: Raw*, avoiding the political drubbing Clinton took for his "briefs" admission at a '94 MTV youth town-hall meeting.

OCTOBER: BENNETT and his moral allies call for much-needed soul-searching among TV talk-show hosts Ricki Lake, Jenny Jones, Sally Jessy Raphaël, and Jerry Springer (see October's low).

JUNE: OLIVER STONE rightly calls DOLE on his armchair movie reviewing (though he goes a bit far by branding Dole's attacks "a '90s form of McCarthyism").

JULY: Critics savage NEWT GINGRICH's WWII novel, *1945*, with such raspberries as "a desert of grindingly awful hearty male dialogue." And just when he was starting to loosen up.

**OCTOBER: Daytime talk-show producers and hosts powwow for two days in New York on how to cut back on the sleaze. No discernible changes in programming were forthcoming.

DECEMBER: Call it a truce of sorts: Radical director **STONE's** *Nixon* resurrects conservative icon Tricky Dick and makes him seem...misunderstood and human.

Route 295 for Howard Stern, keeping a campaign promise made in return for the shock jock's support.

MARCH 28

After only 21 months of marriage, Julia Roberts and Lyle Lovett announce they are separating.

APRIL 7

Dishy models Elle Macpherson, Claudia Schiffer, and Naomi Campbell open Fashion Cafe in New York City.

APRIL 9

Matsushita sells 80 percent of MCA to Seagram. Liquor scion Edgar Bronfman Jr., 39, spirits the $5.7 billion deal.

APRIL 11

Marcia Clark's new straight 'do makes *head*lines around the nation.

CONTINUED ON NEXT PAGE

Mighty

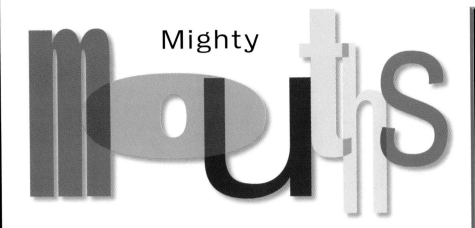

FOR TRASH TALK SHOWS, 1995 just plain stunk. William Bennett blasted them as "cultural pollution." **Sally Jessy Raphaël** got a tongue-lashing from the press when a teen en route to her show disappeared for three weeks. A judge slapped antifur protester **Ricki Lake** with community service for storming designer Karl Lagerfeld's offices. To soften this annus horribilis, EW offers the genre some rare honors. **THE HUGH GRANT REMORSE AWARD: Oprah Winfrey**, who forswore sleaze in favor of more uplifting fare while dissing her raunchy colleagues and tearfully confessing that, 20 years ago, she smoked cocaine. **THE DON'T-QUIT-YOUR-DAY-JOB PLAQUE: Jerry Springer**, who

BONADUCE RODE AGAIN

took time out from egging on transvestites to record *Dr. Talk*, a country-music CD. Sample verse: "There's Oprah, Phil, and Sally/And Jerry Springer, too/A little dose of a talk-show host/You won't seem quite as blue." **THE STATUETTE FOR BEST ACTORS IN A COMEDY TALK SERIES:** The Blockheads. In February, these Canadian comics got on *Jerry Springer*. One, posing as the husband, remorsefully confessed to his "wife" that he'd slept with the babysitter. The hoax didn't amuse the host, who's suing for an undetermined amount. **THE MAKES-US-HAPPY AWARD: Danny Bonaduce**. His past reads like a list of tawdry talk-show topics ("Ex–Child Stars Gone Bad!" "Sunset Strip Junkies!"), so it's fitting that the former *Partridge* got his own mike.

TRUE CONFESSOR WINFREY

And—surprise!—Danny was one of the savviest new hosts, even if he did slip on fishnets for a "drag race." **THE DON QUIXOTE RIBBON:** *Night Stand*, a new Saturday night series that satirizes daytime talk shows. With topics like "Celebs Who Stalk Their Fans," *Night Stand* could squeeze out some laughs—just not as many as the over-the-top **Richard Bey. THE DR. FRANKENSTEIN MEMORIAL GOBLET:** The granddaddy of trash talk, **Phil Donahue**. When Donahue's ratings couldn't compete with his own spawn's, New York's WNBC dropped him for Sally Jessy. **THE CLEAN-UP-YOUR-OWN-BACKYARD PLAQUE:** Procter & Gamble. The hygiene giant pulled its ads—worth an estimated $20 million a year—from some daytime yakfests, claiming it was offended by the high raunch. This from the company that produces the hormone-drenched *Guiding Light* and *As the World Turns.* —*A.J. Jacobs*

THE HOAX WAS ON SPRINGER

The Stars get it

READING CIRCLES HAVEN'T replaced power lunches at The Ivy, and **Jim Carrey**'s $20 million take for playing a cable guy still dwarfs what he'd make as Puck. Still, 1995 was the year of the highbrow remake, with scads of studios breathing new life into such old works as **Jane Austen**'s *Persuasion* and *Sense and Sensibility* and **William Shakespeare**'s *Othello* and *Richard III*. Some chestnuts didn't fare so well, such as **Nathaniel Hawthorne**'s *The Scarlet Letter*, which **Roland Joffé** adapted, turning **Demi Moore**'s puritan Hester into a proto-feminist heroine. But with big- and small-screen versions of *Romeo and Juliet*, *Hamlet*, *Emma*, *Pride and Prejudice*, *Jane Eyre*, and *Moll Flanders* due in '96, Hollywood's rush to the

SCARLET FEVERISH

shelves shows no signs of letting up—especially now that slacker studs like **Keanu Reeves**, who tried his hand at Hamlet, have started brushing up on their iambic pentameter. "This is why we all became actors in the first place," says former *L.A. Law* hunk **Harry Hamlin**, who took top billing in the Shakespeare Theatre's production of *Henry V* in Washington, D.C. "It wasn't just to do TV movies-of-the-week."

Or even mainstream blockbusters, if you're **Annette Bening**, who followed her role in *The American President* by playing Queen Elizabeth in *Richard III*. "Most people around me understand that as an actor sometimes you have to take a role because it *feeds* you," says Bening. But in a year when bloated budgets hindered film profits, there was clearly something else feeding the trend. "It makes sense financially," explains Gareth Wigan, executive VP of production at Columbia Pictures. "You can make a classic for $10 million, earn $30 million at the box office, and even if everything turns against you, you still won't lose much."

Unless you've overspent and played fast and loose with the story— two strikes against Joffé's $50 million *Letter*, now the industry prototype for a classical bust. "You can call anything *The Scarlet Letter*," says Castle Rock Pictures president Martin Shafer, who greenlighted both

HAMLIN'S REGAL MATTER

Othello, starring **Kenneth Branagh** and **Laurence Fishburne**, and Branagh's upcoming *Hamlet*. "But these movies have to stand on their own." Branagh added that they must have a vision strong enough to make them "meaningful to a modern audience." But *Letter* stands as a cautionary tale to those who might interject too many a modern theme; sometimes less is Moore. —*Erica K. Cardozo*

MAY 27

Christopher Reeve is paralyzed from the shoulders down in a riding accident. Two months later, he is able to drive a wheelchair by puffing air through a plastic tube.

JUNE 16

Playing at one out of five U.S. theaters, *Batman Forever* wings in with $52.8 million, the biggest opening ever.

JULY 11

Baseball's All-Star Game scores its lowest prime-time rating since 1968.

JULY 19

La Toya Jackson files for bankruptcy.

JULY 31

Disney announces that it will acquire Capital Cities/ABC for $19 billion. The next day, Westinghouse says it will acquire CBS for $5.4 billion.

AUGUST 4

Sylvester Stallone muscles a three-picture, $60 million deal with Universal.

CONTINUED ON NEXT PAGE

The biz

WHEN IT COMES TO bragging rights, Hollywood executives usually boast about who has the biggest movie, the top-rated TV show, the hottest CD. But in 1995 even the biggest smashes yielded mere chump change. This year, the mega-moguls competed to see who had the biggest...company.

BIG: MCA Inc., parent of Universal Pictures, MCA Records, and the Putnam Publishing Group. Estimated '95 revenues: $6 billion. ◆ **THE MOGUL:** Seagram Co. president and CEO **Edgar Bronfman Jr.** ◆ **THE**

BRONFMAN

DEAL: Bronfman, 39, stunned Hollywood in April by plunking down $5.7 billion to buy MCA Inc. from Matsushita, the Japanese electronics firm that bought the company in 1990 but was happy to unload after the $100 million albatross *Waterworld*. ◆ **POWER PLAY:** Failing to lure Creative Artists Agency superagent **Michael Ovitz** to MCA as president, he did woo Ovitz's partner **Ron Meyer** to the job. ◆ **BONUS POINTS:** Bronfman grabbed home-video and foreign distribution rights to future movies from DreamWorks SKG, the entertainment company formed in '94 by **Steven Spielberg**, **David Geffen**, and ex–Disney Studios chairman **Jeffrey Katzenberg**, who leveraged their initial $100 million investment into a $2 billion war chest—thanks to deals like a $500 million investment from Microsoft cofounder **Paul Allen**. ◆ **WHAT TO WATCH FOR:** Can Bronfman shake up conservative MCA and form the strategic alliances—with a network and a cable company—his company lacks? Will Seagram liquors show up in Universal films?

BIGGER: The Walt Disney Co. and Capital Cities/ABC. Estimated combined '95 revenues: $18 billion. ◆ **THE MOGUL: Michael Eisner**, chairman of

MEYER

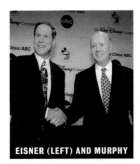
EISNER (LEFT) AND MURPHY

the Walt Disney Co. ◆ **THE DEAL:** In July Disney's $19 billion takeover of Capital Cities/ABC (captained by **Thomas Murphy**), the 1994–95 season's top-ranked network, redrew the entertainment map. The merger allowed Disney momentarily to claim the biggest American media company title— as well as international bragging rights for bringing together global cable services, the family-friendly Disney Channel, and the all-sports ESPN. ◆ **POWER PLAY:** Eisner's coup, which he seemed to pull off with ease, was all the more remarkable given his recent bad luck: the loss of his lieutenant **Frank Wells** to a helicopter crash and Katzenberg to DreamWorks, and his own quadruple-bypass surgery. With his move on ABC, he became generally acknowledged as the most powerful man in Hollywood—especially when the previous titleholder, Ovitz, accepted the Disney presidency. ◆ **BONUS POINTS:** By contrast, Westinghouse Electric's simultaneous $5.4 billion purchase of **Lawrence Tisch**'s embattled CBS Inc. seemed puny. ◆ **WHAT TO WATCH FOR:** Will Disney TV shows dominate ABC lineups? Whither once-fearsome CAA, which took major hits after Ovitz's departure sparked the defections of such superstars as **Kevin Costner**, **Sylvester Stallone**, and **Steven Seagal**?

BIGGEST: Time Warner and Turner Broadcasting. Estimated combined '95 revenues: $19.8 billion. ◆ **THE MOGUL: Gerald Levin**, chairman of Time Warner. ◆ **THE DEAL:** In September Time Warner bested Disney when Levin unveiled a $7.5 billion merger with Turner Broadcasting System. With Warner Bros. studios and such Turner movie holdings as New Line Cinema and Castle Rock Pro-

TURNER (LEFT) AND LEVIN

ductions joined, and HBO aligned with Turner's CNN, Time Warner–Turner may well emerge as king of all media. ◆ **POWER PLAYS:** By brokering Time Warner's marriage with mercurial **Ted Turner** while appeasing cable giant **John Malone**, who could have nixed the deal, Levin trumped his rivals. And by adding stewardship of the Warner Music Group to the duties of Warner Bros. cochairs **Bob Daly** and **Terry Semel**, he

FUCHS

quelled a year of turmoil at the record division— but not before chairman **Doug Morris** was ousted (and later named head of MCA's Music Entertainment Group). Other departures: Esteemed former Warner Bros. Records head **Mo Ostin** eventually went to DreamWorks; and **Leslie Moonves**, the successful president of Warner Bros. TV, became president of CBS Entertainment. ◆ **BONUS POINTS:** Levin eliminated potential rival **Michael Fuchs**, the HBO and Warner Music Group chairman who was once rumored to be his possible successor should Time Warner stock fail to rally. After allegedly opposing the Turner merger, Fuchs was shown the door—with an estimated $60 million in his pocket. ◆ **WHAT TO WATCH FOR:** Can Levin win the approval of the FCC, which could balk at the company's owning multiple broadcast channels and cable systems? Will Warner mascot **Bugs Bunny** and his nemesis **Elmer Fudd** take over as the battling ideologues on CNN's *Crossfire*? *—Gregg Kilday*

---

magazine, *George*. A bare-midriffed Cindy Crawford as Washington graces the cover.

SEPTEMBER 10

At the Emmys, among those cited for best supporting roles are Christine Baranski, David Hyde Pierce, and Julia Louis-Dreyfus' gown.

SEPTEMBER 15

Nearly one million copies of Colin Powell's *My American Journey* make the trek to the nation's bookstores.

SEPTEMBER 16

Television viewers vote to keep the Miss America swimsuit competition, helping to buoy ratings.

SEPTEMBER 19

The U.S. Congress slashes funding for the National Endowment for the Arts by nearly 40 percent.

SEPTEMBER 22

Time Warner and Turner Broadcasting System agree to a $7.5 billion merger.

The New

grind

EXPOSING DEEPLY PERSONAL matters has long been **Barbara Walters'** stock-in-trade, but viewers of *Late Show With David Letterman* on Nov. 16 saw just how far she could take things—off, that is. In response to a Letterman comment about her satiny, belted trench coat, the pioneering *femme* journalist began a striptease. As Paul Schaffer and Co. set the proper mood, Ms. Walters shed the trench coat, flaunting a

low-cut dress, beautiful legs, and some underreported cleavage as well. Walters' attack of modesty when asked about her stab at burlesque a few weeks later—"I took off a coat to show a long-sleeved dress. Is that what they call stripping nowadays?"—seemed hardly necessary by year's end, when the list of women who'd taken something off for Dave had grown to include **Drew Barrymore**, **Demi Moore**, **Carol Burnett**, and **Elizabeth Berkley**.

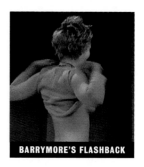

BARRYMORE'S FLASHBACK

Although the *Letterman* disrobings had many marveling at Dave's way with his female guests, what seemed well on its way to becoming a new *Late Show* franchise was, in fact, only a reflection of a more widespread fascination with stripping. As the formerly fringe spectacle danced out of seedy joints and into newfound respectability, actors **Bruce Willis**, **Woody Harrelson**, **Sean Penn**, and **Charlie Sheen** rubbed elbows with the likes of dancers named Busty Dusty and Niki Knockers at upscale clubs. Hoping to cash in on the trend, moviemakers showcased scenes featuring exotic dancers in such movies as *Exotica*, *Kiss of Death*, *The Crossing Guard*, and *Leaving Las Vegas*. "At the '95 Cannes

A TABLE FOR TWO IN *EXOTICA*

Film Festival in May there were countless ads for movies that had stripping as a central theme," says Steve Newman, vice president at Vegas Productions, the company behind the unabashedly NC-17 *Showgirls*, which had it all—gratuitous sex, stripping, and flashy Vegas dance numbers. "It certainly was the latest trend," he says, noting, however, that it may be waning. "There isn't as

CAGE'S *VEGAS* LOSER

much of a fascination with the theme now as there was six months ago." And *Showgirls*' highly publicized flop explains, in part, why. No amount of publicity, nor director **Paul Verhoeven** and screenwriter **Joe Eszterhas**' vows to deliver enough T&A to offend an army of religious reactionaries, could help this dud shine once reviewers took aim and fired. Writing in *The New York Times*, Janet Maslin called the movie "not so hot," adding that "the absence of both drama and eroticism turns *Showgirls* into a bare-butted bore." Moviegoers agreed: *Showgirls* topped out with a sorry domestic gross of $20.2 million, a debacle that Eszterhas and Verhoeven seemed to walk away from relatively unscathed, leaving Berkley to shoulder much of the blame. She may yet land on her feet, though, having nabbed a role—albeit as the other woman—in the upcoming *The First Wives Club*, starring **Goldie Hawn**, **Bette Midler**, and **Diane Keaton**. Yet the strip show must go on. With Demi Moore still to collect on the $12.5 million she'll earn for *Striptease*, a movie about a stripper working to fund her court battle to retain custody of her daughter, we must wait until late May to see whether Moore can make sleaze more palatable than Berkley did. (The fact that Moore's character strips for a cause may help.) Also in the works is Columbia's Larry Flynt biopic, *The People vs. Larry Flynt*, starring Woody Harrelson as Flynt and Hole front-woman **Courtney Love** as Althea Leasure, the—yes—stripper who captivates and eventually marries the *Hustler* publisher. Given

SWING AND A MISS FOR BERKLEY

Leasure's ultimate death from AIDS, this may be the first of these films to bring the not-so-exotic side of these dancers' lives into focus.

The film portrayals of stripping in 1995 generally shied away from such harsh realities, with the exception of the downer tour de force—and winner of the New York Film Critics Circle and Los Angeles Film Critics Association awards for Best Picture—*Leaving Las Vegas*, which stars **Nicolas Cage** as a down-on-his-luck, alcoholic screenwriter who falls

MOORE'S LITTLE NUMBER

in love with a prostitute played by **Elisabeth Shue**. Cage's character's brief encounter with a stripper helps illustrate the depths of his alienation: As a woman gyrates before him, he downs a bottle of hard liquor as if it were Evian, falling into a stupor that ends in the theft of his wedding ring. Seedy and disturbing, the strip scene is a far cry from the glossed-over caprice that showed up in the Canadian import *Exotica*, writer-director **Atom Egoyan**'s critically acclaimed psychological drama about a strip-club patron who seeks an emotional proxy for his dead daughter in a young table dancer. Egoyan admitted in an interview to taking some creative license with *Exotica*'s stylized venue, noting that while real strip clubs are dingy, his was pure fantasy.

Late Show antics aside, if the trend of taking it all off is to have any legs of its own, filmmakers should heed Verhoeven's discovery that not even sex could sell *Showgirls*: "We miscalculated the interest. I realize that mainstream Americans are not willing to see it." —*Casey Davidson*

Five days later, Johnnie Cochran signs his own deal with Random House—for a reported $2.5 million.

NOVEMBER 17
Tony Randall, 75, who plays an older newlywed in *School for Scandal*, marries a 25-year-old understudy in the Broadway show.

NOVEMBER 20

The British royal family is throne for a loop as Princess Diana describes her bulimia and infidelity in a BBC interview.

NOVEMBER 26
In a seeming imitation of a scene from the Wesley Snipes–Woody Harrelson film *Money Train*, robbers set fire to a Brooklyn subway token booth, killing the clerk inside.

DECEMBER 12
Frank "Ol' Blue Eyes" Sinatra turns 80.

DECEMBER 31
Calvin and Hobbes take their last comic sled ride down childhood's puzzling slope.
—*Marlene McCampbell*

—LET'S GO EXPLORING!

Style

STYLISH STARS EMBRACED each of 1995's trends, from satin to rubber, from Gucci to Prada, from Caesar cuts to chrome domes. Mannequins opened both New York's Fashion Cafe and Cleveland's Rock & Roll Hall of Fame. And—fans be damned—Brad Pitt shed his lovely long hair. —*Degen Pener*

MANY BALDLY GO WHERE PATRICK STEWART'S GONE

MADONNA, LOST IN A GUCCI REVERIE

CHRIS O'DONNELL'S ROBIN WAS A RUBBERY HARDBODY

CALVIN'S KIDS GOT THROWN OFF THE BUS

DONNA KARAN'S GREEN PIECE

GEORGE CLOONEY RENEWED THE CAESAR'S SALAD DAYS

SEE LEGS: THE HOT LEATHER PANTS AND JELLIES

UMA, PRADA— PRADA, UMA

JENNIFER ANISTON'S SHAG ATTACK

VH1'S TOP MALE MODEL TYSON BECKFORD IN THE TRENCHES

CLAUDIA SCHIFFER HITS THE FASHION CAFE WALL

ANNA SUI COMES UP SHORTS

SHOWGIRLS' GINA GERSHON'S CIGAR IS JUST A CIGAR

STEVEN TYLER IS A DRAW FOR BETSEY JOHNSON

THE ROLLING STONES, A HEAD OF EVERY ONE, AT THE ROCK & ROLL HALL OF FAME

PITT'S LOCKS HIT CUTTING ROOM FLOOR

COURTNEY LOVE'S TATTOO FOOTS THE BILL

THE DKNY TUBE CAN'T BE TOPPED

NAOMI CAMPBELL TAKES A SHINE TO ANNA SUI'S *AVENGERS*' RETRO LOOK

CHANEL'S VAMP NAILS MADONNA

A HAIR TREND SPOTTED AT THE FASHION CAFE

BAYWATCH'S PAMELA LEE BURNS RUBBER AT CANNES

GENERATIONS OF MANNEQUINS GATHER IN ONE ROOM AT CLEVELAND'S R & R HALL OF FAME

SATIN CLONES COURTNEY LOVE AND AMANDA DE CADENET IN OSCAR'S COURT

OPRAH'S FLOWING GOWN: A REAL OSCAR SWEEP

45

Soundbites

"OH, I'M SORRY. DID MY BACK HURT YOUR KNIFE?"

—**Rachel** (Jennifer Aniston), accusing best friend Monica (Courteney Cox) of betraying her on *Friends*

"WHEN WERE YOU PLANNING ON TELLING ME—ON OUR HONEYMOON? OUR FIRST ANNIVERSARY? WHEN THE KIDS STARTED FLYING AROUND THE HOUSE?"

—**Lois** (Teri Hatcher), after she found out would-be fiancé Clark (Dean Cain) was Superman, on *Lois & Clark*

"MY MOM ALWAYS SAID MEN ARE LIKE LINOLEUM FLOORS: LAY 'EM RIGHT AND YOU CAN WALK ALL OVER THEM FOR 30 YEARS."

—**Grace** (Brett Butler) on *Grace Under Fire*

"FORMER VICE PRESIDENT DAN QUAYLE...ANNOUNCED THAT HE WOULD NOT RUN FOR PRESIDENT IN 1996. HOWEVER, HE SAID HE HAS NOT ENTIRELY RULED OUT RUNNING FOR PRESIDENT IN 1997."

—**David Letterman** on *Late Show*

"I'M BEGINNING TO FEEL LIKE THE RODNEY DANGERFIELD OF JUDGES."

—**Lance Ito**, after lawyers kept disregarding his warnings not to argue during opening statements

"YOU HAVE NO STUDIO AUDIENCE. THAT'S A RELIEF. I JUST THOUGHT YOU WERE BOMBING."

—**Garry Shandling** to Tom Snyder, on *The Late Late Show*

"THIS IS REALLY COOL TO BE NOMINATED TWICE IN THE SAME CATEGORY, AND TO WIN FOR *DUMB AND DUMBER*. BUT I REFUSE TO BELIEVE THAT I'M A BETTER ACTOR THAN MYSELF."

—**Jim Carrey**, also nominated for *The Mask*, on *The 1995 MTV Movie Awards*

"A NEW STUDY SHOWS THAT ONE OUT OF EVERY FOUR DRIVERS HAS FALLEN ASLEEP AT THE WHEEL WHILE ON THE ROAD. AND FOR HALF OF THOSE, THE LAST THING THEY REMEMBER HEARING IS, AND NOW HERE'S A NEW ONE FROM JOHN TESH."
—**Dennis Miller** on *Dennis Miller Live*

"WHEN YOU SEE *CASABLANCA*, DOES IT DEPRESS YOU THAT ALL THE PEOPLE IN IT ARE DEAD?"
—**Roger Ebert**, challenging Gene Siskel's comment that Hugh Grant's real-life fiasco influenced his impression of *Nine Months*, on *Late Show With David Letterman*

"SOMEONE EDUCATE ME. WHAT ARE BEAVIS AND BUTT-HEAD?"
—**David Brinkley** on *This Week*

"THAT IS THE OLDEST-LOOKING MOSH PIT I'VE EVER SEEN. I THINK I SAW MY STOCKBROKER IN THERE."
—**Jon Stewart**, surveying the crowd, on *The Concert for the Rock & Roll Hall of Fame*

"YOU SHOULD HAVE PUT A GUN OVER THE BUTTOCKS."
—**Tim Robbins**, telling director Robert Altman how to get the MPAA to approve *Ready to Wear's* seminude poster, on *Donahue*

"OUR OLD FRIEND SHIRLEY MACLAINE HAS A BIRTHDAY TODAY. SIXTY-ONE YEARS OLD. AND ALSO 185, 496, 1,278."
—**David Letterman** on *Late Show*

"I DON'T WANT TO SUGGEST THAT AL [ROKER] IS LARGE, BUT WHEN HE WAS A KID HE COULD ONLY PLAY SEEK."
—*Good Morning America's* **Spencer Christian**, dissing his *Today* competitor, on *America After Hours*

"HOW'S ELECTROSHOCK GOING? IT CERTAINLY HAS PUT AN ATTRACTIVE CURL IN YOUR HAIR."
—**Sydney** (Laura Leighton) to Kimberly (Marcia Cross), on *Melrose Place*

"THE WIND DOESN'T BOTHER ME. I'M IN THE U.S. SENATE."
—**Bob Dole**, campaigning on a breezy day, on C-SPAN

Scene

JOHN TRAVOLTA WASN'T the only one saying "Look at me!" this year. The comeback king's demand in *Get Shorty* was echoed by Hollywood partygoers as they smoked, joked, and heated up all the major events and some minor ones, like Kate Moss' book—yes, *book*—party. —*Degen Pener*

GOLD-AND-SILVER STONE AT CANNES

DIRECTOR MIKE NEWELL AND HUGH GRANT GET CHEEKY

JENNIFER TILLY'S OSCAR REACH

QUENTIN TARANTINO ARRIVES ON SPEC AT THE ACADEMY AWARDS

BOB DYLAN AND BRUCE SPRINGSTEEN IN A HARMONIC CONVERGENCE AT THE R & R HALL OF FAME CONCERT

A FACE IN THE CROWD: *EW* AT THE EMMYS

DAPHNE ZUNIGA AND HEATHER LOCKLEAR GIVE A SPIRITED TOAST AT THEIR BASH FOR *MELROSE PLACE*'S 100TH EPISODE

SALLY FIELD AND JANE FONDA GREET AND GASP POST-OSCARS

GLITTERATI JOHNNY DEPP AND KATE MOSS TURNED LITERATI AT MOSS' BOOK PARTY

NEWLYWEDS NICOLAS CAGE AND PATRICIA ARQUETTE MAKE IT FORMAL AT CANNES

MEL GIBSON AND SECONDHAND-SMOKING ERIQ LA SALLE

EMMA THOMPSON'S CANNES-DO

TRAVOLTA'S POST-OSCAR PUFF PEACE

48

JIM CARREY AND LAUREN HOLLY AT REVLON'S FIRE & ICE BALL

MELANIE GRIFFITH AND ANTONIO BANDERAS AT THE BLOCKBUSTER AWARDS

ANNE RICE SIGNS BOOKS AND CHANNELS BAD TASTE

TORI SPELLING, UP CLOSE AND PERSONAL AT THE EMMYS

NICOLE KIDMAN STORMS CANNES

JULIE DELPY BUNDLES UP BEFORE SUNSET AT SUNDANCE

JULIA LOUIS-DREYFUS SCOOPS THE EMMYS

ICED OUT AT SUNDANCE

RHEA PERLMAN, DANNY DEVITO AT THE *GET SHORTY* PREMIERE

JANET JACKSON AT THE MTV VIDEO MUSIC AWARDS

MELISSA ETHERIDGE GRIPS HER GRAMMY

MORGAN FREEMAN HANDS IT TO OSCAR

DOWN ON THE RIVIERA, CANNES PARTYGOERS TWIST AND SHOUT

GREAT GODFATHER JAMES BROWN AT THE ROCK & ROLL HALL OF FAME CONCERT

hotSheet

BY JIM MULLEN

1 FRIENDS The most unusual thing about this show? They found six twentysomethings who don't live at home.

2 GEORGE John F. Kennedy Jr.'s new political magazine. How will he get politicians to read something without a centerfold?

3 THE LYLE-AND-JULIA SPLIT Who saw it coming? They seemed to be so happy apart.

4 WATERWORLD A public relations nightmare. You know it's bad when the best blurb you can find is "It's not the *worst* movie of all time!"

5 POCAHONTAS Early settlers sang, danced, cut down trees, and exploited little fuzzy animals for profit. Sounds as if they founded the first Disneyland.

6 THE BEATLES The highest-paid band of 1995. They sat down for interviews and opened the vault. Stop, guys, before you turn into workaholics.

7 HUGH GRANT Had oral sex with a hooker while dating a model. Hard to believe he's still single.

8 THE BRIDGES OF MADISON COUNTY Most men went to this movie only because they thought Clint Eastwood was going to blow up bridges.

9 THE ROCK AND ROLL HALL OF FAME Pete Rose would have no trouble getting in here on the first ballot.

50

10 O.J. SIMPSON Some Americans refused to get caught up in all the tedious details of the nine-month trial. They're called jurors.

11 *ER* Where no one signs forms or waits for hours. No wonder it's so popular.

12 THE INTERNET People are worried about online porn. It's the endless "Who's better, Kirk or Picard?" threads that should scare them.

13 MARTHA STEWART The domicile doyenne has legions of followers armed with glue guns. When's the government going to raid her?

14 JIM CARREY The human cartoon now gets $20 million a movie. Imagine what Daffy Duck could make with a better agent.

15 COLIN POWELL What a smart guy. He knows you can be the most admired man in America or you can run for President. You can't do both.

16 *CENTRAL PARK WEST* They say you can't lose money underestimating the intelligence of the American public. They're wrong.

17 *TOY STORY* The first animated feature to be created entirely on a computer. Now it wants a three-picture deal and a chance to direct.

18 RUSH LIMBAUGH Some of his listeners aren't happy with his new line of neckties—they clash with militia uniforms.

19 PRINCESS DI She gave the BBC an hour-long interview. And what did she say about her mother-in-law? "Who died and made her queen?"

20 MICHAEL JACKSON He enjoyed his hospital stay. He thought all the people in gloves and surgical masks were fans.

ILLUSTRATIONS BY
Barry Blitt

entertaines

of
the

year

THE CAST OF
FRIENDS

It's not *Melrose Place*. That's what it comes down to. Past the ratings and the Emmy nominations and the T-shirts and the billboards and the theme song playing at every stop on every radio dial and the 14, 15, 16—we've lost count—magazine covers and the endless Internet discussions about the show. It's not *Melrose Place*. It's a half-hour sitcom about the people who might watch *Melrose Place*—and then sit around and talk about it. It's about people who do not know Heather Locklear or Laura Leighton or anybody who ever plotted to blow something up, people so wrapped up in the exquisitely mundane details of their lives—job interviews, weight gains, old crushes, new PowerBooks—that you almost believe the characters are sitting watching you, laughing at your jokes. That's why they're *Friends*. In 1995 the pop-culture landscape was overrun not by dinosaurs or by Quentin Tarantino's ultracool urban savages or even by Batman, but by Ross the cute paleontologist pining for Rachel the aimless waitress, Joey the physically blessed but IQ-challenged actor, Chandler the adorable data processor, Monica the job-seeking bombshell chef, and Phoebe the lovely rocket scientist, er, folksinger. People like you, or the way you were or will be or might like to be for at least a half hour every week—young and laughing a lot and weeping a little and living in Manhattan in an interesting apartment with interesting neighbors.

Rachel: "Guess what?"

Chandler: "Okay, the fifth dentist caved. Now they're all recommending Trident?"

Even the backlash against *Friends*, that it's too facile, too good-looking, too white ("I'd like y'all to get a black friend," Oprah Winfrey told the cast when they appeared on her show. "Maybe I

52

THE CAST OF
FRIENDS

could stop by") indicates how close *Friends* has cut to the hearts and minds of the post-baby-boom generation, desperate to be seen as more than slackers. "We've taken the marring label off of Generation X," says Matt LeBlanc, who plays Joey. *Friends* is, in fact, the first successful Hollywood offering in which Gen Xers aren't the nihilistic, self-doubting pop cultura-holics of films like *Clerks*, *Reality Bites*, and *Slacker*. *Friends* are blooming in their 20s, with Ross (David Schwimmer) already married, divorced, and a daddy. Yes, Phoebe (Lisa Kudrow) writes silly folk songs, but—as we learned in the first season—she does it to deal with her mother's suicide. Our *Friends* are working, learning, growing. Monica (Courteney Cox) on feeling old: "Oh my God! I just had sex with someone who wasn't alive during the Bicentennial."

But we get the feeling that these *Friends* are going to be okay. That's infinitely reassuring—for teens, parents, and Xers themselves. "When David goes out," says Cox, "it's like the Beatles just arrived."

Just one year after it was described as a *Seinfeld* knockoff, it now nuzzles *Seinfeld* in Nielsen's top three almost every week. But is it groundbreaking TV? Well, no. Jerry Seinfeld (and George Burns before him on his 1950s TV show) showed that a trip to a refrigerator has as many comic possibilities as a trip to a fat farm. But *Friends* has something extra: sex. Not that these young things are hopping into the sack with each other (haven't we said it's not *Melrose*?). Not even Ross and Rachel (Jennifer Aniston) have engaged in more than a chaste chase, but never has a TV show ignited as much who's-cuter debate across more age and gender lines, in more offices, dorms, and high school cafeterias than *Friends*. Of course, the six costars are remarkably well put-together. But the appeal is compounded by the reliable *Brady Bunch* cast structure—three healthy women and three rowdy men in close quarters.

Joey to Phoebe: "When I first met you, you know what I said to Chandler? I said, 'Excellent butt, great rack.' "

Phoebe: "Really? That's so sweet. I mean, I'm officially offended, but it's sweet."

One *Friends* legacy is already with us: the Rembrandts' theme

FEEDING *FRIENDS*: The young cast are no sophomore slouches

song, "I'll Be There for You." But the show's potential contribution to moviedom looks most promising. All of the cast are signing contracts that will keep most of them busy for several summer hiatuses to come. Notable among them: Matthew Perry's $1 million deal to star in Columbia's *Fools Rush In*, which begins shooting next April, and Schwimmer's multipicture deal with Miramax. "I had $11 when I auditioned for *Friends*, and now I own a home," says LeBlanc, who spent his '95 hiatus shooting Univer-

sal's *Ed*, a comedy about a man and his monkey, sort of a '90's *Bedtime for Bonzo* (meaning LeBlanc is now on his way to becoming President). And though the cast of *Friends* still socialize with each other occasionally, they spend a fair amount of their downtime on the set in retreat in their dressing rooms talking to their publicists and managers. "I'm the one person in the cast who doesn't have a personal assistant yet," says Schwimmer.

"Sometimes I worry about overexposure," says Cox, who is now jetting between *Friends*' Burbank soundstage and the New York location of *Commandments*, a comedy for Universal in which she plays an attorney. But right now, we're still getting to know our *Friends*. "There are so many places to explore," says Aniston. "Joey's family, Phoebe's family. And our relationships and how those affect the group, and if Ross and Rachel get married." Ah, but can Rachel forgive Ross for that personality pro-and-con list he composed with her name on it? Will Monica get a job that makes her happy? Will Phoebe get singing lessons? Please?

Some Internet groupies have even begun a letter campaign to get *Friends*' producers to admit that the female-free Chandler is gay. A spokesperson for the show says Chandler isn't, but Perry, who plays him, thinks the audience should get as close to *Friends* as possible. "The thing I hope for is to get some *Friends* toilet paper going," he says, "with little pictures of all the characters on each paper." He laughs. For now. *—Jess Cagle, with reporting by Dan Snierson*

SANDRA BULLOCK

2

ASK HALF the population, and they'll tell you: Sandra Bullock is a woman's woman. With her loopy grin, goofy demeanor, and screen penchant for sweatpants, she's the gal you can introduce to your boyfriend with no fear you'll be going home alone. But ask the other half of the human race, and they'll tell you Bullock was invented in the same heaven as football. That smile, silliness, and resolute lack of glamour only underscore her perfection. "Men treat me like someone they feel comfortable with," she says. "And I'm a good voice for women." An equal-opportunity goddess, and this was her year to reign. Beginning what Bullock calls her "book of surprises" was the role of a lonely token-booth clerk in last spring's $81 million hit *While You Were Sleeping*. The next chapter involved fighting computer kamikazes in *The Net*, filming the comedy *Two if by Sea* with Denis Leary, and a lucrative $6 million supporting role in the Joel Schumacher legal thriller *A Time to Kill*, based on John Grisham's best-seller. Bullock may not emit the sleek chic of a Sharon Stone, but she doesn't have to; audiences want her to keep her underwear on. So does Hollywood, which recently awarded her $10.5 million to star in Richard Attenborough's *In Love and War*. "The day I found out about the money, I also found out that a small film I produced [*The Mailman*] was going to Sundance," Bullock says. "Life is good, *big time*." —*Rebecca Ascher-Walsh*

3 HOOTIE & THE BLOWFISH

THE HISTORY of Hootie & the Blowfish began 20 years ago, when they were mere minnows. In 1975, *The New York Times* had these words for *another* laid-back, roots-rocking troupe that sold zillions of records: "As long as one can accept the notion of pleasant music without much import beyond its pleasantness, the Eagles are a pretty nice band." Hootie, like the Eagles, occupies a time-honored space in the spin cycle of rock: The *nice* band. The critics and combat-boot crowd may write them off as bland, status-quo party boys, but the Blowfish swam defiantly upstream, selling 11 million copies of *Cracked Rear View* and joining the top debuts of all time. In other words, nice guys finish first. In one year, these wholesome veterans of the keg-party circuit—guitarist Mark Bryan, 28; frontman DariusRucker, 29; bassist Dean Felber, 28; and drummer Jim Sonefeld, 31—morphed into a Gumpish emblem of 1995. They blanketed VH1; they were satirized on *Saturday Night Live*. An episode of *Friends* swirled around a Hootie concert where Courteney Cox scored a hickey from an unseen Blowfish. Rucker even lent his baritone to the World Series, where he sang the national anthem. Imagine Courtney Love howling "The Star-Spangled Banner," and you get the gist of Hootie's apple-pie appeal. —*Jeff Gordinier*

4 JOHN TRAVOLTA

LOOK AT HIM. No, *look* at him. That icy stare John Travolta taught Danny DeVito in *Get Shorty* wasn't merely the year's most memorable piece of eye contact—it was the power glower of a genuine superstar.

Last year, Travolta, 41, revived his near-comatose career with an Oscar-nominated turn in *Pulp Fiction*, and *Get Shorty*, his first post-*Pulp* flick, was one of this year's biggest hits. As gangster-gone-Hollywood Chili Pal-mer, Travolta proved he could play smart every bit as winningly as he once played dumb, even when tossing a thug down a staircase. When he said, "Look at me," you *looked*. His fee for John Woo's thriller *Broken Arrow*, due in February, was a reported $7 million. He's said to be getting $8 million for playing a gas station attendant–turned–genius in Disney's *Phenomenon*; $10 million as an angel in Nora Ephron's *Michael*; and $16 million plus for Roman Polanski's *The Double*, in which he'll play a man and his doppelgänger. His current asking price: an unheard-of $21 million a picture. "Even at my hottest point, I don't think I'd been offered more than three or four scripts a year, sometimes one a year," he marvels. Does he worry that his latest comeback might disappear? "If I had to look over my shoulder," he says, "I couldn't do what I needed to get done. I'm so busy." —*Benjamin Svetkey*

DAVID
DUCHOVNY

5

HALFWAY INTO a conversation, the phone wigs out and David Duchovny's voice becomes a fuzzy cross between radio hiss and a violin. "That's just an *X-Files* thing," he demurs. "It's probably the FBI." Seconds later, the sound vanishes on cue. Which is a perfect way to explain Duchovny's quiet appeal. Every week on *The X-Files*, Duchovny plays Fox Mulder, an FBI agent who peers into a paranormal realm of giant worms, psychos, and psychics and stays calm. In a world gone topsy-turvy, Mulder is our rock. "People feel safe with Mulder," Duchovny says, "aside from the fact that he always loses his gun and gets his ass kicked." That too is vintage Duchovny, whose steely facade hides the soul of a stand-up comic. Ask about his latest *X-Files* adventure: "I'm being upstaged by mechanical roaches." Ask what it's like to be surrounded by kooks: "I don't want to talk about my growing up."

Educated at Princeton and Yale, Duchovny started acting after a close encounter with a Ph.D. in lit crit. It's not a sphere famous for producing prime-time hunks, but Duchovny, 35, has become one. "I'm not really exposed to it, to be honest with you," Duchovny insists. "Occasionally, my assistant will bring a pair of underwear into my trailer, but it's usually mine." —*JG*

JIM CARREY

6

SOMETIMES, riddling well is the best revenge. "Val Kilmer took three parts from me when I was a nobody," recalls Jim Carrey. "But I never resented him. I admired him." It's easy for Carrey to claim no hard feelings, since his manic portrayal of the Riddler upstaged Kilmer's low-key debut as the Dark Knight in *Batman Forever*, 1995's biggest box office hit and Carrey's third straight $100 million–plus smash, after *The Mask* and *Dumb and Dumber*. Striking while the iron was *ssssmokin'*, Carrey quickly turned out *Ace Ventura: When Nature Calls*, a follow-up to his 1994 breakthrough vehicle, *Ace Ventura: Pet Detective*. With a $40 million opening, it set a record for a non-holiday November weekend and has grossed—and we do mean *grossed*—in excess of $100 million.

Besides launching another spate of catchphrases ("Spank you very much," "Re-e-e-e-e-*eal-ly*"), *Nature* proved superstardom hasn't tamed Carrey's wild side. Unlike Eddie Murphy, he'll still do anything for a yuk—let a loogey dribble down his chin, do a Tarzan yell with his butt, you name it. "There are different levels of need in this world," says the actor, whose wacky physical shtick appeals to our unruly inner child. "And my need for attention is great." What's the secret of his success? "I just work hard," he says. "There's something about me that people like." Re-e-e-e-e-*eally*. —*Bruce Fretts, with reporting by Dana Kennedy*

7 NICOLE KIDMAN

THE MOST AMAZING thing about Nicole Kidman's performance in *To Die For* wasn't the Aussie actress' perkily perfect American accent. It wasn't that wicked rain dance she did for Joaquin Phoenix. It wasn't even her character's uncanny ability to switch from sweet to savage with a mere flip of her strawberry blond mane. No, the most amazing thing about Kidman's performance in *To Die For* was that she made it easy to forget she's Mrs. Tom Cruise.

That's not nearly as simple a trick as it sounds. When Kidman, 28, wed Cruise in 1990, skeptics assumed she was just another gorgeous Hollywood wannabe. There have been hints, in various films, that she could actually *act*, but nothing prepared audiences for her tour de force as *To Die For*'s Suzanne Stone, a small-town weather girl who would do anything to get ahead—including murder. "I've noticed a *huge* change in the way people view me," Kidman says in London, where she's just finished playing Isabel Archer in Jane Campion's adaptation of Henry James' *The Portrait of a Lady*, a role coveted by just about every under-35 actress in Hollywood. "I'm getting scripts night and day now. I can't believe it."

And how is Tom adjusting to his wife's new superstar status? "He's been so supportive," Kidman says. "He's been here the whole time, taking care of the children. He's been great." Just don't call him Mr. Kidman. —*BS*

JOHN **WELLS**

8

IF THE WORDS "Get me a CBC, chem 7, stat!" mean anything to you, you have John Wells to thank. As executive producer of *ER*, he's made such esoteric medical jargon a concern of 30 million to 40 million viewers each week and, in doing so, has jolted television prime-time dramas back to life. Now drawing a phenomenal 40 percent share of viewers, *ER* should finish the season as TV's No. 1 show. Not for 25 years—since *Marcus Welby, M.D.*—has a doctor drama worked such miracles.

If it weren't for Wells, *ER* might have wound up in the morgue. Michael Crichton wrote the first episode as a film script in 1974, then let it languish for years, doubting that TV could do a true-to-life-and-death drama. But in 1993, Crichton met with Wells, who knew a thing or two about realistic TV from his tour of duty as coexecutive producer on the Emmy-winning *China Beach*. "John not only realized the important qualities that were in the pilot," says Crichton, "but has week by week, hour by hour expanded them."

Wells has proved equally adept at keeping the large cast and crew from jumping—either off the show or all over one another. "With storms constantly brewing," says NBC entertainment president Warren Littlefield, "he rises above them all." "His door is always open if something feels wrong," says Anthony Edwards (Dr. Mark Greene). "He isn't a pushover, nor is he unreceptive to your feelings."

Wells, 39, toils on *ER* seven days a week, and he's about to get busier—NBC just signed him to a multimillion-dollar deal for five new series. It may barely leave him time for his wife, Marilyn, or his hobby: raising orchids. "I should say I kill orchids on a regular basis," Wells admits. Has he tried a CBC, chem 7, stat? —*Bret Watson*

BRAD**PITT**

YOU COULD argue that Brad Pitt **arrived** by making sure Geena Davis did too. It was 1991 and Pitt was fresh from cheesy TV gigs when he played the sexy hitchhiker in *Thelma & Louise* who took Davis' Thelma to bed and showed her that men were good for something after all. Pitt was onscreen for less than 14 minutes, but his buff grifter was so memorable he could have easily made a career out of playing sensual pretty boys.

Instead, Pitt went off the dreamboat grid whenever possible. This year his choices paid off with two hits, *Legends of the Fall* and *Seven*, and a turn as a madman in Terry Gilliam's *12 Monkeys*. "Only you know what you got in you," he once said.

Pitt, 32, has plenty in him. He's filming Lorenzo Carcaterra's *Sleepers*, has signed on to do *Devil's Own*, with Harrison Ford, and will play a fugitive mountaineer in *Seven Days in Tibet*.

Despite his penchant for character roles, Pitt's legions of female fans continue to grow. Courtney Love boasted that she received a valentine from Pitt. (She didn't.) And lesbian superrocker Melissa Etheridge has been so vociferous about her crush on him she might have called her last album *Yes I Am—Except When It Comes to Brad Pitt. —Dana Kennedy*

10 JANE AUSTEN

SHE DOESN'T GO to the see-and-be-seen parties. She's reticent with the press. There are nasty rumors that she engaged in an incestuous relationship with her sister. And frankly, she could use a makeover. But in this year alone, four of her novels have been adapted for the big and small screens. And with numerous World Wide Web sites devoted to her glory, she holds her own with pinup Brad Pitt. Not bad for a British broad who's been dead for 178 years.

Jane Austen's musings on the manipulations of the 19th-century landed class may involve more talk than action, and yes, they're formulaic, but that only suits Hollywood all the more. When *Clueless* director Amy Heckerling said that Cher, Alicia Silverstone's mall-manic Valley Girl, was based on Emma, the protagonist in Austen's 1816 novel of the same name, purists rolled their eyes. For them, Gwyneth Paltrow will play Emma herself in a film version of the novel, due out next year. And there was this fall's arthouse hit *Persuasion*. And the current *Sense and Sensibility*, starring Emma Thompson and Hugh Grant. And January's A&E and BBC presentation of *Pride and Prejudice*.

Does this onslaught mean Hollywood is going by the book? Maybe not, but with no options to buy and no contentious authors around to throw fits, Austen offers a bang for the buck. And that, in Hollywood's eyes, is pretty damn sexy. —*RAW*

TOM**HANKS**

11

IF TOM HANKS' career obeyed the laws of Hollywood physics, his latest movie would have plummeted like a faulty rocket booster. Instead, he's one of the Entertainers of the Year. Since his 1990 Überflop *The Bonfire of the Vanities*, Hanks, 39, has been on a gravity-defying ride. Consider: *A League of Their Own* ($107 million domestically); *Sleepless in Seattle* ($127 million); *Philadelphia* ($77 million, a Best Actor Oscar); *Forrest Gump* ($330 million, *another* Oscar). In 1995, Hanks gave voice to Woody, *Toy Story*'s cowboy doll (anticipated grosses: infinity and beyond). And as astronaut Jim Lovell, he launched *Apollo 13* into a $172 million phenom. Maybe this shouldn't surprise us. Hanks boasts a long history of defying Hollywood rules. Not only did he go from silly sitcom cross-dresser to gut-wrenching thespian, but he lacks an entourage, has no major addictions, and yes, he's a nice guy. Maybe someday his career will fall back to earth. If that happens, though, he can always rejuvenate it with *Bosom Buddies: The Movie*. Says Hanks, "I'd do [it] only if Peter Scolari agrees to a smaller trailer than mine." —*A.J. Jacobs*

COOLIO

BY NOW IT'S unwritten rap law that every gangsta du jour will offer up an apologia about how his first-person accounts of murder and mayhem in the hood are just street journalism; never mind if they sound like good soldier-of-fortune fun. But Coolio's chilly "Gangsta's Paradise" tells its tale so morosely that you actually buy it as a cautionary one. Wrapping up his bum rap by muttering that his young life "is outta luck...*fool*" (sounding self-

loathing, but definitely pissed off at you, too), the bitter cub reporter here is a loser. And it isn't just "paradise" lost but—imminently, perhaps—his own life.

So however did *this* grim piece of work end up the single of the year? Chalk it up to Coolio's moxie at shifting expertly between drollery and despondency, from bad blood to the best of intentions in his seriocomic characters. On his latest album, also called *Gangsta's Paradise*, he aimed to

add even more dimension to his Compton-inspired panorama: "I highlighted some of the good points of the ghetto and some of the bad—and all the in-betweens. But it's a little more positive than the last one. You know, it was different when it was just my kids, but now it's other people's children looking up to me, too, so I have to be careful." A rapper with a sense of responsibility to go with his street cred? That's...cool. —*Chris Willman*

rookies
of the Year

ALICIA **SILVERSTONE**

1 "ROOKIE OF THE YEAR? What's *that* all about?" asks Alicia Silverstone over the phone. You can almost hear her roll her eyes. "Honestly, this felt like every other year. Busy, very busy."

As *if*! The 19-year-old blond with saucer eyes and pneumatic lips has, granted, been busy in the past. She tossed her hair in a trio of early-'90s Aerosmith videos, and a generation of Beavises swooned. She curled her lip in 1993's thriller *The Crush*, and the Internet nearly melted down. But this was the year Alicia Silverstone charmed even that part of America no longer battling acne. This year, she starred in the surprise comedy hit *Clueless* as an Alaïa-obsessed Valley Girl named Cher. Part adorable puppy, part sex kitten, her deftly calculated comic portrayal proved she could truly act as well as jazz teenage hormones.

Hollywood got the clue. Columbia Pictures gave her a $10 million deal to star in and produce two movies. Yes, produce. ("I've taken a *million* meetings," she sighs.) Next up is *Excess Baggage*, a road tale of a girl who kidnaps herself. It's rumored she'll glide onto the next *Batman* as Batgirl. And the press is lavishing buckets of ink upon even her smallest projects—like *The Babysitter*, a newly released straight-to-video drama she did pre-*Clueless*.

Still, in real life, Silverstone continues to play the part of insecure teen. She insists on describing herself as "a klutz and a goofball." She says she got "a really bad stomachache" while watching *Clueless*. And she confesses that acting terrifies her. "Every time I step into something, I'm convinced I'm going to fail, and it's really horrible. But it's also what keeps me going." We have a feeling she'll keep going for a long time. —*AJJ*

ED **BURns**

HIS LIFE HAS changed, but writer-actor-director Ed Burns, 27, is determined not to let his independence vanish. Which may be a trick, now that his Irish-American family comedy, *The Brothers McMullen*, has recouped its $25,000 cost with $10 million at the box office and made him an overnight success. "I'm not interested in writing for anyone else," Burns says in a raspy, common-sense voice that makes you feel like you're swilling Guinness with a pal. "Despite offers, I'm not going to act in somebody else's romantic comedy about an Irish guy from New York." Instead, he plays an Irish guy from New York in his *own* romantic comedy, *She's the One*, due in '96. Was it rough stepping up to a $3 million budget and high-profile costars like *Frasier*'s John Mahoney? "I get anxiety attacks," Burns says. "I don't wanna be a big star; I want to be a storyteller." After a year like this, he should have no problem on either count. —*Steve Daly*

ELASTICA

WAS IT THOSE fast, ardent songs about sex? Was it the way they conjured up a lost '70s world of leather, safety pins, and vinyl? Or was it those *lips*? Elastica's leader, Justine Frischmann, has the kind of full, taffyish mouth that can smirk at a bloke too blotto to perform, sneering "Is there something you lack when I'm flat on my back?" and somehow make him love every harsh word. Whatever the reason, the foursome that formed Elastica—(left to right) bassist Annie Holland, 29; drummer Justin Welch, 23; guitarist Donna Matthews, 27; and Frischmann, 26—leapfrogged over their macho British brethren, snagged a Lollapalooza spot, and put out a self-titled debut album that whipped American kids into a lather. Frischmann's life is tabloid fodder in London, but now "I get recognized as much here as I do at home," she muses. Hmm. Maybe it's the lips. —*JG*

ALANIS **MORISSETTE**

WE ALL have revenge fantasies, but few of us ride our peeved daydreams to the top of the charts. This year we delegated that task to Alanis Morissette, a 21-year-old Canadian whose scorching single "You Oughta Know" turned an otherwise banal experience—getting dumped—into the banshee howl of a jilted goddess. Revenge is sweet. Not only did the song hurl her *Jagged Little Pill* toward platinum sales—despite critical scorn (see 1995's *worst* albums, p. 132)—but it justified Madonna's Maverick Records and made it kinky to go to the theater. So who is Alanis? Black hair blurs her face; her tunes flirt with café folk, raunch rock, hip-hop. At her core, she's a tough-gal belter from the old school: Pat Benatar for the age of anxiety. —*JG*

KEVIN **SORBO**
LUCY **LAWLESS**

THANK ZEUS for those few TV shows free of latté bars and Manhattan apartments. In other words, thank Zeus for buff thespians Kevin Sorbo and Lucy Lawless, who lord over *Hercules: The Legendary Journeys* and *Xena: Warrior Princess*, two syndicated hours of Bronze Age camp. This year, Sorbo's Fabio-length locks and deadpan delivery snagged him both colossal *Hercules* ratings and a seven-figure movie deal (he'll star in *Kull the Conqueror*). It's a breakthrough, says the veteran commercial actor, that seemed centuries in coming. "I've paid my dues," sighs Sorbo, 37. "It's not like I was an accountant and all of a sudden I said, 'Hey, I want a series.'" Much less one so popular that it yielded a spin-off starring Lawless, 27. The kung fu–chopping actress says she "turned green" with jitters after learning Xena would get her own series but soon got comfy in those dominatrix boots: "I guess it's the culmination of 35 years of feminism. Women can be as badass as any man." —*AJJ*

HARMONY **KORINE**

THE FIRST SIGN THAT Harmony Korine is a born storyteller: You can't tell when he's making stuff up. In conversation the 21-year-old screenwriter might tell you, with supreme nonchalance, that he knows a woman with hair on her tongue—or that he's leaving his apartment because right-wing extremists are spying on him. Tall tales aside, there was nothing phony about *Kids*, based on his grim script about teens slogging through sex and sedation in Manhattan. Forget its fling with controversy; the film confirmed Korine's gift for street talk and grunge drama—skills he'll apply to *Ken Park*, a California counterpart to *Kids*. In March, he directs *Gummo*. After *that*? "I've been thinking about quitting," he says. Don't believe it. —*JG*

SALMA **HAYEK**

REMEMBER THE rubbernecking appearance Jayne Mansfield made in 1956's *The Girl Can't Help It*? Well, Salma Hayek one-upped her, 39 years later, in *Desperado*. Already a soap star in her native Mexico, Hayek, 25, sashayed into the American eye this year, leaving in her wake an on-screen fender bender caused by two gawking admirers. Ever since Hayek pulled off the impossible—namely, outsmoldering costar Antonio Banderas—her Filofax has been filled. Next, she reteams with *Desperado* director Robert Rodriguez in the vampire flick *From Dusk Till Dawn* (due in February). "Robert wants me to only be in his films," she laughs, "but I have to eat." Then comes the doom-struck romance *Breaking Up*. While the weeper may not have *Desperado*'s explosions and bullets, Hayek will still be packing heat. The girl just can't help it. —*Chris Nashawaty*

CHRISTINE **BARANSKI**

ROOKIE? ONLY ON a technicality. The actress playing *Cybill*'s hilariously bombastic rich bitch, Maryann, arrived in Hollywood last season with a scrapbook of raves (and two Tonys) for stage work as sparkling as one of Maryann's Cartier bracelets. Yet now, at 43, the new girl in sitcomville has finally won mass applause—not to mention an Emmy. Playing a dastardly divorcée addicted to gin fizz and revenge ("If I had a nickel for every time my ex-husband

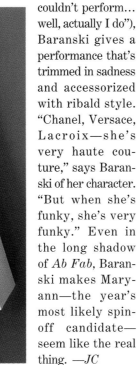

couldn't perform… well, actually I do"), Baranski gives a performance that's trimmed in sadness and accessorized with ribald style. "Chanel, Versace, Lacroix—she's very haute couture," says Baranski of her character. "But when she's funky, she's very funky." Even in the long shadow of *Ab Fab*, Baranski makes Maryann—the year's most likely spinoff candidate— seem like the real thing. —*JC*

DAVID **GUTERSON**

TALK TO DAVID Guterson and it'll make you drowsy. Not only is his voice hypnotically soothing, but he'll tell you that for much of the eight years he spent writing his first novel, *Snow Falling on Cedars*, he rose before 4:30 a.m., wrote for an hour and a half, headed off to teach high school, returned to home-school three of his four children, and retired at midnight. "I'm fortunate in that I can get by on less sleep than a lot of people," says Guterson, 39, whose best-selling *Cedars* made *nobody* drowsy. The racially charged courtroom drama won praise for its Pacific Northwest atmosphere (Guterson and his wife, Robin, live on Seattle's Bainbridge Island), received the PEN/Faulkner prize, and became a surprise paperback best-seller. Today he's at work on his second novel. "The plot keeps changing. All I know is that [*Cedars*] was full of salmon fishing and strawberries, and the new book is full of apples." Sounds delicious. —*Dave Karger*

BABE

GO AHEAD AND CALL him a pig. Unlike other Hollywood players who have earned the moniker, this mud-wallowing, garbage-eating, follicularly challenged specimen is our idea of hog heaven. In his debut role as a porker who thinks that he's a dog and hangs out with sheep, Babe hammed it up and left the herd far behind, grunting his lines with grace and dignity as he embarked on a journey of self-discovery. Sure, he wore a hairpiece and needed a little help when it came to expressing himself, but then, so did Burt Reynolds in his heyday. *Babe* has so far earned $55.9 million thanks to this newcomer's meaty performance—and all of Hollywood is now swining and dining him—but whatever his future may be, one thing's for certain: Fame behooves him. —*RAW*

The

Best of

_of_

Entertainment WEEKLY

NO.1

WITH A BULLOCK

MAY 5, 1995. *Excerpted from* ENTERTAINMENT WEEKLY.

1 **LEARN TO LIKE THE TRANSIT SYSTEM.** Sandra Bullock gets attention in the oddest places. There she was in the winter of 1993, sitting behind the wheel of an L.A. County bus, day in, day out, looking at the same scenery and living in the same costume—one baggy rayon dress she'd picked out but grew to hate in the first week. On a bad day, she worried that she was suffering from

BY REBECCA ASCHER-WALSH

SANDRA'S 10 TIPS TO SURVIVING THE COUNTDOWN TO BIG-TIME FAME

carbon-monoxide poisoning, and that the kink in her neck—which she'd got by constantly turning around to talk to the people sitting behind her—was the first stage of cancer. On a good day, she managed to fixate on these things and still swerve, scream, and smile—that loopy, only-Julia-Roberts-does-it-wider grin—in all the right places. There must have been a lot of good days, because when *Speed*, which, not incidentally, costarred Keanu Reeves, was released in June 1994, Sandra Bullock became famous faster than she ever drove that careening bus. "I was out of the country" when *Speed* opened, Bullock, 28, says 10 months later, nestled in a couch at the Four Seasons Hotel in New York City, with a pillow between her knees and another curled under her arm like a teddy bear. "So I wasn't part of the animal I created. When I came back, it was like there was a whole other me. It was very interesting."

Since the release of *While You Were Sleeping*, the new fairy-tale romantic comedy in which she stars, things have become even more interesting for Bullock. The film premiered at No. 1 last weekend, with a $9.3 million box office gross, proving Bullock can carry a romantic comedy and open it as well.

That Demi Moore was originally in line to play Bullock's part would be heady for any young actress. But Bullock, who is dressed in a cute-as-a-button pink matching sweater set and is still wearing her napped-in *Live With Regis & Kathie Lee* makeup, insists Moore doesn't need to watch her back: "There's this one list, and then there's another list, and I'm somewhere in the middle of the second list, and she's on the other list, so we're not on the same list." (Not to mention that Moore would have earned 10 times Bullock's $1.2 million salary.) She pauses. "I just want to thank her, thank her for being busy and letting me have this," she says seriously. But then that slow-spreading, ear-to-ear grin appears: "I'm so grateful, I gave her half my check. She bought a new dress."

2 EMBRACE YOUR DARK SIDE.
"There's one thing that puts people at ease, and that's humor," she says. "I'd say 50 percent of my humor is because I feel great, and the other 50 percent is because I want to make others feel comfortable so I can get comfortable. It's definitely a control zone. You look at the funniest person in show business, and I'll show you someone who's been through a lot of garbage."

When Bullock began filming *While You Were Sleeping* in Chicago last fall, she'd just ended a four-year relationship with actor Tate Donovan (with whom she costarred in *Love Potion No. 9*), and she was no longer an ingenue whose only task was to exceed others' expectations. "There were scenes that I dreaded, because I would have to go to that horrible dark place in myself," she says, sinking farther into the couch. "A lot of things went down in a year and a half. My career happened, and something that I had built for four years went away. One rug was pulled out from under me, and another one was put in."

3 KNOW YOUR PHOBIAS.
Make that rug a flying carpet. Almost immediately after finishing *While You Were Sleeping* in December, Bullock jumped into Irwin Winkler's *The Net*, a thriller in which she plays a reclusive and unhappy

SPEED-ING BULLOCK: In overdrive with Reeves

computer wizard who gets into serious trouble when her identity is erased. Bullock says she might not have been able to play a character like this a few years ago, but now, "the one thing I've become more comfortable with is showing my weakness and my vulnerability. It's the hardest thing. But it's given me confidence to say, 'This is who I am.' My biggest fault is that I was playing the martyr a lot, saying 'No, no, as long as you're happy,'" she intones in worried-Yiddish-grandmother-speak. What she realized from her breakup was that "the foundation wasn't solid. And the foundation wasn't solid because of my fear. Total fear."

4 THINK BLUE-COLLAR.
"I'm afraid of actors. I don't understand actors," she says without irony. But isn't she one of this scary breed? "I do consider myself an actor," she demurs. "But with more of a blue-collar mentality...I understand people who work with their hands," she insists. "Those are the people I'm not afraid of."

5 AVOID SCARY FANS.
Despite constantly working, she's experienced the seedier side of fame only in the last few months. "I realized things were different when a flashbulb came over the stall door when I was peeing," says Bullock, who promised the camera owner that she could take a picture once the actress was safely out of the stall. Bullock now books herself into ho-

tels under a pseudonym and occasionally hangs out with a friend who doubles as a bodyguard. "But yesterday was the first time I was incredibly overwhelmed," she says. "I can handle anything, but I have to know it's coming, and this I didn't expect. We were doing *Letterman*, and there was a whole side of the street filled with people. I looked out the car window, and I said, 'What are these people doing here?' and [my friends] said, 'These people are here for *you*.'"

6 STAY ON YOUR TOES. There's one place Bullock finds total peace. "Salsa dancing!" she exclaims. Robert Duvall taught her how to merengue on the set of 1993's *Wrestling Ernest Hemingway*, but it was the film's director, Randa Haines, who taught her about the finer points of flamenco. Since then, she's found a dance club wherever she's working. "When I'm dancing is when I'm most comfortable with myself, the most free and expressive," she says. And while she claims she's not yet at ease with the idea of playing a femme fatale, she does love the salsa uniform: "Tight, short skirts, high heels. There's a whole section of my closet devoted to this wardrobe."

7 DO IT YOURSELF. Her usual ensemble? Overalls, Calvin Klein anything, and a rainbow of sweatpants and J. Crew sweaters that hang below her knees. Dresses rarely see the light of day: Bullock's idea of a good time is grouting. Retiling, to be precise. "I've subcontracted some of the work in my home in L.A.," she says reluctantly, "but I'm doing most of it myself....My parents and I ripped down the kitchen. We had out our sledgehammers, and it was like, 'Remember that time...' and then *crash*."

8 KEEP YOUR FOOT ON THE GAS. It looks as if the rest of the renovation will have to wait: Bullock will wing from project to project in the next year like a hummingbird on adrenaline. She's in Nova Scotia beginning rehearsals for the Denis Leary comedy *Two if by Sea*. In September, she may be playing a supporting role as a law student in the thriller *A Time to Kill*.

And next spring, she's coproducing and starring in screenwriter and friend Steve Rogers' project *Kate & Leopold*. Miramax bought the script, about a time-traveling 18th-century nobleman, on Bullock's recommendation; Carrie Fisher is doing a rewrite.

The actress' schedule sounds like a recipe for a breakdown as much as a guide to success. But Bullock claims that "all I need is weekends off."

9 KEEP YOUR EYE ON THE ROAD. Bullock's got a couple of weeks off this summer. Her idea of a dream vacation? "I want to take a road trip with friends," she says. "I've seen very little of the United States. I want to get in an RV and stay in some Motel 6s. I want to go to Graceland, cheeseball central. I want to hear Tom Jones play in Las Vegas." When met with disbelief, Bullock says with sincerity, "He's my *idol*."

SLEEP-ING HIT: Pullman and Bullock team up

10 DON'T FORGET HOW TO SPELL 'BITCH.' Bullock is the kind of person who says things like "What goes around comes around" and "I'm a very good person" without looking the least bit self-conscious. But that does not imply she lacks passion. "I rarely lose my temper, and only then when someone talks down to me, or when I see people treating other people with disrespect," she says. "But I let loose—I get angry and I just can't control it. I get scared of how violent I become," she says, motioning with arms so skinny it's hard not to laugh at what seems like bravado. "On *Speed*, I lost it."

She was talking with an extra on the tarmac (where the climactic scene was filmed), and he complained about the noise. Bullock went to an assistant director to ask if the extras could get earplugs. "He said to the extra, 'Don't talk to her, don't ever go up to her,' and I said, 'Don't you *ever, ever* tell someone not to talk to me. *You get them earplugs*,'" she roars. "I sat there thinking, I'm the biggest B-I-T-C-H that ever lived." They got earplugs.

"You don't own your power," she adds. "You just have it." She pauses, relishing the thought for a brief moment. "You have it, and you do not question it." Lesson learned. ◆

BULLOCK CAN SAY THINGS LIKE "I'M A VERY GOOD PERSON"
WITHOUT APPEARING THE LEAST BIT SELF-CONSCIOUS

AMERICA SEES SHADES OF GAY

BY JESS CAGLE

SEPTEMBER 8. JUST AS ELVIS and his ilk plumbed African-American musical traditions and turned them into mainstream rock & roll in the '50s, moviemakers, TV producers, media people, and rock stars have turned entertainment on its head by mining the gay culture for its sarcasm and style, its glitter and grit, its secrets and celebrations. In 1995, the gay stream flows freely into the mainstream.

Just look around—look *everywhere*. Gay characters are multiplying on screens big and small. Comedy's most popular styles now utilize the gay sensibility—a reliance on irony that's omnipresent in performers and products as varied as Letterman (not *him*, just his raised eyebrow) and *The Lion King* (in which Timon and Pumbaa are…well, whatever you want them to be). The old-fashioned gay-baiting humor of Eddie Murphy and Andrew Dice Clay has been rendered obsolete by gay-*friendly* entertainment. On *Frasier*, the hero inadvertently asks a guy for a date. On *Roseanne*, the heroine was quite purposefully kissed by a girl. On Broadway, gay-themed works are the most dominant genre, and for three seasons, gay-themed plays by gay playwrights (Tony Kushner's two-part *Angels in America* and, most recently, Terrence McNally's *Love! Valour! Compassion!*) have won Broadway's top honors and scored movie deals for their authors.

The revolution has happened two ways: gradually and suddenly. As recently as 1984 Harvey Fierstein shocked the world by publicly thanking his lover on the CBS Tony Awards telecast. At this year's Tonys, many such expressions of gentle demonstrativeness went almost unnoticed. In 1978, it seemed unthinkable that the charming French farce *La Cage Aux Folles*, about a nightclub owner and his drag-queen lover, could reach beyond audiences who didn't mind subtitles. But in 1983 it became a hit Broadway musical, and next year it will become a major American movie—*The Birdcage*, starring Robin Williams and (in the dress) Nathan Lane. And in music, record and movie mogul David Geffen and artists like Elton John, k.d. lang, and Melissa Etheridge have done what was unthinkable until very recent memory: They've come out and not only continued to work but thrived.

But gay culture has brought about even more basic changes—sometimes changes as fundamental as how things *look*. The erotic male form once strutted only in marginal venues—either below the mass-culture radar (all-male pornography) or above it (the walls of art museums). Now it's right up there at your local mall, helping sell tickets to the year's top-grossing film, *Batman Forever*. Chris O'Donnell's batsuit features a strikingly commodious codpiece; and are we wrong, or does the Riddler have a little crush on Bruce Wayne? *Batman Forever* is, in fact, emblematic of the new, mutual inclusiveness—the *give* and *take* and *take back*—of gay and straight audiences. Its sex appeal bids for the attention of all sexual persuasions; so do its jokes, and the screen winks broadly in all directions.

What force roiled this sea change? A mission by Hollywood to (a) eradicate all forms of bigotry and homophobia, or (b) to destroy the values upon which society rests? Not on your lifestyle. Quite simply, gay sells. As the success of *both* drag-queens-on-the-

A **ONCE-INVISIBLE** GROUP FINDS THE SPOTLIGHT IN TODAY'S SOCIETY AND SEIZES THE **OPPORTUNITY**

road films *The Adventures of Priscilla, Queen of the Desert* and *To Wong Foo, Thanks for Everything, Julie Newmar* shows, gold lamé on a man is as good as gold. So it's no accident that advertising was at the vanguard of the gaying of America as the first business to realize that homosexuals comprised a very desirable demographic. Not the largest demographic, but one with powerful handfuls of disposable income.

The most striking and omnipresent outgrowth of that awakening has been the mass marketing of erotic male images. Calvin Klein pioneered the movement more than a decade ago by plastering Times Square with an enormous, indelible Bruce Weber billboard of a hunk in his underwear, hands creeping precariously close to his nether regions. Then, during the proliferation of daytime talk shows throughout the 1980s, male strippers began gyrating in middle-class, middle-American living rooms on a daily basis. Now straight men are expected to be just as moussed and buffed as their gay counterparts; and they are subtly pressured to emulate the exhibitionistic sex appeal of models like Marky Mark and Michael Bergin, who have posed seductively in ads intended to sell shorts not just to gay men, but to all men.

Heterosexual women have long been inveigled to buy lipstick worn by gorgeous models in advertising, but now Versace targets them with overtly homoerotic ads. Chalk it up to "lesbian chic," a trend that was spawned as Madonna and Sandra Bernhard flirted in 1991's *Truth or Dare*, grew as playfully ambiguous style arbiter Ingrid Casares began showing up in paparazzi photos everywhere, and crested with Cindy Crawford shaving k.d. lang's face on the August 1993 cover of *Vanity Fair*. This curious media trend may have passed, but lesbians have kept their media cachet. Says Sarah Pettit, editor of the lesbian and gay newsmagazine *Out*: "Straight women are looking around

OUT, LOUD

A sampling of the pop-culture leaders in the gay revolution. From top: lang, who came out on her own terms; teen role model Cruz from TV's *My So-Called Life*; Etheridge, who became more popular after coming out; Geffen, the billionaire producer and entrepreneur.

thinking, 'Is *she* one? Am *I* one?' And they're kind of titillated by it."

Gradually, the entertainment industry realized that gay can sell a niche-market art film (such as the minor summer hit *The Incredibly True Adventure of Two Girls in Love*) and help sell a film with crossover appeal (*Four Weddings and a Funeral*). Androgyny chic has ushered in a new brand of movie star: Johnny Depp, Leonardo DiCaprio, and Keanu Reeves would once have been called sissies. In music, Nine Inch Nails' Trent Reznor and R.E.M.'s Michael Stipe use sexual ambiguity as a marketing tool—enigmas wrapped in mysteries, they're all things to all persuasions.

Nowhere is gay assimilation more evident than in the proliferation of gay characters in film and TV. And no longer are these characters solely the province of one "very special episode" per year. They populate *Roseanne*, and have for a while. NBC's smash *Friends* features a recurring lesbian character (David Schwimmer's intensely sympathetic ex-wife) and her lover. The short-lived *My So-Called Life* featured a gay character who was played by an openly gay actor, Wilson Cruz. *NYPD Blue*'s gay male replacement receptionist (whose boyfriend happens to be a cop) proved so popular last season that the show's producers are bringing him back. And the most conscientious writers and producers pride themselves on making these characters real—not just real funny. Explains David Lee, the gay cocreator of *Frasier* and director of last season's accidental-date episode, "There was humor in the situation [the characters] found themselves in, but you weren't laughing at anyone because he was gay." The episode sparked high ratings and is up for Emmys both for its script, by gay writer Joe Keenan, and its direction.

The revolution has been slower to take hold at movie studios, which all but banned gay characters after the dismal failure of *Making Love*, the oh-so-serious

IN 1995, THE GAY STREAM FLOWS FREELY INTO THE MAINSTREAM VIA TELEVISION AND THE BIG SCREEN

1982 drama in which Michael Ontkean left Kate Jackson for Harry Hamlin (actually, audiences shied away from the film because it stank). Still, by the early 1990s, it seemed almost every movie hero or heroine had a lovable gay neighbor—a lovelorn friend in *Frankie & Johnny*, a flower-toting sissy in *The Prince of Tides*. But not until 1993 did a major studio, TriStar, release a film hinging on gay characters—*Philadelphia*, which was criticized within the gay community for playing it safe and never giving Hanks and his lover, Antonio Banderas, an on-screen kiss. Didn't matter. The $197 million it grossed worldwide was the sound of cash registers ringing: The right stars could sell tickets whether they were playing gay or not. (Anyone who believes that playing a gay character can hurt a career should note the recent résumés of Hanks and Banderas.)

It is, in fact, the AIDS epidemic that has exponentially increased the visibility of gays in the mass media. Indeed, a disproportionately high number of gay men in films are depicted as suffering from AIDS, whereas the issue of coming out to one's friends and family—a crucial aspect of every gay person's life—has never been satisfactorily dealt with in movies or on TV. The sexual side of gay life is still an area that Hollywood tends to treat awkwardly at best; although portrayals of gay men as sexual predators (as in 1980's *Cruising*) tend to be a thing of the past, more often than not, gay characters are neutered, limited to longing looks and chaste kisses.

But just as negative pop stereotypes of black characters in old Hollywood (*Gone With the Wind*) gave way to dull black plaster saints in the 1960s (*Guess Who's Coming to Dinner*), and then, finally, more realistic treatment, so will gay characters and themes and punchlines evolve. And the voices opposing this cultural shift—whether political, personal, or just nervous—are being drowned out. Not by the sound of disco, or the roar of drag queens, or the relentless engine that drives Hollywood. But by consumers at Tower Records in Seattle, by moviegoers at cineplexes in Buffalo, by TV viewers in their Amaril-

OUT THERE

From top: *To Wong Foo*'s Patrick Swayze; Hanks, who won the Oscar for *Philadelphia*; Roseanne, who tests tolerance in prime time; R.E.M.'s Stipe; the sexy cover of the *Out Classics* CD

lo living rooms—all of whom are putting their time and money where their interests lie. An ENTERTAINMENT WEEKLY/Gallup poll shows that 63 percent of 18- to 29-year-olds, perhaps the most avid purchasers of entertainment, don't mind seeing a same-sex kiss on screen when they go to the movies, and nearly 18 percent would like to see more gay characters and situations. In short, this revolution is the only kind Hollywood can trust—one driven by the marketplace.

As performers like Elton John, Etheridge, and lang have come out, other doors of acceptance have opened. MTV viewers wrote hundreds of letters each week to Pedro Zamora, last year's *Real World* gay resident, as he battled AIDS. And as coming out became more common, there was a crucial shift in the perception of those inveterate culture consumers, the baby boomers: According to the ENTERTAINMENT WEEKLY/Gallup poll, 71 percent of 30- to 49-year-olds say they count a gay person among their relatives, coworkers, or friends.

The gay sensibility was born from the plight of the disenfranchised—gay people are aware, as much as anyone, that life according to *The Brady Bunch* exists nowhere outside a Hollywood soundstage. At its most outrageous, the aesthetic flares into camp—a comedy genre that ridicules with both affection and anger—and is personified by drag queens. But today, camp isn't simply an in-joke among gay audiences; it has gone mainstream. Last spring's send-up *The Brady Bunch Movie* (in which a gay teen had a crush on an oblivious Marcia) was a triumph of the new camp, a shiny subversion of mainstream Americana that proved a hit with mainstream Americans.

At this point, the commercialization of gay culture seems like more than a passing fad—after all, the closer you cut to the heart of consumerism, the more acceptance, if not outright enthusiasm, is revealed. Even those who think the novelty will wear off may find themselves in a different world when it does. It may well be a more tolerant and compassionate place, at least for one minority. ◆

JULY 21. HUGH GRANT IS MOTORING his snow-white BMW convertible slowly along Sunset Boulevard. He hangs a right onto a secluded residential street, wheels up a winding hill, and pulls to the curb. "Very impressive, isn't it?" he asks, grinning coyly at the stranger sitting in the passenger seat. "Quite lovely, no? A bit smaller than expected,

though, don't you think?"

Okay, wipe that filthy smirk off your face. Grant is talking about Cary Grant's old house—a stunning Deco edifice perched high above Hollywood—and his car mate on this late-June day is just a magazine reporter with an enviable, though now ironic, assignment: Cruise around Los Angeles with England's hottest new screen sensation and let him riff on the town that's about to make him a megastar. We've even brought along one of those cheesy tourist maps of celebrity homes for inspiration.

But four days after our grand tour, the 34-year-old actor was caught taking a cruise of an entirely different sort. The details of his awfully embarrassing adventure are by now

WHAT'S A GUY LIKE HUGH DOING IN A PLACE LIKE THIS?

BY BENJAMIN SVETKEY

a ball, with Letterman offering a Top Ten list of Grant's future movies (No. 1 was *Poca-hooker*).

The timing could not have been worse: just two weeks before the July 12 opening of *Nine Months*, by far the most important movie of Grant's career. If last year's *Four Weddings and a Funeral* was the film that got Grant noticed in Hollywood, this was to be his first shot at a genuine blockbuster. Directed by hitmaker Chris Columbus (*Home Alone*), it casts Grant as a happily unmarried man who goes off the deep end when his girlfriend— played by Julianne Moore (*Vanya on 42nd Street*)— announces she's pregnant. Disarmingly witty, beguilingly bumbling, handsomely mop-topped,

well known: On June 27, at about 1:30 a.m., Grant was arrested for inviting a Sunset Strip prostitute named Divine Marie Brown (above) into his BMW, driving to a secluded residential street, and engaging in what the LAPD discreetly described as "an act of lewd conduct." Within hours, it was the bust heard round the globe. Grant's bummed-out mug shot was plastered on front pages on both sides of the Atlantic. CNN and local news programs played the story as if it were the capture of the Unabomber, complete with up-to-the-minute bulletins. And, of course, the late-night boys had

the character was shaped as the perfect vehicle to launch Grant into the stratosphere of stardom.

But, of course, that was "BS" (Before Scandal).

"It's all very weird," admits Columbus. "We're perplexed and wondering what effect it will have on the movie…."

"At least," Columbus says, "it wasn't an animal."

Two weeks later, a few hours before taping his July 10 guest shot on The Tonight Show—*his first post-arrest public appearance—Grant is talking on a phone from his hotel room in Los Angeles. "Well, I*

"NONE OF IT HAS BEEN THE KIND OF PRESS YOU REALLY WANT," GRANT SAYS. "NONE OF IT IS WHAT YOU MIGHT CALL NICE."

can't pretend that these have been the best couple of weeks of my life," he says contritely. "To be honest with you, none of it has been the kind of press you really want. None of it is what you might call nice. Curiously, though, the suffering one goes through in these circumstances—you don't mind it too much. I almost feel as if I deserve a good whipping."

It would be juicy to report that there were ominous signs of things to come during our drive around L.A.—an empty bottle of tequila rolling around the car floor, an old copy of *Swank* sticking out of the glove compartment. But no such luck. Grant was a total gentleman, an irresistible charmer. He's the sort of chap who doesn't just knock on your hotel room door— he raps to the tune of "Shave and a Haircut." Jolly English exclamations—"Easy-peasy!"— sweeten his sentences like tasty verbal toffees. The man is so smoothly amusing, so suavely appealing, he makes you glad there'll always be an England.

MAIN SQUEEZE: "We love each other," Grant says of Hurley

Still, Grant insists that playing cute has taken him years and years of practice to perfect.

"I was nicer as a child," he says as we take a drive-by peek at Telly Savalas' Polynesian-style ranch house in Brentwood. "Then I became a pretentious, overeducated, hoity-toity teenager at Oxford. I buttoned my shirt up to the top and smoked a lot of cigarettes and wore two V-neck jumpers and wrote excruciatingly embarrassing theater reviews for a university paper. After I left [Oxford] and became a failure as an actor, I got nice again."

The failure part didn't last long. After a brief stint writing ad copy, he landed a leading role in Merchant Ivory's 1987 *Maurice*, playing a sexually ambivalent turn-of-the-century aristocrat. That led to a string of mostly mediocre TV gigs and a couple of feature films, including 1991's *Impromptu*, in which Grant slipped into a Polish accent and party-size wig to play the prissy composer Chopin. And then came *Four Weddings*, the first movie to truly tap into Grant's slick Brit shtick. Made for about

$6 million (Grant was reportedly paid only $100,000), it grossed $250 million worldwide, making it one of the most profitable films ever released. And Grant sealed his new on-screen image with two similar roles, an endearingly baffled clergyman in the Elle Macpherson artsy nudie flick *Sirens* and an endearingly baffled nouveau pervo in Roman Polanski's *Bitter Moon*. By the end of the year, he was being heralded in the press as Cary Grant incarnate.

"I was in L.A. about a year ago," he says, "and I went to all the studios, shaking everybody's hands. People were saying things like 'We want to be in the Hugh Grant business.' Disney was my favorite. There was this guy at the studio who took me out of my car and into the building. And as we were walking through the parking lot he said, 'So, how are you doing today?' I told him, 'I'm fine, thank you very much.' He walked me into the building and turned around and said again, 'So, how are you doing today?' I told him, 'Well, like I said, I'm fine, super, thanks.' We went in the lift and halfway up he turned around and said, 'So, how are you doing today?'" Grant makes a gargoyle face. "Really frightening."

For months, rumors of his next move kept car phones buzzing all over Hollywood. Ultimately, he picked *Nine Months*, mainly because of Columbus. "I especially admire the *Home Alone* films. I think they're clever, clever, clever. Especially No. 2," he says, astonishingly in earnest. "I know Americans think small-budget English films are fascinating, but I'm always yawning my head off. I've always had a soft spot for big-budget American movies."

"My friends from Nine Months *have been incredible," Grant continues on the phone. "And not just them, but people I've never met, both in show business and outside of it. Big stars—and I shan't name names—have been faxing and calling, saying 'Hang in there.' And there have been thousands of letters. That, really, has helped put this ghastly business in perspective. Because a lot of people*

"I THINK YOU KNOW WHAT'S A GOOD THING AND WHAT'S A BAD THING," HE TOLD JAY LENO. "I DID A BAD THING."

who've written in have been through trauma so much worse than mine. I mean, when they say, 'I've had epilepsy for 16 years,' you realize that this has been bad but not that bad."

Grant is very clever at dealing with the press. He feeds reporters such heaping gobs of quotable chitchat that by the end of an interview, the tape recorder is practically burping and begging for an Alka-Seltzer. Still, you can find an occasional fracture in the Kevlar lining of his charm. For instance, there's Grant's ugly bathrobe dream. "I used to dream about Gorbachev before he lost power," he confesses. "I'd panic because I was meeting him and had nothing to wear. I'd ask my brother what to do, and he'd tell me to wear my dressing gown. I'd say I can't. He'd tell me to wear his as well. So I'd meet Gorbachev wearing two dressing gowns. What would a psychologist make of that?"

Whatever one makes of the dream, from now on, Grant's words will get a new, more salacious scrutiny. And journalists will be forever twisting his most innocuous pre-arrest quotes into obnoxiously tittering sound bites. Uh-oh, here comes one now:

"Elizabeth is the dish of the day," Grant says of his supermodel girlfriend. "She works with such great makeup and styling people, she just keeps getting better and better. And when she does magazine shoots, they give her a different look every time, so a new girl comes home every night. It's dead sexy."

On the phone, Grant takes his girlfriend much more seriously. "I've been with Elizabeth for eight years, through thick and thin. She's an incredible person. We love each other and we're going to try to get over this. We're going to try to make the best of it. And it's not at all easy because I've taken the trust away, which is quite a big foundation stone of a relationship. I can't tell you everything is rosy—that would be completely phony. Nor is it the case, which I saw reported today, that we've split up. That's just one of the many inventions of the British press."

Grant takes a wrong turn on the way to Nicole Simpson's house and for 15 minutes we're lost in

Santa Monica. The double-murder crime scene is the last stop on our Hollywood tour—"the grail," Grant calls it—and it's clearly the one spot he's most thrilled about visiting. As we finally reach the Bundy Avenue shrine—still shrouded in yellow police tape—Grant recalls a murder story from his own early years growing up in west London.

"A man who lived nearby when I was a child was accused of killing his wife," he says. "She was found in various pieces on a golf course. Everyone thought he'd done it except my mother, because she's the nicest person [Grant's mother, Finvola, is a teacher; his father, James, a retired carpet salesman]. She insisted we be polite to him. She'd say, 'It's wrong to have prejudged him.' We shared candy with him. Turned out he had done it. He chopped her up and left her head in the lost luggage department at Waterloo Station. It was a seminal experience for me."

PERFORMANCE ANXIETY: An ad for *Nine Months*

Grant's Tonight Show gig is the single most important public appearance of his career—and he's looking forward to it about as much as an aneurysm. For two weeks, photographers have been camped outside his London flat and his country home. The tabloids were merciless—one even ran a lengthy exegesis on the prostitute's assessment of his sex organ. Now, after jetting halfway around the globe, he's about to face the world head-on for the first time since his Divine madness began. "I'm just going to hope for the best," he says on the phone. "I'm just going to wing it."

A few hours later, when Leno announces his name, Grant nervously pushes himself on stage. He looks so excruciatingly uncomfortable—fidgeting, taking umpteen sips of water—that you're tempted to click to Dave. But finally he settles down and starts doing what he does best—laying on the class.

"I think you know in life what's a good thing to do and what's a bad thing," he tells Jay. "I did a bad thing, and there you have it." He gives the studio audience (and an estimated 18.5 million viewers—one of Leno's biggest draws since he took over Tonight) a stumbly, bumbly smile. They give him back a burst of redemptive applause. Easy-peasy. ◆

UPDATE: Nine Months *went on to gross $69.6 million domestically.*

COOL, COLLECTED X-FILER DAVID DUCHOVNY EXPLAINS HOW HE BECAME TV'S MYSTERIOUS NEW PINUP BOY

SEPTEMBER 29. GARRY SHANDLING has sent David Duchovny a note—"Enjoy this, you big queer"—along with a videotape of Duchovny's recent appearance on HBO's *The Larry Sanders Show.* As is customary on that reality-bending talk-show send-up, Duchovny guest-starred as himself—sort of. "I told [the writers] I wanted to be as objectionable as possible," he explains. "Garry kept telling me, 'People are going to think this is really you, that you really are a jerk.' But I just said, 'Who cares?'" Duchovny was so perfectly rude and obnoxious on the program—"When I get back to my hotel room, there better be a big f---ing fruit basket," he sneered at Larry during one commercial break—that he and Shandling instantly became pals. "David is actually a very funny guy," Shandling says. "He should do more comedy. Not that *The X-Files* isn't extremely funny."

"I'm finally beginning to understand star trips," Duchovny (above, with costar Gillian Anderson) says. "I've heard about stars doing insane things and I've been, like, What is their problem? But I obviously have that in me too. I've felt myself having those Hollywood feelings, these infantile rages, mostly because I can get away with it. So now that I'm finally beginning to understand it—to see it in myself—I wanted to play it. That's why I did the thing with Garry."

But Duchovny's willingness to play snotty on *Larry Sanders* hints at more than merely the actor stretching his range. This is a star who obviously enjoys the subtle absurdities of fame, who can put some intellectual distance between his life and his public image.

"I *think* it was Roland Barthes," he says, biting into a yam at Vancouver's Yam Café. "He wrote that the camera eroticizes whatever it looks at, just by making it the focus of its gaze. Being photographed gives you a certain energy in other people's eyes, a certain buzz. I'm the focus of millions of eyes every Friday night because the camera is photographing me. That changes the way people see me. But it has nothing to do with me—it has to do with the camera.

"That's the thing about fame. Ultimately you realize you're being appreciated for something that doesn't have that much to do with you. So it's not satisfying," he says. "It's perfume. Nothing goes inside. It doesn't give you anything deep or meaningful. You get Knicks tickets—that's about it.

"It's weird. To me, the show is like a wave, and I'm on top of it looking down. And right now it's a *biiiig* wave, so sometimes it's scary. But mostly I'm just detached from it all." Still, he's not worried. "I feel I've got 10 more years of playing the guy. When I'm 45, I'll start thinking about what else I want to do." ◆

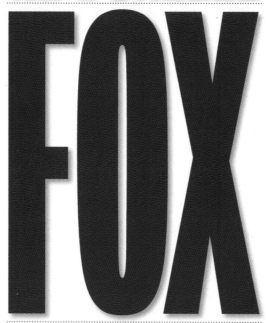

NO WONDER HE'S CALLED FOX

BY BENJAMIN SVETKEY

JERRY MAGNOLIA

SUGAR GARCIA

BY CHRIS WILLMAN

JERRY GARCIA TRIBUTE.
JEROME JOHN Garcia didn't cling to any of the ethnic heritages that were his to claim—not the lineage of his Spanish-immigrant father, nor the Irish-Swedish ancestry of his mother and the maternal grandparents who largely raised him. Jerry Garcia was an *American* beauty. Though most of the skittish parents of the '60s weren't tripping over each other to recognize it, the Grateful Dead's bushy-haired frontman fit any number of fairly patriotic paradigms. Musically, as much as pharmaceutically, Garcia was a real don't-fence-me-in kind of fella. Here was a one-man melting pot who could absorb every kind of music, from old-timey bluegrass or Tin Pan Alley standards to modern jazz or psychedelia, with blithe osmosis, then make jolly alchemy out of 'em, arriving at a stew as indigenously American as...well, as American as Jerome Kern,

for whom Garcia's bandleader dad named the boy.

The artist formerly known as Captain Trips, Garcia was an accidental guru whose very visage symbolized agitation, then consolation, to successive generations of the Establishment. Last year, no less a mouthpiece for The Man than *Forbes* listed the collective Dead among the country's 20 best-compensated entertainers, and a line of expensive Garcia-label silk neckties derived from his artwork included even the nation's President and VP as proud customers. These are the sorts of capitalist lapses nomadic Deadheads could easily forgive, given how little their heroes had actually done to court success over four ragtag decades. In Garcia was your basic youthful no-account who happened into a middle-age accounting bonanza through not too much design of his own. He got rich, true to great American form, as the culture and the counterculture enacted their own corporate merger.

If most folk finally "got" Garcia, Garcia didn't get straight—at least not for any great stretch before the final month of his life, which he spent in

DEATH

and out of rehab. However the autopsy report might read, it's clear the none-too-skeletal figurehead of the Grateful Dead died of consumption—that is, an inability not to consume, in mass quantities. And certainly, that too is all-American in its fashion.

His addictive personality may have been his best and worst quality: The same restless, sense-famished compulsiveness that kept drawing him back to drugs, to a three-pack-a-day cigarette habit, and to junk food also made this high-school dropout a zealous student of virtually every kind of fine art (he painted throughout his life), literature, and music. Even during the years he was using heroin, a drug that kills the lust for life in most longtime users, rarely would a day go by without Garcia starting and finishing a book ("My life would be miserable if I didn't have those little chunks of Dylan Thomas and T.S. Eliot," he once said) or spending hours practicing scales and trying to learn complicated licks off old records. Whistling Gloria Grahame's refrain into and beyond the Nancy Rea-

gan epoch, he was the quintessential boy who *cain't say no*—to the eternal detriment of his health and to the undying benefit of grateful Deadheads, who got the good end of his endless assimilations.

Not everyone hailed the late conquering hero. Conservative pundits were quick to assail a not-quite-cold Garcia for leaving a legacy of libertine shame. Rush Limbaugh figured the outpouring of good will for someone who "destroyed his life on drugs" proved "our priorities are out of whack, folks." While admitting he'd never heard a Dead song, William F. Buckley Jr. conceded Garcia must have made a lot of folks happy but emphasized that, by never publicly denouncing drug use, "he also killed…a lot of people."

After a counselor found Garcia dead in the early morning hours of Aug. 9 at the Serenity Knolls rehab center in Marin County, where he'd checked in just two days earlier, the country's Greek choruses and armchair psychoanalysts struggled to find the gentle patriarch's dark side. Underneath that placid, publicly reticent, legendarily Buddha-like

OF THE DEAD

exterior, it wasn't easy to locate. "The guy was a f---ing saint," says David Grisman, the famed mandolinist who recorded three extracurricular albums of acoustic music with his friend of three decades. "He was smart and very funny and had an awful lot of depth and compassion and soulfulness."

Still, some friends caught glimpses of an underlying loneliness beyond the outer merriment. Whatever melancholia Garcia suffered probably was first formed when, at the age of 5, he witnessed the drowning death of his father, Jose, in a Northern California river. "The major focus of Jerry's heartache was the loss of his dad," says Linda Conklin, who met Garcia when he decided to check out her Kid Street Theatre in Santa Rosa before pledging it funds from the Grateful Dead's Rex Foundation. "Jerry got involved [with us] pretty much from our slogan, 'The healing begins when the smallest hand has been touched.' And one of the things Jerry said was, 'Where were you when I was a kid?'"

A LONG STRANGE TRIP: Garcia (bottom center) and the Dead

After his father's death, his overwhelmed mother, Ruth, sent the young, asthmatic Jerome to live with her parents for five years. His grandmother's love of the Grand Ole Opry proved a source of post-traumatic comfort as well as considerable influence: Jerry was a bluegrass fanatic for life. Bill Monroe's sway gave way to Chuck Berry's—momentarily, at least—as Garcia got hooked on the upstart subgenre, rock, after moving back in with his mother and stepfather, who were running a San Francisco fishermen's bar. His mother got him a guitar when he was 15—the same year, coincidentally, that he shared his first joint.

Garcia quit high school and joined the Army, which—nine months and an unconscionable number of AWOLs later—quit him. It was during his Army stint, ironically, that he really got serious about the guitar he'd smuggled on base, as well as the five-string banjo. In spite of having had the middle finger of his right hand cut off at age 4 by

his only sibling, brother Tiff, in a wood-chopping accident, Jerry proved a fingerpicking natural. Not long after his dishonorable discharge from the Presidio, he was living out of his car in Palo Alto, where he met fellow auto dweller Robert Hunter, soon to be part of a bluegrass band with Garcia and later to be the Dead's foremost lyricist. There he also met Sarah Katz, with whom he formed the short-lived folk duo Jerry and Sarah and an almost as brief marital union.

A bluegrass band Garcia started, the Wildwood Boys, gave way to Mother McCree's Uptown Jug Champions, which quickly evolved into the blues-rock bar band the Warlocks—and ultimately the Grateful Dead, when another group named the Warlocks was discovered. Initial gigs, circa mid-'65, were as humble as Garcia. "The first time I saw the Dead, they were backing up a stripper," says Peter Albin, former bassist for Big Brother and the Holding Company. "It was goofy. But after a while, looking at the stripper became kind of boring, so everyone started concentrating on Jerry's licks."

From 1987 to the present, the Dead have toured as many as 300 days a year, ranking among the top five touring groups, with annual concert grosses in the $35 million to $55 million range—not including merchandising, estimated to gross another $7 million or more annually. And though the band officially operated as a democracy, there was no doubt Garcia felt the pressure of being, in most people's eyes, the CEO. There were some contentious band meetings along the way, but for the most part, the Dead's cooperative vibe was still thriving. Jerry's body, much less so. In 1986 he lapsed into a diabetic coma, an illness so serious that friends had to teach him to play the guitar again during his recovery. And in 1991 he entered a hospital after collapsing from exhaustion and was told he had an enlarged heart as well as damaged lungs. Recent years found Garcia alternating between genuine

"JERRY WAS THE EMOTIONAL CONTENT OF THE GRATEFUL DEAD. HE WAS THE GUY WHO WAS MAKING THE ATOMS MOVE."

health-and-exercise kicks and backsliding binges.

Lately, though, he'd acquired new motivation for moderation. On Valentine's Day of last year, Garcia, a tux-clad but tieless groom, wed filmmaker Deborah Koons, 45, whom he'd first dated in the mid-'70s but had only fallen head over heels for in 1993. Admittedly a "mediocre" dad in earlier years (a result, friends say, of treating the band's camp as his primary family), Garcia was now also enjoying more intimate relationships with his grown daughters from his first two marriages—Heather, 31 (Sarah's daughter); and Annabelle, 25, and Teresa, 21 (daughters of second wife Carolyn Adams, more famously known as Mountain Girl)—as well as taking an active part in raising his youngest girl, Keelin, 7 (whose mother, Manasha Matheson, he never married).

But in recent concerts, the music—which always veered between Shinola and its opposite—was suffering more noticeably from Garcia's ill health, as was, apparently, his marriage. "Jerry knew that drugs were in the way of his being an artist, and having the relationship with his wife that he wanted, and in some respects having relationships with a number of people," says Sattinger. "There was a frustration with members of the Dead, that he was the only person still on this trip. But Jerry himself had the desire to go into rehab. If he didn't, his way would be to say, 'F--- you, stay out of my life.' "

In early July, Garcia checked into the Betty Ford Center. Why exactly he checked out after only two weeks remains a mystery at least publicly; some speculate that the Center's rigid work regimen and philosophy didn't agree with Garcia's laidback temperament. But he hadn't given up being serious about sobriety. Just two days later—right after his 53rd birthday—he told friends he was going scuba diving (a new passion) in Hawaii but instead checked into Marin County's more secluded Serenity Knolls, closer to home than Betty Ford, in geography as well as in spirit.

At the private funeral in Belvedere on Aug. 11, Deborah Koons Garcia told the mourners her husband had died with a smile on his face—not always the most credible of eulogistic assurances, but not wholly unbelievable in the case of the perpetually

TOUCH OF GRAY: Garcia "died with a smile," his widow said.

smirk-prone Garcia. At the official farewell for Garcia, his girls proved themselves their father's daughters by nudging the reverence level down several notches. "He may have been a genius, but he was a s——y father," said a smiling Annabelle at the private service, more or less echoing her dad's own characterization of his parenting skills. Two days later, at the public memorial in Golden Gate Park, she told the 20,000-strong crowd: "We love each and every one of you because you put us through college. And we didn't have to work at Dairy Queen." Clearly, their father left a legacy of sardonicism.

Those remaining behind are left to speculate further still on how a guy seemingly so bent on submerging his personality to the greater good ended up inspiring such a rabid cult of personality. When original Dead member Ron "Pigpen" McKernan died in 1973, the band was left without a single volatile or even particularly mobile stage presence; rather than boring audiences, this seemed to make them more attentive. Even a trace of a smile from Garcia would throw a crowd into the kind of paroxysms usually reserved for pelvic thrusts.

His refusal to talk on stage was explained as nervousness over having anything he might say received as holy writ. "I always have stage fright," he said in an unpublished interview scheduled for the CD-ROM magazine *Launch*. "I don't feel I have the personal energy to address that large a crowd. It's a special thing that requires a hugeness of being I don't feel I've got. I feel more like the guy who's the apex man on the human pyramid; I'm up there, but I'm up there because everyone else is pushing."

The question remains: Can the Dead live without him? Some of those not willing to give up the exodus hope so. But a pal as partial as Grisman, for one, is doubtful: "He was the emotional content of the Grateful Dead, and most of the musical content as well. He was it. You have to be blind and deaf not to see that. That's what you remember about the Dead, that guitar playing, that voice. He was the guy who was making the atoms move." *Requiescat in pace*—Jerry Garcia, gone fission. *(Reported by Heidi Siegmund Cuda, Chris Garcia, Steve Hochman, Carolyn Littleton, Vicki Jo Radovsky, Jessica Shaw, Russ Spencer)* ◆

MARCH 31. BECAUSE YOU ARE a young man, you recognize her face in an instant. The elevator doors fly open, and there she stands. You know those eyes, brimming wide as teacups. You know those lips, glistening and upturned like a wedge of tangerine. Alicia Silverstone greets you with knock-kneed exasperation, as-suming for a split second that she has wound up on the wrong floor. "Oh, my God!" she says in a whis-pered flurry. "I'm sorry."

Were you a decade older, you might not know her name, and the thought might pass through your brain with-out much consequence: "Pretty girl. Probably an actress." You might take the Memory Lane exit back to high school—Ali-cia Silverstone, after all, is only 18 years old—and recall that cheerleader in your Spanish class, the one you never had the guts to talk to.

But you'd be wrong. Here at the Four Seasons Hotel in Beverly Hills, you're sharing an elevator with *power.* "Huge," casting director Marci Liroff says of Alicia Silverstone. "She's a huge movie star."

Of course, so far Miss Huge has conquered only a corner of the world—the part known in demo-graphic parlance as *guys.* Among those males who frequent fraternity houses and video arcades, the name Silverstone carries more weight than Streep, thanks to her kitten-eyed coup de théâtre in what might be the most popular trilogy of videos in the short history of MTV: Aerosmith's "Cryin'," "Amazing," and "Crazy." In another era, the mak-ing of the girl of the year required at least a few hours to let the dough rise; now you punch a but-ton on the microwave, wait 30 seconds, and serve.

The rest of the world got the news about Alicia Silverstone in June '94. That's when the actress, as *The Crush*'s scheming nymphet, took home two MTV Movie awards for Best Breakthrough Perfor-

THE MAKING OF
ALICIA
SILVERSTONE
BY JEFF GORDINIER AND A. J. JACOBS

mance and Best Villain. Suddenly, Silverstone was more than a video soubrette. "I truly loved doing the videos," she says with a practiced air, "but it's been hard hearing all the time that you're just the Aero-smith chick." Fear not. En route to theaters are *True Crime,* in which a Catholic schoolgirl turns gumshoe, *Le Nouveau Monde,* a Gallic coming-of-age story, and, most notably, *Clueless,* a teen comedy described by its creators as a Rodeo Drive version of Jane Austen's novel *Emma.*

The thing is, Silver-stone is still a teenager, and from time to time she acts like one. Over lunch, she encounters a piece of ligament in the slices of her chicken sandwich. She scrunches up her face, reaches into her mouth, retrieves the meat, and flicks it on a plate.

"They're like morsels or something," she says.

Morsels of what?

"Probably like chicken muscle or something."

Thus it's breathtaking, moments later, when you ask what directors she'd like to work with and she mentions the man responsible for the psychosexual manifestos *Last Tango in Paris* and *The Conformist.*

"Well, I just met Bernardo"—she stumbles a bit with the surname—"How do you say his name?"

Bernardo Bertolucci?

"Yeah, him," she says. "Bernardo Bertolucci."

You just met him?

"Upstairs," she says with a coy laugh. "It would be nice to work with him. He's very brilliant.

"I want to do more classic things," she continues. "I'd love to do Helena Bonham Carter's roles. I've heard her say in articles—and I don't know if they're real, because I don't believe articles any-more—but I've heard her say that she'd like to do contemporary things. So, maybe we could swap." ◆

UPDATE: *See Silverstone's Rookie of the Year en-try on page 66.*

HOLLYWOOD'S RULES HAVE CHANGED. SO WHO'S TO SAY
THAT VIDEO'S LOLITA CAN'T TANGO WITH BERTOLUCCI?

HOLLY

BY ALBERT KIM

OCTOBER 13. LEGEND HAS IT that movie mogul Jack L. Warner banned the appearance of TV sets in all Warner Bros. movies, a desperate symbolic act made to ward off an inevitable sea change in entertainment. Lately, you kind of know how old Jack felt. Yesterday, you were sitting in your den, somnolent and content amid your CD collection and videotape library, awash in the glow of your 50-channel TV. Today, you're a casualty of the digital revolution, one of those odd statistics in *USA Today. Number of people who haven't surfed the Net, who don't have a CD-ROM, and who in general will be left behind when tomorrow comes: You.*

But Hollywood learned its lesson from Warner all those years ago: Wishing something away only makes the eventual shock of reality that much worse. According to InfoTech, a Vermont-based research firm, there were 1.2 million CD-ROM players worldwide at the turn of the decade; this year, there are an estimated 46 million. In that same period, the number of subscribers to online services (primarily America Online, CompuServe, and Prodigy) exploded from 1.7 million to 11 million, according to estimates by the market research firm SIMBA Information. By 1999, that number is projected to hit 26.3 million.

Actually, the concept of multimedia was banging around in our collective consciousness long before computers entered the picture. It's a term first used in the '60s to describe educational projects that combined audio, visual, and textual materials. Then, in the '70s, rock promoters lured dreamy-eyed teens to laser light shows set to psychedelic music by trumpeting the whole shebang as a multimedia extravaganza. But in the early '90s, around the time Hollywood executives adopted the PowerBook as a fashion accessory, multimedia took on a new dimension. A new technology, CD-Read Only Memory, entered the equation, and with it, that novel but fuzzily defined concept, interactivity.

Then an old Cold War artifact came into play: a sprawling computer network, begun as a Defense Department experiment, called the Internet. Suddenly multimedia was no longer the sole province of geeks and trippers. The press, ever in search of a zeitgeist-friendly trend, pounced and began spreading word of the digital revolution, a.k.a. the Information Age, a.k.a. the Bit Bang. Next thing you know, cable systems and telephone companies and movie studios were scrambling to get in bed with each other, and Newt Gingrich was droning on about cyberspace being the "land of knowledge," and Dennis Hopper was doing his trademark bad-guy act, but this time in a videogame.

Every movie company, record label, book publisher, and television network worth its silicon now

WIRED

Edwards, who hosted a nationally broadcast infomercial for the product; the Rolling Stones, who licensed out "Start Me Up" for Microsoft's TV spots; and basketball's star rapper Shaquille O'Neal, who has his own chat room on Microsoft's new online service.

Software as celebrity: By reflection, celebrities as software shouldn't be such a strange notion. In 1993, past-his-peak actor Corey Haim filmed a few scenes for a forgettable CD-ROM game titled *Double Switch*, and publications from *Billboard* to *The San Francisco Chronicle* took notice. This year, hardly an eyebrow was raised when an interactive movie called *Ripper* began shooting. Its cast includes Karen Allen, Ossie Davis, Oscar nominee Burgess Meredith, and Oscar winner Christopher Walken. Sometime in those two years, between *Double Switch* and *Ripper*, Hollywired was born.

For now, at least, the medium may be more compelling than the message, which still consists mainly of promotional or repackaged programming. But be patient. The future, as they say, is just a matter of time. "I've had the good fortune to twice be placed in history at the beginning of a wonderful new technology," says Charlton Heston, who recently completed work on the CD-ROM *Charlton Heston's Voyage Through the Bible*. "With TV in the '40s, and now with multimedia. In both cases, the new media represented the future of the moving image."

The future of the moving image... One hundred years ago, French audiences sat in a darkened Parisian basement and screamed in terror at the vision of a train rushing toward them, a scene from the Lumière brothers' *L'Arrivée d'un Train en Gare de la Ciotat*, the world's first commercial motion picture. A century later, the future of the moving image again hurtles inexorably toward a wary audience. And if the metaphor grabs you, heed this note: Stop screaming—the train is already here. ◆ *(Additional reporting by Lisa Milbrand and Ken Neville)*

sports a new interactive division, as well as a plot of virtual land on the Internet's World Wide Web. But more importantly, the digital revolution has affected the Hollywood ethos in a fundamental sense. In August, Microsoft released Windows 95, its new operating system, and enlisted a phalanx of celebrities for support. No one so much as blinked at what would once have seemed a laughable incongruity: stars and software. Among those unafraid to plug the event unabashedly (for a fee, of course) were Jay Leno, who emceed the launch party; *ER*'s Anthony

FROM SPIELBERG ON CD-ROM TO SHATNER ONLINE, CELEBS IN TINSELTOWN ARE PLUGGING INTO MULTIMEDIA

JULY 14. OVER LUNCH AT A QUIET middlebrow restaurant in Los Angeles, Kevin Costner is talking a blue streak. For weeks, he has been caged in editing rooms, trying to make sense of the sometimes thrilling, sometimes sprawling *Waterworld* footage, racing toward a July 28 release date. He's the star of the show, a producer, and now—in the wake of some brutal battles fought during production—an investor in the film and its surrogate director. "I'm not doing this

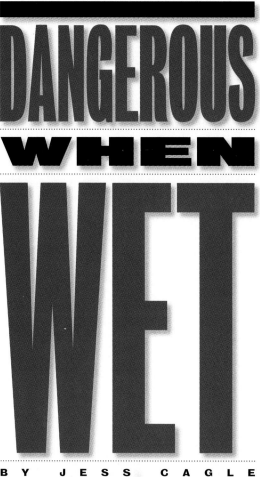

because I love this," he says. "I really wanted to be in the mountains fishing this summer and hunting. I did not want to be in the editing room. That wasn't my job. It wasn't something I signed on for. I didn't want it. *I don't know how to make that any clearer.*"

How'd it come to this?

The answer will explain how *Waterworld* gobbled up a record budget, generating a record amount of ink on, variously, reports of the volatile Hawaiian weather that plagued the production, rumors that an on-location affair led to Costner's decision to divorce while filming last October, and gossip about the runaway cost—estimated conservatively at $160 million, liberally at $180 million. Even *The Wall Street Journal* hit the pool, announcing—*quel scandale!*—that there were no bathrooms on the atoll set. The answer will also explain how the film began without a finished script and finished off, perhaps once and for all, the star's rocky 10-year friendship with director Kevin Reynolds, who jumped ship after Costner took over editing duties. "In the future, Costner should only appear in pictures he directs himself," says Reynolds. "That way he can always work with his favorite actor and his favorite director."

"All I know is that I'm going to work every day trying to fix problems, trying to make a movie for people spending seven dollars to go see and enjoy," Costner says.

Waterworld's byzantine history began nearly a decade ago in the fertile brain of a 1983 Harvard graduate named Peter Rader. In 1986, Rader, an aspiring director, had two meetings at the production company New Horizon. He was first told that if he wrote the script, he could direct. He arrived at his next meeting bright-eyed and hopeful: "I've got this brand-new spin. What if we set the entire thing on water?"

"Are you crazy?" they replied. "A movie like that would cost us $5 million!"

New Horizon passed, and Rader decided to write the script on spec. In 1989, Lawrence Gordon's Largo Entertainment purchased *Waterworld* for a price in the mid–six figures and asked for rewrites. There were seven drafts over the next two years, and then, in 1991, a miracle happened. Costner phoned Lawrence Gordon's brother Chuck, who had a production deal with Largo. "What's this thing called *Waterworld*?" Costner asked. Gordon sent him the screenplay, and Costner called to say he was interested.

Within days, Kevin Reynolds called: "What ever

HOW IN THE 'WATERWORLD' DID KEVIN COSTNER'S EPIC GET TO BE SO OVER BUDGET, OVER SCHEDULE, AND OVERWROUGHT?

happened to that project *Waterworld?*"

"Funny you should mention it," Chuck Gordon told him. "A giant movie star is interested in it."

Reynolds and Costner had already met.

Sixteen years ago, Kevin Reynolds, now 45, was a golden boy. Steven Spielberg had produced his 1985 feature debut, a road comedy called *Fandango.* Reynolds auditioned Costner, now 40, and gave him his first starring role, and they hit it off. Both are principled—some would say stubborn—men who like to have their way with their vision of a film.

When Costner was making his directorial debut on *Dances With Wolves*, Reynolds stepped in to help with some of the more complicated scenes. In his first flush of superstardom, Costner hired Reynolds to direct *Robin Hood: Prince of Thieves* (1991). Then their relationship went sour. They played creative tug-of-war over Costner's insistence on trying an English accent and squabbled over script and editing changes. Reynolds walked off the film during the editing. The two stopped speaking.

"I'm not interested," said Reynolds when Gordon disclosed the identity of the giant movie star who had set his sights on *Waterworld.*

"I'm not going to do it," Costner told Gordon. "But I really think [Reynolds] is the right guy to direct it."

Gordon finally persuaded the two Kevins to meet in Lake Tahoe, where Costner was shooting *The Bodyguard.* There they resolved their differences—"I *thought* we did," says Costner—and agreed to try working together again.

Reynolds, Costner, and Gordon's first order of business was to overhaul Rader's script. They kept his basic concept—a future in which the polar ice caps have melted and the earth is underwater. Reynolds put gills on the Mariner (Costner's character), one of the first human beings to mutate and adapt to this wet new world, while Costner pushed for him to be something more than a standard action hero. So he became a grizzled loner reluctantly saddled with a beautiful woman and her adopted daughter, whose tattoo of a map to dry land makes her a target of the villainous Deacon.

But early on, the old conflicts between Costner and Reynolds resurfaced. "Kevin Reynolds saw this as a movie that could redefine '90s action," says Marc Norman, who composed three drafts of *Wa-*

WATERLOGGED: Costner as the Mariner

terworld. "Costner also wanted that kind of action, but not at the expense of character."

Reynolds had planned on polishing the script further before shooting. But Costner—worried about the June 1994 start date—took it into his hands, ordering his own writers to work on it. Reynolds claims Costner took control of the script when they "were still months away from shooting."

"Kevin [Reynolds] said, 'If you were director, would you let somebody do what you're doing right now?'" Costner recalls. "And I said, 'No, but *I* wouldn't *be* in this position.'"

Crags of black lava line the way to Kawaihae Harbor on the island of Hawaii, where most of *Waterworld* was shot. Kawaihae means "warring waters."

In May 1994, the cast joined the 500-plus crew on the island. Jeanne Tripplehorn (*The Firm*) would play the Mariner's sexy atoll passenger. Tina Majorino (*Corrina, Corrina*) beat out Oscar winner Anna Paquin as the tattooed tyke. Dennis Hopper signed on as the Deacon after shooting began. Throughout June, *Waterworld*'s crew built the trimaran—the Mariner's 60-foot sailing vessel (two were built, costing at least $500,000 each); a floating "slave colony"; and the atoll, a doughnut-shaped metal jumble that would become a metaphor for the gargantuan production itself. Originally budgeted at $1.5 million, the atoll, constructed of 1,000 tons of steel, ultimately weighed in at $5 million.

On June 27, 1994, the adventure began. "The winds were terrible," says one crew member. "Some days we couldn't shoot at all." Shots were often ruined by other boats on the horizon, and angles from inside the atoll sometimes caught glimpses of mountains in the distance—a *Waterworld* no-no. An effects crew, operating in an expensive postproduction crunch, had to correct the glitches by computer.

The two Kevins eased into a truce, but now it was Universal's turn to make noise. For one thing, high-profile crew members kept leaving. Peter Chesney, the designer who helped create the atoll's elephantine gates, was reportedly forced off the set in August, along with effects liaison Kate Steinberg. Gone by Labor Day was frustrated first assistant director Alan Curtiss, who production sources say had tried to convince the studio from the start that the picture couldn't be finished in the

96 originally scheduled days. Curtiss thought it needed 135; it eventually took 166.

By the time Curtiss quit, the budget had risen to $135 million, and a production scheduled to end before October's hurricane season had no end in sight.

In October, hurricane season arrived—though the biggest storm was Costner's announcement that he and his wife, Cindy, the mother of his three children, were divorcing after 16 years of marriage. The announcement only whetted the appetite of the press, already hungry for details from the set, which had been closed to journalists. Costner even banned the tabloids themselves from the set after he saw a crew member with one that carried his photo on the cover. "This doesn't help me at all to have this sitting here," he told the worker. "I'm really happy you have time to read this. I wish I had the time." And when Hopper tried to show Costner a tabloid article, Costner got up and walked away. "I don't ask for a lot on the set," he says. "Be quiet, don't read my tabloid headlines to me."

By the time the production moved to L.A. early this year, the bill was up to $150 million.

Back on dry land, Reynolds shot underwater city sequences in tanks at Huntington Beach and scenes of the Deacon's tanker (a replica of the *Exxon Valdez*) on a field south of L.A. Footage of the 110-foot tanker miniature had already been shot in the Mojave Desert, so the filmmakers started on postproduction, producing such elaborate visual effects as a computer-generated ocean and creating a giant sea creature from scratch.

STORM: Costner's marriage collapsed

Meanwhile, whatever détente the two Kevins had reached was icing over in the editing room. Costner predicted that the cuts Reynolds would choose would leave the film with nothing but "wall-to-wall action, which the movie couldn't sustain. It's not *good* enough to be wall-to-wall action."

"[Costner's] biggest concern was the Mariner," says Reynolds. "Mine was the story. I wanted a coherent tale from beginning to end." Says screenwriter David Twohy, "There should be one director on a movie, one clear voice. When you have a star as talented and powerful as Kevin, it leads to pushing and pulling. Sometimes that can hurt a film."

Reynolds took Universal's suggestions on the condition that he'd also prepare his own version for a Directors Guild of America screening—a standard part of postproduction. He says the producers agreed, but that Costner and Chuck Gordon wanted "a day or so" to edit the film. "A week later, they were still cutting," says Reynolds. When the producers said there was no longer time for him to preview the movie for the DGA, "I finally said, 'I'm not going to work like this.' That's when I left."

Ten days later, on May 9, the lights went down on a test screening of the producers' rough cut in Sacramento. The audience had been invited to "a new action movie with a major Hollywood star." At 7:25 p.m., they were told it was *Waterworld*. "I want my money back!" shouted one man. "I *knew* it would be this f---ing movie!" The print received lukewarm to bad reviews. As of late June, camera crews were on Catalina island, still working, taking shots of the ocean.

These days, the two Kevins are once again not speaking. Reynolds says his next project is to move to Seattle with his wife and daughter. "I'm taking some time off," he says. "Next year I want to do a really small movie, more personal." Starring who? "Starring nobody."

At the end of *his* interview, Costner, still in a gentlemanly good mood, boards his big white Chevrolet and heads back to work. He idles in traffic on a bridge that spans a small gully. A woman has parked on the side so her little girl can get out and gaze over the guardrail at the water.

"I keep thinking that woman is going to toss that kid over," says Costner. He pulls the great white vehicle forward and thinks on this further. "I'll have to jump in and save her." Now he's smiling again, and he laughs at himself. "I hope the music's playing when I go." ◆ (*Additional reporting by Gregg Kilday, with Pat H. Broeske, Michael Szymanski, and Jeffrey Wells*)

UPDATE: *Waterworld's U.S. gross was $82.5 million, about half of what the movie cost to make.*

"IN THE FUTURE, KEVIN SHOULD ONLY APPEAR IN PICTURES THAT HE DIRECTS HIMSELF," SAYS DIRECTOR REYNOLDS OF COSTNER

MARCH 17. THE IRONIES RAN DEEPER than the lines of fans who camped out overnight for R.E.M. tickets. Seven weeks into the band's almost yearlong world tour, Bill Berry, the group's congenial drummer, was talking about how happy he was to be back doing what he loved best—playing amp-pulverizing rock & roll. "It can't get too loud for me," he said in his soft Georgia drawl. "If I had the hair for it, I'd be in a metal band." Sipping soup in a chilly backstage

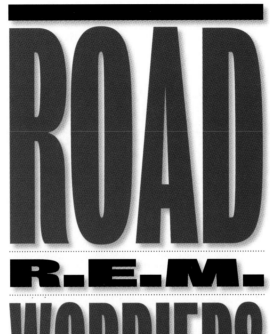

ROAD
R.E.M.
WORRIERS
BY DAVID BROWNE

area in Rome, Italy, Berry, 36, spoke of how much he had matured in the five years since the band had temporarily retired from the road. "I was 30 on the last tour, and I had the brain of a 20-year-old," he admitted. "The tours would end, and it was like, hey, the party keeps on. On the last tour, I was a mess. I was drinking too much. That's not gonna happen this time."

It was clear that the members of R.E.M., no strangers to a bit of rock & roll high life, were taking better care of themselves. Guitarist Peter Buck, 38, had shed some of his extra poundage and was joined on the road by his new wife and their 9-month-old twins. The group had bought a treadmill machine for exercising before shows, while Berry and bass player Mike Mills, 36, brought along their golf clubs. ("When we're in the States, they'll probably be up before *me* to play nine holes," cracked tour manager Dave Russell.) When not on tour, Berry lives quietly in a restored colonial house outside of R.E.M.'s home base, Athens, Ga., with his wife, Mari. Says longtime band friend Jim Herbert: "The guy was never affected by fame."

A week later, all that preparation amounted to zip. On stage in Lausanne, Switzerland, on March 1, the drummer was seized by a massive headache and

left the stage. Back at the band's hotel, doctors examined Berry and assumed the problem was a migraine. When the headaches continued, he was checked into a local hospital, where it was discovered that he had suffered a ruptured aneurysm (a burst blood vessel) on the right side of his brain. On March 3, Berry had a craniotomy for not one but two aneurysms—the one that had ruptured and one that could have.

Three days later, Karen Moss, a vice president at Warner Bros., the band's label, reported, "They're saying he'll make a 100 percent recovery, but they can't tell how soon that will be"; and on March 6, the band announced it was canceling all its European tour dates through April 20. On the eve of returning as conquering heroes, R.E.M.—who hadn't toured since 1989 in order to save themselves from the rigors of the road—ironically found themselves victims of something worse than backstage food. One of the year's most awaited tours became that much more anticipated—but for all the wrong reasons.

THE IRONIES don't end there. According to Michael Stipe, the group's lead singer, it was Berry who initially goaded them into hitting the concert circuit again. "Bill was the first one to pick up on the

IN A WORLD GONE ALTERNATIVE, R.E.M. ARE ROYALTY, ALBEIT ROYALTY WEARING T-SHIRTS AND CONVERSE SNEAKERS

"WE WERE EITHER GONNA BREAK UP OR EXPLORE NEW OPTIONS," SAID DRUMMER BERRY. THEY OPTED FOR THE LATTER.

ROMAN HOLIDAY: Stipe admits the group almost quit the road after their grueling 1989 *Green* tour

fact that as a band, we were a little bit falling apart," said Stipe, 35. "We realized we were not going to be our idea of a band if we didn't tour again. In a way, it was a little bit of an effort to pull us back together."

What kept R.E.M. off the road all that time were memories of their grueling 1989 *Green* tour, the already-established band's first foray into actual arenas. "It got to be really routine, like a job," recalled Mills of those concerts. Added Berry, "We were either gonna break the band up or explore some new avenues." They opted for the latter, which included two relatively unconventional albums (*Out of Time* and *Automatic for the People*), a lengthy break from the road, few interviews—and, ironically, combined album sales of 6.5 million.

The rewards of such unintentional mystique building were evident when tickets for the band's

1995 U.S. tour went on sale over the Jan. 21 weekend: In all 18 cities, concerts sold out in roughly an hour. An R.E.M. insider said the cost of mounting the tour would be "several million dollars"—not counting lost revenue from the canceled European shows—yet industry observers predicted it would easily be one of the year's top earners, with the potential to gross at least $50 million. In a world gone alternative, R.E.M. are royalty, albeit royalty given to wearing T-shirts and Converse sneakers.

On the road, the changes in their status were evident in more ways than fiscal statistics. There were the six massive equipment trucks, the nine buses (including one per band member), the four chefs who whipped up delectable Thai or Mexican meals every night, the 47-person road crew. There was the Ping-Pong table and the backstage room where Buck and backup multi-instrumentalist Scott McCaughey would drop off their children. "Nobody wants to ride on my bus, because I have kids," said Buck, "and I don't blame them. It's not exactly rock & roll Valhalla. On a real big night, I get to listen to one CD."

R.E.M. themselves strive to maintain their street cred despite arena status. In Rome, the band stopped into a tiny basement club to see a Sicilian rock band, where they signed autographs and allowed stunned clubgoers to take photographs—an almost unimaginable gesture for a band of their stature. Yet they raised eyebrows bigger than Berry's continuous one when they opted to use Ticketmaster, especially since Bertis Downs, the group's lawyer, had testified against the company during last year's Pearl Jam-instigated congressional hearing. "Ticketmaster as the only company is bad for business, but it left us with no choice," Downs said in Rome. "It feels hypocritical, and we've taken some heat for it, but we want to play shows."

When the discussion turned to Green Day's charging a maximum $15 per ticket (as opposed to R.E.M.'s $35 average), Buck added, "That's a great thing. But then again, they haven't exactly gone out and played 15 years. We did low-budget shows, and lived low budget, for years, and I'm not gonna throw away money to prove a point."

R.E.M. played their first shows in Athens when Jimmy Carter was President, and as men approaching 40, they *have* earned the right to a good salary—and a little extra glory. "You know when it hit me?" Berry said, pondering the band's new status. "When we played 'Losing My Religion' in Madrid and they sang the first two words, 'Oh, life,' it was louder than the band. That was the difference between what we were in 1989 and being like Bruce Springsteen or Michael Jackson. But it was a great feeling, I must say."

YET ANOTHER IRONY—or omen, if you will—came the night of R.E.M.'s first of two Rome concerts at the sports arena Palaeur, exactly a week before Berry's collapse. One verse into the opening song, "What's the Frequency, Kenneth?" the sound

MAN ON THE MOON: Berry suffered an aneurysm on tour

and lights twice went dead. Then, during "Man on the Moon," it happened *again*. "What the f--- is going on?" said Stipe from the stage, his soft murmur of a voice flashing a twinge of anger. "Did someone put a curse on us or something?"

The crowd didn't mind, nor did they care that the sound system reduced much of the music to a wind tunnel with a beat, or that the intimacy of songs from *Automatic for the People* was swallowed up in the cavernous space. They didn't even seem concerned that the two-hour show concentrated heavily on the band's last three albums, omitting early hits like "Fall on Me" or "The One I Love." They greeted the recent hits (and the arty films behind the band) with cigarette-lighter salutes and a lusty, aerobics-class abandon.

What *was* evident from the Rome concerts is that R.E.M. are both the most natural and least natural arena band on the planet. Mills, looking like a Hollywood cowboy, worked the front rows as if he were perfectly at home. Stipe, coming off like an underfed white hip-hop kid with his shaved head and wool hat, addressed the crowd with oddball, deadpan comments ("We're going to play a song, and then another song after that") and sang "Country Feedback" with his back to the audience. The following night, as part of their plan to stave off boredom, they replaced 30 percent of the set list with different songs, including a rare performance of "S. Central Rain (I'm Sorry)."

Back at their hotel—the same one, strangely enough, where Kurt Cobain had attempted suicide 11 months before—the band and a few friends and family members commandeered the bar. In light of the double-whammy power outage (caused, it turned out, by a fluctuation in the venue's house power), Berry, Buck, and Mills truly needed to chill out.

"You feel like a total d---head, but you keep playing," Buck said as he unwound with a glass of wine. "If you don't accept a few bumps in the road, there's no point in doing it." Berry, standing nearby, grinned his consent and grabbed a beer. In retrospect, it was an eerie coincidence in a situation loaded with them. ◆

UPDATE: *The recovered Berry finished R.E.M.'s foreign and U.S. tour dates, which ended in November.*

JOHN GRISHAM

EXPOUNDS ON THE PRICE OF FAME, BAD REVIEWS, AND HOLLYWOOD

ATTORNEY'S PRIVILEGES

BY MARK HARRIS

MAY 5. JOHN GRISHAM's *The Rainmaker* isn't an autobiography, but the title—jargon for an attorney able to generate gigantic cash windfalls—couldn't be more applicable to its creator. Immediately upon publication, Grisham's sixth novel, a darkly funny story about an impoverished young lawyer doing battle with a corrupt insurance company, shot to No. 1 on hardcover bestseller lists, while his 1994 death-penalty novel, *The Chamber*, has topped paperback lists since March. Grisham's Midas touch extends to Hollywood as well; movies made from his previous novels *The Firm, The Pelican Brief,* and *The Client* have been major successes, and the coming year will bring films of his 1989 courtroom saga, *A Time to Kill*, which set a record with its $6 million-plus movie sale, as well as *The Chamber*. In addition, CBS has just finished filming the pilot for a television series based on *The Client*, starring JoBeth Williams. On a recent trip to New York from his home in Oxford, Miss., where he lives with his wife Renée (above), Grisham spoke about his critics and his movies.

ENTERTAINMENT WEEKLY: *You're getting great reviews for* The Rainmaker. *How sensitive are you to bad ones?*

GRISHAM: I was pretty uptight about them at first. The only place where *A Time to Kill* got reviewed was the Memphis paper—my home paper—and they trashed it. That was a deep wound that has never healed. Then *The Firm* came out, and most reviews were pretty good. *Pelican* was painful from coast to coast. I'd read a bad review and want to go out and kill people. *The Client* was next, and it got trashed—the reviews started talking about the fame and the money. Pat Conroy [*The Prince of Tides*] told me, "Your life is a whole lot easier if you stop reading reviews." So I stopped reading almost all of them.

EW: *What kind of control would you like to have over your movie adaptations?*

GRISHAM: I'm still scared of Hollywood. I've been lucky. I've had three films—all very enjoyable, all commercially successful. I got to meet the stars, and then I went back to my farm to coach Little League where I belong. And after three movies, that's still the way to do it. Now *A Time to Kill* is different, because I have script approval and I have the right to be consulted on casting. I'll get script approval with *The Rainmaker*, or I won't sell it.

EW: *What's going on with* The Chamber?

GRISHAM: We sold the film rights [to Universal, which had originally hoped to have Ron Howard direct] based on an idea. I thought they were crazy, offering me $3.75 million for a book that I had not written—and I thought, Well, I might just be stupid enough to take it. Now I wish I hadn't sold the rights before I wrote the book, and I'll never do that again. It's a lesson I learned. Ron and I talked about the story all the way through. And I said, "I won't tell you how to make the movie; you won't tell me how to write the book." We laughed about that. But some of the studio people had ideas about what should be in the book, and it was infuriating.

EW: *And what would you like to accomplish next as a writer?*

GRISHAM: I don't know. I'd love to write great literature. I'd love to be a great writer. I'd love to write really good, serious books. And I'd want them to sell. ◆

OCTOBER 20. YOU'RE BORED. You could drive to the cineplex to see Sylvester Stallone and Antonio Banderas run around in *Assassins, or* you could stay home and watch Rachel pine for Ross on *Friends*. What do you do? If you're smart, you stay home. Sure, great movies still come along, and TV still shows junk. But as a rule, you've got a greater chance of finding something good on TV than at the movies. Cynical? Read these 10 reasons why the small screen is superior.

TV SAVES THE WORLD

BY BRUCE FRETTS

AS THE YEAR'S MOVIES FELL FLAT, **TV** SOARED HIGH!

1 WOMEN THRIVE ON TV. With *Roseanne, Grace Under Fire, Murphy Brown, Caroline in the City,* and *Ellen* near the top of the Nielsens, there's no shortage of strong TV women. No wonder *seven* Oscar-nominated actresses joined TV series this season alone: Christine Lahti (*Chicago Hope*), Mercedes Ruehl (*Frasier*), Elizabeth McGovern (*If Not for You*), Mariel Hemingway (*Central Park West*), Cathy Moriarty (*Bless This House*), and Madeline Kahn and Mary Tyler Moore (*New York News*). Now look at the scintillating parts for women in some of the year's movies: Gwyneth Paltrow cooks supper for Brad Pitt and Morgan Freeman in *Seven*; Julianne Moore plays a cat-loving "surveillance expert" who snuggles up to Stallone in *Assassins*. Are TV execs feminist and movie execs sexist? Nope. It all comes down to money. The key to huge opening weekends for movies is young men; they're also the most likely to give a film repeat business. As a result, says McGovern, "parts in movies for women tend to be less interesting." On the other hand, she adds, "TV advertisers go after women, and women have the need to see themselves reflected in interesting, dimensional characters."

2 WE CARE MORE ABOUT TV CHARACTERS. Most movie characters are one-night stands. TV characters are long-term friends. For example, we've spent 11 years with Dr. Frasier Crane. "Because the audience is well acquainted with Frasier, there's a whole world of history we can draw on," says Kelsey Grammer. "This is somebody they *know*." On the big screen, characters are often larger-than-life figures caught up in extraordinary situations, with their personalities secondary to the story lines. Even after all these years, do we really *know* James Bond? Roseanne, however, has spent seven years wringing big laughs out of the eminently relatable struggles of an average American family.

3 TV DOES BETTER WITH DRAMA. While primetime TV has entered a new golden age of dramas, movie studios seem less interested than ever in the genre. Why? Because it's hard to sell overseas, appeals to older audiences less likely to go to the movies, and rarely generates blockbusters.

POWERFUL WOMEN! DEEPER CHARACTERS! TONS OF DRAMA!

GREAT DAMES: TV OFFERS MEATY ROLES FOR ROSEANNE (WITH LECY GORANSON, LEFT) AND **HOPE**'S LAHTI (RIGHT), BUT MOVIES ARE THE PITTS FOR **SEVEN**'S PAL-TROW (BELOW LEFT)

THE SMART SET: JIM CARREY (CENTER) REFLECTS ONE **DUMB**-ENSION, WHEREAS **FRASIER** (BELOW) AND HBO'S **LARRY SANDERS SHOW** (FAR RIGHT) ARE MORE COMPLEX COMEDIES.

DRAMA CLUB: WHILE QUALITY SHOWS LIKE **MURDER ONE** (WITH DANIEL BENZALI, NEAR LEFT) ARE ALL OVER THE SMALL SCREEN, SERIOUS FILMS LIKE LAST YEAR'S **QUIZ SHOW** (RIGHT, WITH PAUL SCOFIELD AND RALPH FIENNES) ARE BECOMING AN ENDANGERED SPECIES.

"There's an argument that says, 'Why bother going to a theater to see a small character drama?'" says Twentieth Century Fox Films chairman Peter Chernin, former head of the Fox TV network. "People say, 'Yeah, I think I'll wait to see that on video.'"

A few years ago, TV execs had all but written off dramas as commercially unviable, too. Then *NYPD Blue* took an in-depth look at the human condition and hit the top 20. And *ER* took an inside look at the human body—and hit No. 1. Suddenly, TV dramas have a pulse again.

4 IN TV, THE WRITER RULES. As *ER* executive producer John Wells explains: "The train leaves the station on the first day of a series, and you have to continue to provide material. The person who makes that happen is the writer." Like Wells, TV's true auteurs—*NYPD*'s Steven Bochco, *Larry Sanders*' Garry Shandling, *Friends*' Marta Kauffman and David Crane—have never severed their roots as writers. Television "is totally writer driven," says *Roseanne*'s executive producer Eric Gilliland. "If other people get in charge, it's going to be a mish-mash." Which is a good description of most movies today. Studio execs want formula product with feel-good endings, and directors seem more concerned with visual fireworks than coherent stories.

5 TV IS MORE FUN TO TALK ABOUT. Half the kick of *Melrose Place* is watching it with friends and busting on the unbelievably stupid people on screen. That's what led bars like Baja Sharkeez in Manhattan Beach, Calif., and the aptly named Jake's Dilemma on Manhattan's Upper West Side to start *Melrose* nights on Mondays. "It's like a big party," says Baja Sharkeez owner Greg Newman. "A movie theater isn't a big party."

6 TV DEALS WITH "MATURE THEMES" MORE MATURELY. Sometimes censorship can force writers and directors to be more creative. *NYPD*'s tastefully suggestive love scenes are more titillating than *Showgirls*' full-frontal assault. And the horrors of police work are less graphic but more evocative on *NYPD* and *Homicide* than in *Seven* and *Die Hard With a Vengeance*. "We see the aftermath of violence—we see death, but we're very cautious," says *Homicide*'s executive producer Tom Fontana. "Movies can do anything. It's easy to say, 'Let's blow his head off.'"

7 TV IS MORE CONVENIENT. An unscientific survey of moviegoers in New York and L.A. yielded the following complaints: Movies cost too much. You have to wait in line. They sell out. People talk during the show. The seats are uncomfortable. People with big hats sit in front of you. The snacks are too expensive. By contrast, TV is a veritable paradise. It's cheap. There are no lines. It never sells out. You can shush talkers without getting dirty looks. You can sit where you want, wear what you want, and eat what you want—including popcorn with real butter. Best of all, parking is never a problem. "I promised my dad he wouldn't have to go down to the city to see my movies," says Cathy Moriarty of her decision to do *Bless This House*. "He'd be able to watch me in his chair." So *that* explains why she's costarring with Andrew Clay.

8 TV DOES MORE WITH LESS MONEY. HBO's *Truman* cost $8 million; Oliver Stone's *Nixon* cost $43 million. "With TV, there's a limit—spend much more, somebody closes you down," says Frank Price, producer of HBO's *The Tuskegee Airmen* and former head of Columbia and Universal. "It's impossible to get into a *Waterworld* situation." In fact, NBC shut down the James Clavell miniseries *Gai-Jin* early this year when it went over budget. *The X-Files* costs about $1.5 million per hour, a drop in the ocean compared with the $175 million *Waterworld*. Yet *X-Files* creator and exec producer Chris Carter says he gets movie-quality production values by skimping on effects and making maximal use of locations (a Canadian battleship was used for four different sequences last season).

9 JAMES BURROWS DOES TV. Can any current cinematic comedy director match Burrows' TV CV? *The Mary Tyler Moore Show*, *Taxi*, *Cheers*, *Frasier*, *Friends*, as well as *NewsRadio*, *Partners*, and *Caroline in the City*. Maybe the early Woody Allen rivaled Burrows. But Burrows' light farcical touch seems even nimbler when compared with the sledgehammer approach of a filmmaker like Chris Columbus (*Home Alone*, *Nine Months*).

10 YOU CAN CHANGE THE CHANNEL. If a TV show stinks, you can surf around for something that stinks less. But in a theater, you're stuck; you can try sneaking into another movie, but you may get nailed by an usher. In today's "multichannel environment," prime-time network shows can't afford to be less riveting than the Weather Channel. And they have to maintain quality—if a series loses its spark, it risks losing its viewership. Just ask the cast of *Northern Exposure*. ◆ *(Additional reporting by Kristen Baldwin, Steve Daly, Dave Karger, Dana Kennedy, Kate Meyers, Lisa Milbrand, Dan Snierson, Anne Thompson, Gary Eng Walk, and Bret Watson)*

GOOD WRITING! BETTER SEX! SOMETHING TO TALK ABOUT!

WRITE AND WRONG: A SINGLE HALF-HOUR EPISODE OF **FRIENDS** (RIGHT) PACKS MORE LAUGHS THAN THE ENTIRE **FLINTSTONES** MOVIE, WHICH A TOTAL OF 35 SCRIBES TOILED TO MAKE FUNNY.

WITS AND ASS: MASTURBATION WAS TASTEFULLY HANDLED BY **SEINFELD** (LEFT, WITH JASON ALEXANDER), AS **SHOWGIRLS** (RIGHT, WITH ELIZABETH BERKELEY) SHOWED TOO MUCH.

CHATTERBOX: SHOWS LIKE **THE X-FILES** (BELOW) AND **MELROSE PLACE** HAVE OUT-OF-THIS-WORLD BUZZ POTENTIAL AND CREATE WATERCOOLER KLATCHES.

AUGUST 18. YOU HAVE to wonder what Selena would have thought of the vigil outside Craig's Record Factory on the south side of Corpus Christi, Tex., the night her album *Dreaming of You* was released. Assembled in the shopping-center parking lot, teenage girls, dressed and made up in the style of the slain Tejano music queen, were prancing and lip-synching to her beach-blanket anthem "Bidi Bidi Bom Bom," their heroine's 1994 novelty hit. In all, some 4,000 Selena fans had jammed into a roped area meant for 1,500 as searchlights swept the sky. A few wept, but most were there to party. Selena had called Corpus Christi home, and they roared as one at every mention of her name; they held their ground when the pushing escalated to mosh-pit levels. They devoured the free food dispensed by the record store's clerks, and whooped encouragement to the 75 strutting, Selena-swiveling lip-synch contestants, who ranged from toddlers to twentysomethings.

Then, at 12:01 a.m. on Tuesday, July 18, the doors of Craig's flung open, and a well-mannered group began snapping up Selena's musical last will and testament. Thirty-year-old Alice Doria, a housewife from nearby Odem, was the first to buy Selena's posthumous album *Dreaming of You.* "I bought a cassette and a CD," said Doria, who'd been in line since 12:30 that afternoon with her daughter, two nieces, and a neighbor. "I'm gonna put one away and play one till it wears out. Then I'm gonna buy another."

Gunned down March 31 by her fan-club president and boutique manager, Yolanda Saldívar, 34, in a dispute over missing funds, 23-year-old Selena Quin-

SELENA BORN AGAIN

BY JOHN MORTHLAND

tanilla-Pérez was an American-born woman who sang in Spanish and had dreams of topping the charts like Madonna. Four months after her death, she did just that. *Dreaming of You*, an agreeable hodgepodge of pop that includes the four English songs she'd completed, sold 175,000 copies its first day, and 331,000 its first week. Sales of Selena's last album, *Amor Prohibido*, almost tripled, reaching 1.5 million copies; overall, her EMI Latin catalog improved by 2.4 million. Selena's music is suddenly speaking to people who'd previously never heard of *Tejano.*

Selena's crossover dream wasn't hers alone. Though nearly all Tejano artists—who fuse Mexican, pop, polka, and country sounds—are born in the U.S., they sing in Spanish to affirm their common bond. Selena's rock-solid family life and devotion to God made her a role model and more.

Thousands of fans—she has large followings in the Southwest, L.A., and Chicago—made the pilgrimage to Corpus Christi this summer. They make the rounds to their idol's grave (shown above), home, and business headquarters, where they hold vigils or leave flowers. Then they move on to Selena Etc., the boutique that she founded—and that was managed by Saldívar. Families wander through the converted house, admiring the memorabilia and looking through racks of clothing while beauticians calmly fix the hair and nails of customers.

The only thing missing from the flourishing Selena business is Selena herself. ◆

UPDATE: *On Oct. 23, Yolanda Saldívar was convicted of murder and sentenced to life; she plans to appeal the decision.*

THE YOUNG TEJANO SINGER HAD A ROCK-SOLID FAMILY LIFE AND DEVOTION TO GOD THAT MADE HER A ROLE MODEL

movies

NIXON

1

OLIVER STONE PUSHES his hell-bent propulsive sensibility into a new realm of manic truth-telling. In his brilliant, kaleidoscopic dramatization of the life of Richard Nixon, he shows us the Nixon we all know in our bones—the sweaty, stiff-backed paranoiac, his heart black with self-pity—and then takes us deep into the back rooms of postwar history to lay bare how Nixon's pathology, his belief that deliverance was attainable through lies, served and finally extended an ominous shadow government. Using the vertiginous multimedia style he developed in *JFK* and in *Natural Born Killers*, Stone layers 50 years of images into Nixon's snakelike voyage through the corridors of power. He turns history itself into a hypnotic Black Mass, anatomizing the elusive space between public perception and backroom reality, until the notion of "cover-up" takes on dimensions of mystical unease. And Anthony Hopkins, in a towering performance, puts us right inside Nixon's skin, revealing the squirmy, desperate soul behind the neurotic mannerisms. His shambling masochistic righteousness becomes Shakespearean in its fury, as he locks himself off, Kane-like, from the world and turns an entire nation into the mirror of his self-annihilating disgrace. More than just biography, *Nixon* is a dizzying and cathartic spectacle—a free fall through 50 years of American political imagination. Oliver Stone has become the most exciting filmmaker of his time, and *Nixon* is the movie he was born to make, a galvanizing vision of the corruption of America. **BY OWEN GLEIBERMAN**

CRUMB

IT WOULD BE hard to think of a movie experience more memorable than the two hours I spent getting to know the underground-comics artist Robert Crumb and his supremely warped family. Crumb, in his ecstatically exhibitionistic cartoons, draws on the convulsions of his own id, turning his most scandalous fantasies into a trippy grunge burlesque of American life. In Terry Zwigoff's great documentary, he appears before us as a razor-tongued contradiction (imagine Howard Stern in the body of Wally Cox), a perpetual adolescent-outsider nailed to the cross of his own sins. Is R. Crumb a hero or a creep? In *Crumb*, he's both at once, and the movie is a nightmare and a party at the same time. Crumb's two brothers—the mournfully unhinged recluse Charles and the jittery sexual molester Maxxon—are gifted, lucid wrecks, and what's apparent throughout the film is how their spooky

TOYING WITH SUCCESS: Electrifying *Story*

psychotic *otherness* echoes Robert, the celebrity survivor. They are the ghosts within him, and *Crumb*, the most powerful portrait yet from the Age of Dysfunction, lays bare the impossibility of separating the darkest aspects of our families from the deepest aspects of ourselves.

TOY STORY

CAN A MOVIE that's this much fun be a work of art? It can when made with the wit, spirit, and delirious imagination of *Toy Story*. Director John Lasseter uses the eerie hyperrealist magic of computer animation to create the illusion that we're seeing shiny plastic playthings like Mr. Potato Head spring to three-dimensional life. What's every bit as amazing, though, is that the characters are three-dimensional inside, too. And when the movie enters the home of Sid, whose schizoid toys would give Salvador Dalí the shivers, you know you're not in Disney land anymore.

CLOCKERS

SPIKE LEE, in his electrifying adaptation of Richard Price's inner-city novel, broke through years of sclerotic gimmickry and yelling-around-the-dinner-table theatrics to attain true maturity as an artist—and hardly anyone gave a damn. Framing a complex murder mystery around Strike (Mekhi Phifer), a nerve-jangled teenage crack dealer, Lee creates a shattering portrait of a community in breakdown. As Rodney, a stone killer with a mask of a smile, Delroy Lindo reveals how survival can breed betrayal, then murder, then madness. The film presents the tragedy of the American inner city on its broadest, most colorful canvas yet. Still, some dismissed *Clockers* as one "hood movie" too many, as if the dramatic value of certain lives had a statute of limitations.

DEAD MAN WALKING

IS IT POSSIBLE to make a liberal message movie that isn't a preachy, ennobling tract? The miracle of Tim Robbins' wrenching drama is that it moves us to view capital punishment with new eyes by bringing us perilously close to characters a lesser movie would have signposted. The heroine, a nun (Susan Sarandon), receives a letter from a death-row inmate (Sean Penn), and though she isn't sure whether to believe his claim of innocence, she fights to commute his death sentence anyway. *Dead Man Walking* forces us to confront the humanity of someone who may be a brutal killer. At the same time, it shows us the grief of the victims' families and dares to suggest that execution may be a route to absolution. Penn, in a stunning performance, mixes blasé sociopathic viciousness with something terrifyingly frail, revealing that even a heartless man can bleed.

NICE *BRIDGE* WORK: Eastwood and Streep find love in *Madison County*

A LOVELY *BUNCH*: The new and improved '90s Bradys put on a show

THE BRIDGES OF MADISON COUNTY

A GREAT WEEPER: When Clint Eastwood stands abandoned in the Iowa rain, we're watching stone melt. Like *Casablanca*, *The Bridges of Madison County* makes a quick, doomed love affair seem more timeless than a lifelong one. Eastwood, in a beautiful piece of direction, retains the strength of Robert James Waller's novella (don't deny it—the plot worked) but replaces the Whitman-goes-Harlequin treacle with something moodier: a slow dance of wills, as two weary middle-aged souls quietly erase the space between them. And Meryl Streep gives the performance of her career. Now flirting, now brooding, now radiant, her Francesca is every woman who was ever torn between the roles of lover and caretaker.

PRIEST

A YOUNG CLERGYMAN (Linus Roache) who's homosexual, who goes cruising, who listens to a confession of incest and feels bound by his vows not to stop it—in outline, *Priest* seems all but designed to shock. The real shock, though, is that the movie's subject isn't transgression but faith. It shows the anguish of a man who, because he's gay, violates Catholic doctrine with every breath. Yet his devotion to God is so powerful that in the very helplessness of his desire, his sin, he seems to be crying out for a new definition of what it means to believe.

CRIMSON TIDE

IT ONLY LOOKS like a Cold War retread. In Tony Scott's riveting submarine thriller, the prospect of the U.S. and Russia tilting nuclear warheads toward each other has nothing on the white-hot conflict between Gene Hackman, as the sub's martinet commander, and Denzel Washington, as the upstart who leads a mutiny rather than risk Armageddon. (Talk about a new power generation.) The two actors keep working to top each other's fury, making this duel feel palpably alive.

THE BRADY BUNCH MOVIE

NO ONE COULD be less enthusiastic than I at the prospect of seeing the cheese-ball sitcoms of the '60s and '70s turned into feature films. But *The Brady Bunch Movie* is a wonderful surprise. Exuberantly witty, it re-creates the show's polyester suburban utopia down to the last inch of shag carpeting—and then puts the slyest of quote marks around the Bradys themselves, so that the audience's affectionate mockery of the family's too-good-to-be-true wholesomeness becomes a joke the movie is deviously in on. (Gary Cole doesn't just play Mike Brady—he deconstructs him.) As a satire of American teenagers raised on the casual surrealism of consumerist daydreams, *The Brady Bunch Movie* is hipper than *Clueless* and three times as funny.

SAFE

TODD HAYNES, THE most truly independent filmmaker in America (*Poison*), is in top form in this acerbic nightmare about a middle American ditz (Julianne Moore) who finds that she's allergic to the pollution and plastic of modern life. That sounds like a dated theme, but the heart of the movie comes later, when Moore joins a self-help cult run by a "compassionate" guru (Peter Friedman) who's the most insidiously evil character I saw in 1995. The theme of *Safe* is that the cures we take are even worse than the diseases, an eerily ambiguous message that Haynes molds into a work of creepy beauty—a horror film of the spirit.

THE *TIDE* IS HIGH: Washington, Hackman see *Crimson*

The Worst

THE PEREZ FAMILY

1 MEMBERS OF THE Cuban community protested Marisa Tomei, Alfred Molina, and Anjelica Huston's casting as Cuban refugees. Actually, the Screen Actors Guild should have protested. As Dottie, a.k.a. the earthy, noble spirit of the working class, Tomei shimmies, hootchie-coos and spills out of her dress like a peasant Charo. She steamrolls everyone in her path, including the audience, who, in Mira Nair's fiasco, are put through two hours of embarrassingly "colorful" ethnic drama.

HACKERS

2 LEAST RIVETING trend of the year: watching characters sitting in front of computer terminals, typing. In this drab cyberfable, the tedium is compounded by those doing the typing, a bunch of "hip" geeks who christen themselves with names like Cereal Killer. But have no fear—these hackers are saving the world! In their dreams.

HOME FOR THE HOLIDAYS

3 JODIE FOSTER'S second directorial outing suggests that she's better off staying in front of the camera. *Home for the Holidays* is about a family coming apart at Thanksgiving, but it's the movie that comes apart. Foster piles on one fractious, overstaged scene after another, and her "sensitivity" to actors boils down to letting them do anything they please (it's scary to see Robert Downey Jr. without his leash).

DANGEROUS MINDS

4 TEACHER Michelle Pfeiffer brings the ennobling spirit of poetry to the inner city—i.e., she tosses candy bars at her students as if they were dolphins and informs them that Bob Dylan wrote a song about a drug dealer. The real dangerous minds are the ones that think up movies like this.

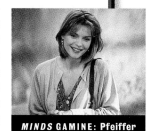

MINDS GAMINE: Pfeiffer

THE USUAL SUSPECTS

5 THERE ARE some who claim to have seen Bryan Singer's crime thriller six times, but if you saw it 600 times it still wouldn't make sense. Singer doesn't draw you into twists and turns: He tells you about twists and turns (through endless, numbing voice-over). He *has* to tell you, since the heists and car bombings don't actually connect to each other. Is it any wonder that the big scene at the end comes as such a relief? (A-ha! That's why I didn't follow it! *It was all made up!*) Message to Keyser Söze: Stop saying your stupid name.

PRIME *SUSPECTS*?: We're not *Usual* fans

The critics' Choices

KILLER B

"SOMETIMES A FILMMAKER gets so far inside the tawdry pleasures of B-movie conventions that the pulp comes out spicy and hot; it can tickle the taste buds of even the most jaded viewer. *Desperado*, a propulsive rock & roll spaghetti Western, is that kind of movie." (#289/290, Aug. 25/ Sept. 1)

ACTING UP

ON *HIDEAWAY*: "Alicia Silverstone—the fetching young ingenue from several Aerosmith videos—knows how to work her best feature, the upside-down teen-doll smirk. Someone ought to cast her as Lolita, but fast. Her talent may not last much past the age of consent." (#265, March 10)

"HUGH GRANT, in *Nine Months*, is playing a guy who can't make up his mind to join the rest of the domesticated world. His scandal reinforces what we see on screen: Grant as a charming brat of insecurity who's in dire need of growing up." (#284, July 21)

"IF *THE BASKETBALL DIARIES* is a mess, it's an energetic, watchable mess, and for a few soul-freezing moments, you get a glimpse of the great actor Leonardo DiCaprio is going to be." (#271, April 21)

ON *COPYCAT*: "The highest compliment I can give Harry Connick's performance is to say that he's very nearly as scary here as he is when he does those Frank Sinatra impersonations on record." (#299, Nov. 3)

ON *UNDER SIEGE 2: Dark Territory*: "Steven Seagal is the dark Buddha of action heroes, the Man with the Velvet Scowl." (#285, July 28)

OUT OF FOCUS

"EXCEPT FOR THE FACT that you can see right through him, Casper might be the Pillsbury Dough Boy's shy cousin—call him Poppin' Dead." (#277, June 2)

"POCAHONTAS is an aerobicized Native American superbabe, and with her long, muscular brown legs, regal shoulder blades, and silky black hair flowing down her waist, she looks ready to host *Pocahontas' House of Style*." (#279, June 16)

ON *THE QUICK AND THE DEAD*: "The plot is just an excuse to line up one badass cowboy (or girl) opposite another and let the eyeball-to-eyeball fireworks fly.... It's *A Fistful of Dollars* meets Wimbledon." (#262, Feb. 17)

FILM? NAH!

ON *VAMPIRE IN BROOKLYN*: "It mixes lame blood-pellet effects with lame gags. Its one lingering image is that of Eddie Murphy trying, and failing, to rise from the dead." (#299, Nov. 3)

ON *IT TAKES TWO*: "Two more reasons TV is better than the movies: The Olsen twins are now big-screen stars." (#302, Nov. 24)

(From reviews by Bruce Fretts, Owen Gleiberman, and Ken Tucker)

If you're having a good blackjack night in Vegas, it means you're cheating. (*Casino*)

....

Never say "F--- you, f---ball" to a man with a gun. (*Get Shorty*)

Scotsmen wear nothing under their kilts. (*Rob Roy, Braveheart*)

....

Julia Roberts and Kyra Sedgwick really *do* look alike. (*Something to Talk About*)

....

The medical term for birthing babies is *obstetrics*, not *obstruction*. (*Nine Months*)

....

Weather girls *do* have brains. (*To Die For*)

—Dave Karger

FRIENDS

(NBC) So popular, so unceasingly amusing, *Friends* is a little miracle: A show that's already survived its hype, its imitators, and its hit-single theme song. That TV's most appealing, sexy cast turns out also to be the funniest is one of those coincidences that makes television our most surprising friend. This sextet of chums comprises a tidy summary of contemporary sitcomic styles: David Schwimmer's Ross is neurotically earnest; Jennifer Aniston's Rachel is slinky, spoiled, and slapsticky; Matt LeBlanc's Joey is a doe-eyed doofus hunk. Courteney Cox's Monica is the lovely fussbudget, while Matthew Perry's Chandler is the ultimate yuppie wise guy. As for Lisa Kudrow's Phoebe—well, as we said in the EW "Cool" last summer, she's the coolest ditz. For a show peppered with salty jokes and glib pop-culture references, *Friends* can be gratifyingly sincere. This season, the pals dealt with an intruder in their midst, as the snippy Julie (Lauren Tom) became Ross' mismatched girlfriend (we know he's made for Rachel). The friends' reaction to Julie—and her ultimate rejection (by Ross and by the *Friends* viewership)—was handled with uncommon realism. Whether the subject is an unarticulated crush, parenthood, lesbianism, the parameters of good-neighborhoodism, or whether Phoebe can turn absolutely *anything* into a Dylanesque folk song, *Friends* is always supremely assured, clever, and often surprisingly touching. The only sitcom I watch in reruns and laugh at just as hard the second time around. **BY KEN TUCKER**

NYPD **BLUE**

(ABC) Television's best drama is relentless, and loved for precisely this quality. Just when we think we have a fix on any one of its characters—whether it's Jimmy Smits' moody Bobby Simone, or Nicholas Turturro's nice guy Martinez, or Justine Miceli's cool customer Lesniak—the series pulls that person in another direction, further humanizing and complicating these cops. The biggest potential pitfall the series had going into this past season was the sentimentalization of the marriage of Andy (Dennis Franz) and Sylvia (Sharon Lawrence), but that was adroitly avoided. Now the ongoing challenge facing the writers is how to turn the romance between Bobby and Kim Delaney's Diane into something more than an extended fling.

HELLO *LARRY*: (L. to r.) Tambor, Sharon Stone, Shandling

THE LARRY **SANDERS SHOW**

(HBO) Difficult to pick out this season's highlight: Was it Brian (Scott Thompson), new assistant to Hank (Jeffrey Tambor), explaining to peerlessly obnoxious writer Phil (Wallace Langham) the intricacies of gay sex? Was it former MTV supporting player Colin Quinn, son of Rip Torn's Artie, calling Janeane Garofalo's tough, feminist booker Paula "babe"? Was it Larry (Garry Shandling), upon hearing the gravelly voice of Brett Butler entering his office, saying "I'd know that voice anywhere. Hello, Dad!"? Shandling's beautifully complicated, inside-baseball showbiz spoof continues to accumulate emotional power as its run continues. Forever, one hopes.

NEWSRADIO

(NBC) Created by ex–*Larry Sanders* writer Paul Simms, *NewsRadio* is cruising through its first full season as one of the most satisfying sitcoms on television, with vividly imagined characters (headed up by Kid in the Hall Dave Foley's marvelously polite yet firm, intelligent yet silly news director) and intricate layers of gags. Special credit to Phil Hartman, who could easily have starred in his own show yet chose this ensemble, where his sly talents are on constant, glowing display.

X-CELLENT ADVENTURERS: Anderson and Duchovny forage for the truth

THE **X-FILES**

(Fox) The most telling phrase uttered this season was by an observer of some paranormal phenomenon under investigation by agents Dana Scully (Gillian Anderson) and Fox Mulder (David Duchovny): "Monsters begetting monsters." Which is to say that in the pure logic of this great series, one thing always leads to another. Coincidences are significant; the truth may be out there, but it's not making itself easily understood. The relationship between these two central professionals is at once collegial, sensual, and unearthly equal.

MURDER **ONE**

(ABC) Based on this series' extraordinary two-hour pilot about a grim, sleazy homicide, I had expected to place it higher on this list. But as the weeks wore on, *Murder One* lost some momentum, mostly due to the intro-

SINGULAR SENSATION: *One*

duction of weak secondary plots that smelled of *L.A. Law* mothballs. Still, as chief defense lawyer, Daniel Benzali has managed to sustain his interpretation of the lead role; he dares to brood slowly, eloquently, as if caught in a Shakespearean tragedy while wearing a pin-striped suit.

SEINFELD

(NBC) Gutting it out in his seventh season, Jerry Seinfeld has transcended the style he created, which now permeates TV (I love *Friends*, but this is where they got the point of view and pacing). Among this season's more inspired notions: Julia Louis-Dreyfus' Elaine as a writer of florid copy for the J. Peterman catalog, and Jason Alexander's George evincing something uncharacteristically close to pity for a clothing-store guard having to spend all day on his feet.

FOUR SCORE WITH SEVEN YEARS: *Seinfeld* and company stay on track

THE BONNIE HUNT SHOW

(CBS) Now officially on hiatus, this brave sitcom—so funny yet so different in its rhythms (slower) and attitude (unironic, idealistic, romantic)—is the year's most underrated show. I concede that in its final weeks, locating a punchline in *The Bonnie Hunt Show* was more than a bit difficult, but by that

BONNIE RATES: Hunt

PSYCHED OUT: *Frasier*'s Grammer, with Eddie, is TV's best session

time, I'd become so fond of Hunt's Chicago TV-reporter character and her charming friends and workmates that I'd happily spend a half hour with them without insisting that they crack me up. Sometimes whimsy is its own reward.

FRASIER

(NBC) Thank goodness they're losing Mercedes Ruehl next month. As Frasier's radio-station manager, she's screwing up one of the best sitcoms with her sour puss and leaden delivery. The rest of the show is just dandy, though. David Hyde Pierce's touch remains light, and if we critics have been showering him with praise, Kelsey Grammer deserves to be doused too: He does the finest slow burns on television. And let's hear it for the underrated Jane Leeves, whose Daphne—frisky and cagey—has managed to make herself an object of desire to Pierce's Niles without ever suggesting that she is aware of her own desirousness.

ER

(NBC) Unlike the *Friends* phenomenon, the *ER* popularity juggernaut was one I resisted for as long as possible: "Too slick, too obvious," I scoffed. For a while. Fact is, *ER* is irresistible, its pace continues to exhilarate, and if its mini-plots are still skimpy, the ensemble has become an emotionally complex collection of distinct individuals.

The
Worst

THE PURSUIT OF **HAPPINESS**

1 (NBC) Comedy writing at its most automatic. The show once used a gay character as a sign of prime-time progressiveness but put that character to such stupid use that what came across was the writers' contempt for progressiveness. A well-deserved cancellation.

DEADLY **GAMES**

2 (UPN) The worst show on a mediocre network, this videogame-comes-to-life dreck couldn't even cash in on the sci-fi trend or pervasive cyberhype well enough to create entertaining junk. Christopher Lloyd, a.k.a. Sebastian Jackal: Between this and the pretentious *Things to Do in Denver When You're Dead*, maybe you should get someone else to pick your future employment.

GAMES OVER: Lloyd

CHARLIE **GRACE**

3 (ABC) This private-eye drama starring ex-Sexiest Man Alive Mark Harmon arrived DOA; the show might have been merely boring and harmless had its literary pretensions (especially the Raymond Chandleresque voice-overs) not been so egregious.

STAND-UP DOESN'T DELIVER: *Foxworthy* fares badly

THE JEFF **FOXWORTHY SHOW**

4 (ABC) Foxworthy is a likable stand-up comic, and his "redneck" shtick can be mildly amusing. But in turning such minor charms into a big-time sitcom, everything has collapsed.

THE **HOME COURT**

5 (NBC) There are, of course, many lousy sitcoms, but this seems even lousier because its star is so notably wasted. Pamela Reed tried hard to squeeze her fine talents to this clunker about a judge and her family; Reed's valiant efforts only made the show even more depressing.

DOWN *HOME*: Reed

The Critics' Choices

TUNING IN

ON *SERVING IN Silence: The Margarethe Cammermeyer Story*: "I suppose this is the point at which, as a member of the hydra-headed liberal media conspiracy, I'm supposed to congratulate NBC for its courage in airing a scene of what still, in television land, amounts to illicit sexuality." (#260, Feb. 3)

ON HEATHER Locklear in *Texas Justice*: "She may not have the glamorous richness of a movie star, but she deploys the sort of sexy superficiality that comes across on the small screen as both excitingly realistic and giddily exaggerated. She is what is commonly called a hoot." (#261, Feb. 10)

"IF I WERE a 10-year-old, I'd bite anyone who tried to keep me away from an episode of *Xena: Warrior Princess*." (#302, Nov. 24)

BOTTOMING OUT

"*GABRIELLE'S* supposedly distinguishing characteristic is that it does out-of-studio remotes during the show, but I call talking to consumers in a Downey, Calif., shopping mall about dating habits a waste of technology." (#294, Sept. 29)

"*RUSH LIMBAUGH'S America* gives the lie to the notion that the media are pervasively liberal; they are, in fact, so instinctively, traditionally conservative that Limbaugh himself had trouble get-

ting heard early in his career because he was perceived as being *too* radical in his rightness." (#263/264, Feb. 24)

ON *SATURDAY NIGHT Live*: "It radiates a contradiction: lazy arrogance mixed with a desperate desire to be liked." (#296, Oct. 13)

ON *LATE Show With David Letterman*: "Dave doesn't stop at butt kissing—in fact, his on-air fondling makes him seem like the Richard Dawson of late night." (#287, Aug. 11)

MIXED SIGNALS

ON *THE Single Guy*: "The view of the single life here is distinctly depressing. I say let's get Johnny stoked on Prozac and set him up on a blind date with Elizabeth Wurtzel." (#295, Oct. 6)

"THE PROBLEM with *Hard Copy's* Hollywood reporting—its bread and butter—is that no genuine star would ever be crazy enough to sit down and talk with them." (#288, Aug. 18)

ON TIFFANI-AMBER Thiessen's *Beverly Hills, 90210* character: "If Valerie is a refreshing spritz of Obsession perfume, the men of *90210* are beginning to smell like fusty Mennen Skin Bracer." (#276, May 26)

(From reviews by Bruce Fretts, Lisa Schwarzbaum, and Ken Tucker)

You can kick a heart across the floor like a hockey puck and still put it in someone's chest. (*Chicago Hope*)

Yasser Arafat will talk to anyone—like Tabitha Soren on MTV.

You can have great sex while you're asleep. (*Mad About You*)

Cats can ride on the backs of motorcycles. (*Beverly Hills, 90210*)

Stucco apartments are much stronger than they look. (*Melrose Place*)

—Kristen Baldwin, Alan Carter, A.J. Jacobs, Jessica Shaw, Ken Tucker, Gary Eng Walk, Bret Watson

books

A CIVIL ACTION

Jonathan Harr (Random House, $25) Harr turns a nine-year lawsuit over two industrially poisoned municipal wells in Woburn, Mass., into a taut, gripping narrative—the best legal thriller we've ever read. His account documents a landmark case pitting eight families against two multibillion-dollar corporations that they accused of poisoning city water wells with toxic waste. The results couldn't have been more horrifying: twelve children with leukemia, six of them living almost next door to one another. And the case appeared to speak for itself—or so the first plaintiff's lawyer thought upon first look at the evidence. ◆ There was never any doubt that the wells were poisoned with an industrial solvent. But when it came to determining how the contaminant got into the water supplies and how much damage it did, lawyers for the defendants—W.R. Grace and Beatrice Foods—were ready to spend not only millions of dollars but much of their adult lives to convince a judge and jury it wasn't the companies' fault. Opposing them is the flawed but idealistic lawyer representing the leukemia-devastated families who drank the well water. Naturally, the book has been snapped up by Hollywood—Robert Redford will produce as well as star in an upcoming movie version. ◆ From a literary perspective, however, the remarkable thing about *A Civil Action* is Harr's ability to turn bitter legal warfare into a compelling story without sacrificing either the complexity of the issues involved or their cost in human lives. A genuine feat of reporting and storytelling. **BY GENE LYONS**

WHAT WE LEARNED FROM BOOKS THIS YEAR

Howard Stern doesn't look any better in a dress...or any worse. (*Miss America*, by Howard Stern)

Big-city career women crave illicit rolls in the hay with denim-clad macho men just as much as rural housewives do. (*The Horse Whisperer*, by Nicholas Evans)

Dealing with health-insurance companies can be a nightmare.... Oh, wait, we knew that already. (*The Rainmaker*, by John Grisham)

THE **LIAR'S CLUB**

Mary Karr (Viking, $22.95) In the "So You Think *Your* Family's Crazy" category, Karr's nonfiction memoir of her East Texas childhood takes the blue ribbon. The boozing "Liar's Club" was how Karr's daddy escaped her momma—herself a drinker, dreamer, and keeper of dark secrets. The author's wit and prose impressed us as much as her refusal to whine.

OUR **GAME**

John le Carré (Knopf, $24) A flaky onetime double agent embezzles millions and runs off to the Russian Caucasus region to buy arms for Ingush rebels. His retired ex-associate must stop him or look like a traitor. An engaging tale from the most literary espionage writer around.

LINCOLN

David Herbert Donald (Simon & Schuster, $35) Donald gives us a Lincoln for the 1990s: A moody, melancholy man prone to brooding and indecision. The Harvard historian even compares Lincoln's nature to—hold on to your hat—Bill Clinton's.

PRACTICAL **MAGIC**

Alice Hoffman (Putnam, $22.95) Magic realism again invades Long Island. Two sisters grow up among witches, yearn for simple love and tranquility, yet find themselves possessed of quasi-supernatural powers. But simple love, in Hoffman's deceptively ordinary world, is always a delusion—and sometimes an enchantment.

AN UNQUIET MIND: A MEMOIR OF MOODS AND MADNESS

Kay Redfield Jamison (Knopf, $22) A brave, brilliantly crafted book by a Johns Hopkins professor who cowrote a medical text on manic-depressive illness—but kept her own struggle with it a secret until now. So strong is the stigma of mental illness that Jamison feared losing face, even with colleagues. Absolutely indispensable for anybody who wants to know how the illness feels from the inside.

DIVIDED **LIVES**

Elsa Walsh (Simon & Schuster, $23) A fascinating account of the ways in which TV correspondent Meredith Vieira, conductor and first lady of West Virginia Rachael Worby, and breast surgeon Dr. Alison Estabrook have made it in a man's world—and the amazingly intimate secrets they were willing to tell the author.

TOM: THE UNKNOWN TENNESSEE WILLIAMS

Lyle Leverich (Crown, $35) The first of two volumes, Leverich's exhaustively documented, insightful portrait looks to become an instant classic. Our reviewer said, "reads like a psychological novel and ends like a cliffhanger."

AFTER **ALL**

Mary Tyler Moore (Putnam $24.95) Moore's life reads like a sweeps week's worth of *Oprah*s: failed marriages, booze, diabetes, adultery, divorce, the deaths of her son and brother, a sister's drug overdose, a stalking fan, etc. But *After All* reads not like a celebrity bio but a real book by a courageous and determined woman.

HIGH **FIDELITY**

Nick Hornby (Riverhead, $21.95) A witty, candid exploration of the lonely nights and lost loves of a 35-going-on-18-year-old London record shop owner who hides from his hurt by reorganizing his record collection. Yet beneath the jokey surface lie haunting emotional truths.

The W o r s t

DRIVING UNDER THE AFFLUENCE

1 *Julia Phillips* (HarperCollins, $24) As a Hollywood gossip Phillips was a knockout. Her first book, *You'll Never Eat Lunch in This Town Again*, trashed some of the town's biggest names. Alas, it appears to have convinced her she was a writer. Big mistake. She has nothing to say, at an absolutely numbing length (321 pages).

I WANT TO TELL YOU:
MY RESPONSE TO YOUR LETTERS, YOUR MESSAGES, YOUR QUESTIONS

2 *O.J. Simpson* (Little, Brown, $17.95) As an old country song goes, if you don't know, we ain't gonna tell you.

THE HORSE WHISPERER

3 *Nicholas Evans* (Delacorte, $23.95) An unhappily married New York magazine editor takes her daughter's hurt horse to Montana and the care of a lean, laconic, sexy rancher. The nag is the only credible character.

IN THE CUT

4 *Susanna Moore* (Knopf, $21) With a reputation based on stylish coming-of-age novels, Moore tried writing an erotic thriller and ended up with a genuinely dirty book.

THE HOUSEKEEPER'S DIARY
CHARLES AND DIANA BEFORE THE BREAKUP

5 *Wendy Berry* (Barricade Books, $19.95) Even if Princess Di and Prince Charles had any secrets left, this twit wouldn't know them. —*Edited by Gene Lyons*

The critics' Choices

BOOKMARKS

ON WINSTON GROOM'S *Gump & Co.*: "When last we heard, Tom Hanks was saying he had no interest in a *Forrest Gump* sequel. Even so, wait for the movie." (#288, Aug. 18)

ON THE PREVIOUSLY unpublished Louisa May Alcott novel: "Maybe if enough readers had studied *A Long Fatal Love Chase* over the years, there would be no need for *Smart Women, Foolish Choices*." (#292, Sept. 15)

ON C. DAVID HEYMANN'S *Liz*: "Taylor was created when glamorous excess meant something. She enthralls because, beneath the purple eye shadow and giant jewelry, we see a remnant of the old Hollywood fantasy that, thanks to dispassionately nosy books like *Liz*, has been shot to hell." (#273, May 5)

ON NANCY SINATRA'S *Frank Sinatra: An American Legend*: "You know a book is in trouble when you look forward to the part where the author records 'These Boots Are Made for Walkin'." (#297, Oct. 20)

ON ROBERT JAMES Waller's *Border Music*: "In the world according to Waller, all men are Adam after the fall, and all women cardboard." (#261, Feb. 10)

"WANT TO READ really shocking stuff? Well, you won't find it in Howard Stern's *Miss America*." (#303, Dec. 1)

(From reviews by Jess Cagle, Vanessa V. Friedman, A.J. Jacobs, Gene Lyons, and Lisa Schwarzbaum)

Tell 'em your presidential plans *after* you sign that multimillion-dollar book deal. (*My American Journey*, by Colin Powell)

T. rex bites aren't as serious as they look. (Corollary: Egghead chaos theorists are tougher than they look.) (*The Lost World*, by Michael Crichton)

Office supplies can be used as booby traps if bad guys are chasing you. (*Vertical Run*, by Joseph R. Garber)

Don't be misled by a book's title. (*My Point...And I Do Have One*, by Ellen DeGeneres)

Classical-music-loving Taoists can be hitmen, too. (*The Juror*, by George Dawes Green)

—*Erica K. Cardozo*

music

JOAN OSBORNE

Relish (Blue Gorilla/Mercury) With Joan Osborne, many easy comparisons come to mind: Sheryl Crow with soul, Bonnie Raitt with longing in more than just her heart, Melissa Etheridge with subtlety and restraint. Yet none of those analogies do justice to this remarkable debut by this Kentucky-born, New York-based hip-shaker. First, there is the voice: rich with a brick-oven smokiness, powerful yet never show-offy, a deeply spiritual and sexual instrument that can leap from a girlish whisper to an afterglow purr to a head-thrown-back wail. That voice transforms "Man in the Long Black Coat," an obscure, late-period Dylan parable, into a smoldering piece of Southern gothic. "One of Us," the album's late-blooming hit, could have been a joke about the Lord living among us; the way Osborne sings it, it becomes a hymn. The music that accompanies her is just as stick-to-the-ribs earthy, dipped in roadhouse soul, folkish ballads, barroom rock, and blues, without sounding like museum-ready House of Blues nostalgia. (Even more astounding, some of her collaborators were members of the Hooters, two-MTV-hit wonders of the mid '80s.) By not condescending to the boozing-and-brawling clichés of the bluesy earth mama, Osborne plays off of, not into, that stereotype, and makes it fresh again. The only things shaky about *Relish* are the junkies, prostitutes, suicidal depressives, and sinners who populate Osborne's songs. But one listen to her comforting, uplifting voice and you know they'll eventually be okay too. **BY DAVID BROWNE**

SIMPLY SMASHING: *Collie* is one of 1995's top dogs

SMASHING **PUMPKINS**

2 *Mellon Collie and the Infinite Sadness* (Virgin) Like that shy grade-schooler who never worked well with others, Pumpkins auteur Billy Corgan has always been out of step with his slacker-rock peers—more ambitious, more driven, more pretentious. Here, he pushes those traits to the limit, using two discs to ponder commitment, self-hatred, his childhood, and romantic redemption. Yet what could have easily been an indulgent therapy session set to grunge guitars is instead a heady musical feast—primal-scream metal, unplugged balladry, even long, trippy pieces that recall the heyday of progressive rock. To Corgan, making music isn't just a job, it's an adventure—one that finds him, and us, rediscovering the thrill of rock at its most audacious and liberating.

MOBY

WRONG IS RIGHT: Moby reels in a win

3 *Everything Is Wrong* (Elektra) If you think techno has hit a dead end, you're right—and thanks to this stunner, you're also wrong. To producer and born-again Christian Moby, techno's computerized pulse can be adapted to any genre, be it punk, dance hall, club music, or Enya-style celestial musings. And he proceeds to do just that on a gorgeous, impeccable sonic landscape. The new spirituality comes to pop, but sweating is still allowed.

COOLIO

4 *Gangsta's Paradise* (Tommy Boy) Everyone's favorite Los Angeles braider uses his second album to wax positive about the ghetto, preaching respect for women and nonviolence. And instead of stark gangsta beats, his producers opt for cushiony grooves (many based on soul and R&B hits) that elevate Coolio's voice and messages to a higher plane.

RAPSODIC: Coolio

PJ **HARVEY**

5 *To Bring You My Love* (Island) When she barks "You wanna hear my long snake moan," it's clear Harvey's not inviting you on a stroll through the zoo. With her fourth album, she finally gets a dramatic yet uncluttered production worthy of her songs, her fresh-razor-edged voice, and her subject matter: sex as catharsis, sex as frustration, sex period.

LOVE SEXY: Sharp-tongued Harvey in a reflective moment

RANCID

6 *...And Out Come the Wolves* (Epitaph) Sure, they sound like the Clash, but these second-generation L.A. punks share a more important element with their predecessors. The year's most bristling rock record, *Wolves* recalls a time when punk was less about safety pins than it was

SONIC BOOM: Toning down the raw power of the early Youth, *Washing Machine* is good for more than a few spin cycles

about blow-the-roof-off anthems. And unlike Green Day, it's hard to imagine Rancid as Saturday-morning cartoon characters.

SONIC YOUTH

Washing Machine (DGC) Downplaying raw power, the aging Youth lock into relaxed, trancelike guitar grooves. Not a major leap forward for a band that continues to lead the underground into the aboveground, but a refinement of a style that still sounds startlingly fresh.

EAT TO THE BEAT: lang serves up a musical buffet

MATTHEW SWEET

100% Fun (Zoo) Who needs a necrophilic Beatles reunion when this guy continues to knock out songs that make even the most tone-deaf want to sing along? Sweet is neither Lennon nor McCartney, but their values—the melodic hook, the deliverance through effervescent pop—live on in his hardest-hitting record. "We're the Same" is the year's great lost hit single.

k.d. lang

All You Can Eat (Warner Bros.) So everyone's favorite chanteuse falls head over heels and realizes that love can still stink. Big deal—except the meticulous, measured melodies and beats only make her yearnings more intense. Subtle and nuanced at a time when subtlety and nuance are not valued pop commodities, it flopped commercially and deserves better.

COUNT BASS-D

Pre-Life Crisis (Work/Columbia) On his debut album, Nashville's first major rapper ignores gangsta and dares to invent lounge rap—a smooth, rolling blend of hip-hop rhymes, loose-limbed jazz rhythms, and crooning. And he never forgets that rappers still have the best senses of humor in pop.

The W**o**rst

WHAT WE LEARNED FROM **MUSIC** THIS YEAR

Superstars shouldn't count on continued success with follow-ups to big albums. (Green Day, Melissa Etheridge, Ace of Base)

Live albums don't sell unless they're called *Unplugged*. (Bonnie Raitt's *Road Tested*, Steely Dan's *Alive in America*, Peter Frampton's *Frampton Comes Alive II*)

The goofier the name, the bigger the sales. (Hootie & the Blowfish, Goo Goo Dolls, Presidents of the United States, Bone Thugs-N-Harmony)

The kids are alright, especially if they're Australian. (Silverchair, Ben Lee, Noise Addicts)

Punk wasn't the grunge of '95,

THANK YOU, BUT NO: Duranosaurus wrecks

LENNY **KRAVITZ**

Circus (Virgin) On the verge of a breakthrough, he shoots and... chokes. Kravitz once had skill and chutzpah to compensate for lack of originality. Here, dispensing platitudes and decrying rock clichés while reveling in them, he constructs a circus that should be run out of town.

ALANIS **MORISSETTE**

Jagged Little Pill (Maverick/ Reprise) The problem with this overnight heavyweight isn't, as some complain, the grab bag crafted by producer Glen Ballard. Ballard knows a solid hook when he constructs it, and only a true crank could deny "You Oughta Know." No, the real nuisance is the frontwoman, whose histrionic yelp reduces honest expression to contrivance and whose lyrics descend to trash-TV topicality. Not for nothing was she once considered the Debbie Gibson of Canada.

DURAN **DURAN**

Thank You (Capitol) Did you hear the one about the lounge lizards who follow up their comeback with an album of covers? And not just *any* covers, but R&B, rap, and new-wave oldie covers way beyond their reach? [Wild laughter.]

BUSH

Sixteen Stone (Trauma/Inter-scope/Atlantic) Silverchair, this year's other leading alterna-posers, can be forgiven since they're just teens imitating their heroes. There's no excuse for Bush, smarmy Brits who plundered every Seattle in-flection and, depressingly, rode it to platinum sales.

EDWIN **McCAIN**

Honor Among Thieves (Lava) Bad enough that Hootie & the Blowfish sound as if they were cloned from ghosts of soft-rock past. Now imagine a *Hootie* clone.

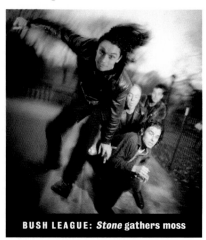

BUSH LEAGUE: *Stone* gathers moss

The critics' Choices

FOOD FOR THOUGHT

On JANET JACKSON's single "Runaway": "A frothy piña colada of a song, but the buzz sure feels sweet while it lasts." (#289/90, Aug. 25)

On THE Pretenders' *Isle of View*: "Like Lulu after too many cigarettes and bourbons. Survival never sounded so luminous." (#298, Oct. 27)

On ACE OF Base's *The Bridge*: "So dorky, you have to love 'em…but for sheer candied pop, this is one pleasurable way to rot your teeth." (#302, Nov. 24)

On CANDLEBOX's *Lucy*: "Every bit as appalling and derivative as their first, with the foursome once again hacking out the kind of generic grunge that works like some Hydrox knockoff of Pearl Jam's genuine Oreo. In fact, it's encyclopedically bad." (#296, Oct. 13)

RAW TALENTS

"SELENA HAS A sob-in-the-throat voice that would have spoken to lovesick teenagers everywhere, but her non-Hispanic producers and songwriters saddled her with greeting-card sentiments and Abdul-lite melodies, exorcising any ethnic flavor." (#284, July 21)

On K.D. LANG's album: "Demureness has rarely been k.d. lang's style, so it isn't surprising that when she calls her new album *All You Can Eat*, she doesn't mean the local buffet-style family restaurant." (#296, Oct. 13)

INSPIRATION, DIVINE

On AL GREEN's *Your Heart's in Good Hands*: "Sweet soul music, whether you're saved or not." (#300, Nov. 10)

…AND NOT SO

On LENNY Kravitz's *Circus*: "In a match he probably considers equal, Kravitz discovers God… he may have seen the light, but the bulb is distressingly dim." (#292, Sept. 15)

SOUR NOTES

On SHANIA Twain: "What do you get when you pair a former resort singer with a Karen Carpenter fixation and a pop producer who thinks it would be fun to work in country? One of the worst records of the decade." (#261, Feb. 10)

On BONE Thugs-N-Harmony: "For all their polish, [they] commit that most unimaginable of sins: They make gangsta rap that's dull." (#286, Aug. 4)

On ANNIE LENNOX's *Medusa*: "She ends up like Rita Coolidge—that '70s cover-version vampire, sucking the life right from the song." (#266, March 17)

On WHITE ZOMBIE's *Astro-Creep: 2000 Songs of Love, Destruction and Other Synthetic Delusions of the Electric Head*: "As for lyrics, the album title says it all." (#270, April 14)

(From reviews by David Browne, Bob Cannon, Jim Farber, Alanna Nash, and Marina Zogbi)

despite the music industry's efforts to the contrary. (Rancid, Dance Hall Crashers)

....

You don't have to be Southern or talented to be a big country star, especially if you're a size 2 and married to a famous producer. (Shania Twain)

....

The mid-'90s are *not* the mid-'60s, and there is not a new British Invasion. (Oasis, Blur, Elastica)

....

Success in one band doesn't guarantee it in another. (Foo Fighters, the Amps)

....

TESH RULES!

—Ethan Smith

multimedia

CHOP SUEY

1 *(Magnet Interactive Studios, CD-ROM for PC and Mac, $34.98)* It wasn't a good year for CD-ROMs. Sales never lived up to the leather-lunged hype, there was no breakthrough title like 1993's *Myst*, and the metastasizing World Wide Web got all the press. Paradoxically, this might be the best thing that's happened to CD-ROMs. Now that expectations have been lowered, multimedia publishers may experiment with what's on the disc instead of jamming out the next life-consuming adventure game. Which means we could end up with more titles like *Chop Suey*. ◆ Created by illustrator Monica Gesue and writer Theresa Duncan, *Chop Suey* is a story disc for girls, but that's okay—*Calvin and Hobbes* is supposedly for kids too. By clicking around a funky folk-art map of a Midwestern town—imagine cartoonist Lynda Barry designing a chamber of commerce brochure—you can tap into the magic-realist lives of two girls named Lily and June Bugg, their Aunt Vera (she's been married three times, and they've all been named Bob), her slacker son, Dooner, and other dreamy souls. *Chop Suey* has a relaxed literary quality (the folksy narration is by National Public Radio's David Sedaris) and a serious sense of the silly (see if you can find the beatnik fireflies and Edgar Allan Posies) that make time spent with it feel like lolling on a lazy summer day. The plangent soundtrack is wonderful, and there's a surprise in every corner, but the reason *Chop Suey* heads this list is that it's one of only two CD-ROMs released this year to offer an honest-to-God sense of place. **BY TY BURR**

WHAT WE LEARNED FROM MULTIMEDIA THIS YEAR

1

"Sex" appeared in 26,132 documents on the Internet. (According to a Lycos search)

You can make a bundle with high-tech stocks. (Netscape) You can lose a bundle, too. (Netscape)

It's a boys' world. (*Doom, Doom II, Ultimate Doom: Thy Flesh Consumed*, etc.)

Misc.activism. militia makes misc.alt.sex look wholesome.

The long arm of the law now extends a bit farther, as student Jake Baker learned after being arrested for posting a rape fantasy online. (Charges were later dismissed.)

THE RESIDENTS' BAD DAY ON THE MIDWAY

2

(INSCAPE, CD-ROM for PC and Mac, $49.95) This is the other one, a multistranded tale of dread and epiphany at a traveling carnival. The graphics have an almost obscenely tactile feel, and the vibrant human tales reek of the best Southern gothic.

THE WORLD WIDE WEB

3

TODAY EVERY shlub with something to say or sell has a home page, and the A.C. Nielsen Co. is compiling Web ratings. But wait a couple of years. Cable modems will ease the aggravating downloading time, and audio, video, and software add-ons will goose the medium's capabilities. For now, the Web is a beautiful Babel.

THE PALACE

4

ONLINE CHAT has become a great way to trade gossip or swap cyberspit, and now at least four outfits offer virtual chat software, but our money's on the Palace (http://www.thepalace.com), owned (like this magazine) by Time Warner. It's easy to move around in, the graphics are deluxe, and the avatars creatively goofy.

SONIC NET
ROCKTROPOLIS
FIREFLY

5

THESE MUSIC SITES on the Web offer tantalizing glimpses of what could be. The amusingly snide Sonic Net (http://www.sonicnet.com) has reviews, live chats with bands, concert info, and sound clips. Firefly (http://www.agents-inc.com) recommends albums based on the ones you like. And Rocktropolis (http://rocktropolis.com) spotlights new releases with full-bore Web gimmickry—and sports Daryl Hannah as a guardian angel.

TOTAL DISTORTION

6

(POP ROCKET, CD-ROM for PC and Mac, $64.95) Joe Sparks' music-video adventure is a dizzying hoot: Futuristic food processors spit meatball sandwiches, rude noises abound, and everything you touch *does* something.

FLUX
THE NETLY NEWS
SUCK

7

THESE ONLINE tip sheets cast an eye on the burgeoning Net stew. The weekly Flux (http://www.hotwired.com/flux)—found on *Wired* magazine's Web extension, *Hotwired*—is the classiest; the daily Suck (http://www.suck.com) is more anarchic and given to pranks; and the Netly News (http://pathfinder.com/Netly), on Time Warner's Pathfinder website, has a bite that belies its corporate parent.

THE SPOT

8

THIS IS THE guiltiest pleasure (http://www.thespot.com) on the Web. It's *The Real World* meets *Melrose Place* meets *Microserfs*: Six alarmingly healthy Californians share a house, an online diary, and assorted lovers, bosses, and pasts. Every day you can access new entries, photos, and sound clips. Wonderfully dopey.

ENHANCED CDS

9

A COMPACT DISC that plays music on your stereo and offers liner notes, videos, photos—anything—on your computer, but the music is mostly reissues and remixes.

THE FILM ZONE

10

THIS SITE is an unsettled mix of promotion and movie-buff journalism (http://www.filmzone.com), but it is perhaps the best of the Web's movie sites.

The Wrst

MR. PAYBACK

1 (*INTERFILM, PG-13*) The first widely promoted interactive film involved (a) joysticks attached to theater seats, (b) color-coded buttons corresponding to plot choices on the screen, (c) yelling and screaming as audiences tried to sway the vote. It might have started a fad if the movie itself didn't (a) offer similar stories no matter which plot thread was chosen, (b) make *Ace Ventura* look like Merchant Ivory, (c) betray an unseemly S&M fixation. After *Mr. Payback*'s brief theatrical run, commercial prospects for interactive films were (a) nil, (b) nada, (c) zip.

ROLLING STONES VOODOO LOUNGE

2 (*GTE Entertainment, CD-ROM for PC and Mac, $49.95*) A lavishly designed interactive disc that just sits there on screen, this lazy entry from the World's Least Dangerous Rock Band helps explain why CD-ROMs had such a bum year.

SPAM

3 THE CONGLOMERATION of Internet bulletin boards known as Usenet covers just about every subject known to humankind, but the amount of "spam" (mass postings, usually commercial, to all newsgroups) has turned this corner of the wired world into chaos.

BABES ON THE WEB

4 ROBERT TOUPS Jr.'s round-up of more than 300 individual women's home pages, all slathered with hubba-hubba "wit." Since it links to some impressive pages, *Babes* (http://www.tyrell.net/robtoups/BABE.html) actually constitutes a service. It's the unbearably smug tone we could do without.

VIRTUAL REALITY HELMETS

5 A LOT OF companies came out with VR headsets—almost all guaranteed to sprain your neck and give you vertigo. The year saw plenty of breakthroughs, but home VR remains a George Jetson fantasy.

The Critics' Choices

TOP OF THE LINE

ON WINDOWS 95: "I, for one, don't need Jennifer Aniston to sell me on Windows 95—though she's certainly welcome to try." (#289/290, Aug. 25)

ABORT, RETRY, IGNORE

ON *ROLLING STONES: Voodoo Lounge* (CD-ROM): "You may be hard-pressed to remember when the Stones were capable of making music so tender and brutal it took your breath away. So completely does this product misinterpret the idea of multimedia—that text, audio, and video can be combined to create a *deeper* experience—that it trashes the band's remaining credibility despite the concurrent release of the acoustic album *Stripped*." (#303, Dec. 1)

ON MICROSOFT'S "social interface" *Bob* (floppy or CD-ROM): "More than a little creepy—*2001*'s HAL reimagined by Martha Stewart." (#270, April 14)

ON NETWORK TV cybersites: "Sounds like a chance for TV to pioneer new projects and programs to take advantage of the creativity and interactivity of cyberia, right? Think again. In fact, think *marketing tool*." (#266, March 17)

(From reviews by Ty Burr, Dana Kennedy, and Bob Strauss)

Some things are worth waiting for, like the three-years-in-the-making, mind-bending, gloriously adolescent, hyper-reactive rock video–adventure CD-ROM *Total Distortion*.

AOL word censors found the word *breasts* offensive, but *hooters* was just fine.

Bill Gates, with celebrity endorsements, talk-show spots, and a best-selling book *and* CD-ROM, may be the *real* king of all media. And in *The Road Ahead*, he took on the Justice Department as if it were any old Microsoft rival: "One area the government should stay out of is compatibility."

—*Laura C. Smith*

Video

THE ART OF BUSTER KEATON

1 *(1920–27, Kino, unrated, $29.95 each; laserdisc Vols. 1 and 3 $99.99, Vol. 2 $139.99)* With each passing year, the world looks more the way Buster Keaton saw it. Technology permeates our lives; we run by clockwork, and the only possible human response is serene, inventive comic rebellion. Copyright issues had kept most of Keaton's silent-era canon from video until this year, when Kino released 10 tapes comprising 11 features and 19 shorts, all in breathtakingly clean prints. If you've never seen a Keaton comedy, we recommend you invite your friends over and gorge on two or three of these tapes at a pop: Where Charlie Chaplin's mix of slapstick and treacle looks mighty creaky these days, Buster's deadpan has a dry, cool wit that ages like wine. Watch *Sherlock, Jr.* if you want to see a hilarious dissertation on movies and identity; watch *Our Hospitality* for its hair-raising stunts; watch *The Navigator* for the distilled Keaton vision of man versus machine; and watch *The General* for epic grace. Behind the films lies a tragic tale of a man's unassuming genius falling victim to studio politics and alcohol; for more on that, read any of the fine Keaton biographies available. In the end, though, the films are all that matter, rivaling Bach or Hopper or Fitzgerald in their technical perfection and humanely comic despair. As civilization grows louder, Keaton's silence continues to pack a kick in the pants. **BY TY BURR**

HEAVEN'S WAIT: It took 50 years to get *Leave Her* on tape

IMMORTAL **BELOVED**

THIRTY-TWO SHORT FILMS ABOUT **GLENN GOULD**

(1994, Columbia TriStar, R, priced for rental, laserdisc $39.95; 1994, Columbia TriStar, unrated, $19.95, laserdisc $34.95) The rebel-with-a-piano genre found new life with these two releases. *Beloved* gave us the life of Beethoven with a well-tempered Gary Oldman as Ludwig, and just the right amount of melodramatic cheese, while *Thirty-Two Short Films* splintered the career of pianist Gould—the James Dean of classical music back in the '50s—into innovative shards. Both boast glorious soundtracks and seriously benefit from hooking the VCR up to your stereo.

HISTORY OF **ROCK & ROLL**

(1995, Time-Life, unrated, tape Vol. 1 $13.48, Vols. 2–10 $23.48, set $159.99; laserdisc set $199.98) These 10 hours of musical history on 10 tapes (or five discs) come as close as possible to covering the generational juggernaut that rock once was, and the demographic kaleidoscope it has become. The series ran in TV syndication earlier this year, but additional archival footage has been added for video, making it a head-spinning crash course in the four-beat basics.

LEAVE HER TO **HEAVEN**

(1945, FoxVideo, unrated, $19.98; laserdisc $39.98) One of the creepiest of the old "women's films" finally makes it to home video. Gene Tierney (*Laura*) uses her wide-eyed beauty to unsettling effect as the all-too-devoted wife of a writer (Cornel Wilde). Refusing to share him with anybody, she lets her crippled brother-in-law drown and throws herself down the stairs to abort their baby. As one of the characters says, "There's nothing wrong with Ellen. She just loves too much."

HEAVENLY **CREATURES**

(1994, Miramax, R, priced for rental; laserdisc $39.99) Wildly stylish, this true-crime tale from New Zealand plunges viewers into the fervid inner world of its teenage antiheroines—frumpy Pauline (Melanie Lynskey) and chic, deluded Juliet (Kate Winslet)—while never muting the grimness of their murder of Pauline's mum.

NATURAL BORN KILLERS: Lynskey and Winslet in *Creatures*

FRESH

(1994, Miramax, R, priced for rental; laserdisc $39.99) Coming as it did, near the end of a cycle of violent inner-city dramas, *Fresh* was overlooked by theatrical audiences. On video, it's harder to turn away from this disturbing story of a 12-year-old drug runner (Sean Nelson) who is smart enough to recognize the destruction his bosses are wreaking, clever enough to turn the tables against them, and wise enough to mourn his own amorality.

FRESH FACE: Sean Nelson

PHOTO FINISH: *Red* (with Jacob) completes Kieslowski's color trilogy

RED

(1994, Miramax, R, priced for rental; laserdisc $39.99) Now that the third and final installment of director Krzysztof Kieslowski's *Three Colors* is on video, you can watch the entire trilogy in sequence. The voyage moves from the chilly pretensions of *Blue* to the poker-faced romantic comedy of *White* to the serene concordance of *Red*, in which the hopes of post-Communist Europe are personified by a young model (Irène Jacob) as she comes to understand a corrupt retired judge (Jean-Louis Trintignant).

BEFORE **SUNRISE**

(1995, Columbia TriStar, R, priced for rental; laserdisc $34.95) A slow starter in theaters, cowriter-director Richard Linklater's third gem in a row (after *Slacker* and *Dazed and Confused*) is finding a starry-eyed following on

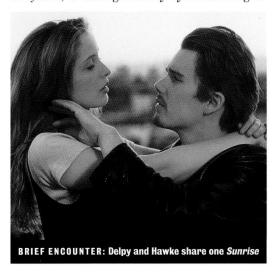

BRIEF ENCOUNTER: Delpy and Hawke share one *Sunrise*

video. If you've ever been young and stunned by sudden love, you'll click in to this tale of an American kid (Ethan Hawke) and a French girl (Julie Delpy) who meet on a train and spend a day and night AWOL with each other. Like youth itself, it's all talk—wonderful, impassioned, end-of-the-universe talk.

THE OLD **DARK HOUSE**

(1932, Kino, unrated, $24.95) The year after James Whale directed 1931's *Frankenstein*, he made the ne plus ultra of the travelers-stranded-in-a-creepy-mansion genre. Charles Laughton is one of the unlucky victims, but it's the eldritch denizens of the Femm household who'll stay with you: Boris Karloff as a mute butler,

THIS OLD *HOUSE*: Whale's creepy classic reaches a new audience

Ernest Thesiger as the bony master of the house, and—weirdest of all—actress Elspeth Dudgeon as the 102-year-old Femm *patri*arch.

BAD **COMPANY**

(1995, Touchstone, R, priced for rental) If you give in to its goofy, cynical chic, this thriller is more fun than almost anything else on video this year. Laurence Fishburne is a former CIA agent drafted by the "Company" to carry out freelance corporate sabotage, Ellen Barkin is his boss, and the two of them rip up the screen in a glorious display of hypersexed nostril-flaring. It's the kind of great trash that Hollywood is too timid to make anymore.

The Worst

O.J. FITNESS: MINIMUM MAINTENANCE FITNESS FOR MEN

1 *(1995, All Works Enterprises, $19.95)* "For men with tight schedules who feel they don't have time to go to a gym," reads the box copy. Actually, this tape (with its provocative outtakes) is for panting courtroom junkies and hopeless cynics. Is it any worse than your average fitness video? Not really. Can it be watched with any kind of objectivity? Come on. Was it the most blatantly exploitative video to be released in 1995? No easy feat, but yes, Your Honor, it was.

CYBER BANDITS

2 *(1995, Columbia TriStar, R, priced for rental; laserdisc $49.95)* Maybe it's too easy to take potshots at direct-to-video action flicks starring has-been celebs. And, true, the participation of Grace Jones, Adam Ant, and *Airplane!*'s Robert Hays wouldn't automatically make this one of the worst. No, *Cyber Bandits* is here because in a year rife with lousy cyberthrillers, it's the only one to use a *dental X-ray machine* as a futuristic prop.

NAKED IN NEW YORK

3 *(1994, Columbia TriStar, R, $19.95; laserdisc $34.95)* When did Congress pass the law that all young directors must make debut movies about the romantic and artistic travails of young directors, and that those movies must all star Eric Stoltz?

Okay, Stoltz portrays a playwright here, but the de rigueur screaming self-indulgence is present and accounted for. Wasted amid the whining: Ralph Macchio, Mary-Louise Parker, Kathleen Turner, Tony Curtis, Timothy Dalton, and a swell pop soundtrack.

EDEN DISORDER: Dana Delany had no *Exit*

EXIT TO EDEN

4 *(1994, HBO, R, priced for rental; laserdisc $34.98)* More depressing than the sight of Rosie O'Donnell and Dan Aykroyd in bondage gear is the notion that someone in Hollywood thought it would be funny. Casting the two as cops who trail smugglers to an S&M retreat, *Exit* stumbled from its kinky Anne Rice source into a weird no-man's-land of unsexy raunch and queasy slapstick.

LOVE AFFAIR

5 *(1994, Warner, PG-13, priced for rental; laserdisc $34.98)* You're a famous movie-star playboy, (Warren Beatty), and you've just settled in with your dream gal (Annette Bening). How better to show your love than producing, and casting yourselves in, a remake of *An Affair to Remember*? Just imitate the earlier movie and throw in Kate Hepburn for sentimental points.

The critics' Choices

Jim Carrey is an amateur: Kino Video's 10-tape set of mostly new-to-video masterpieces, *The Art of Buster Keaton*, proves it.

....

Video is better than TV: Forget those crappy *Jaws* reruns. MCA/Universal's new letterboxed version blows them out of the water...

....

...but even video can go too far: As if *Baywatch*'s plot twists merited more than an hour, LIVE Home Video released *Baywatch the Movie: Forbidden Paradise*.

....

Unbelievably, the Ernest franchise is alive and kicking: After *six* movies, Jim Varney returned in the straight-to-video *Slam Dunk Ernest*.

—*Chris Nashawaty*

AT HITS' END

ON *FORREST GUMP*: "Defenders of director Robert Zemeckis' movie may argue that what makes the brilliantly acted and always diverting *Gump* such fun is its unreality, that despite its use of actual events and historical figures, it's just a fairy tale with no ax to grind. Show me a Brothers Grimm story that refers to Friedrich Wilhelm IV, and I might buy it." (#273, May 5)

ON *CLUELESS*: "Character development this multileveled is virtually absent from Hollywood films these days—how ironic that it should turn up in what's been referred to as an 'MTV movie.'"(#304, Dec. 8)

ON SANDRA BULLOCK in *While You Were Sleeping*: "Giggly one minute, eyes glistening with tears the next, she seems stricken with the Meg Ryan Syndrome: an overestimation of one's own cuteness." (#295, Oct. 6)

CRUISING DIRECTORS

ON *THE LITTLE RASCALS*: "Back in the '80s, a prediction that Penelope Spheeris, the maverick filmmaker whose output consisted of disturbing rock documentaries and violent dramas of alienated youth, would someday helm a feature version of the *Our Gang* comedy shorts might have seemed as far-fetched as John Waters directing a remake of *The Sound of Music*." (#261, Feb. 10)

ON THE FILMS of Barbet Schroeder (*Kiss of Death*, *Barfly*): "Should he ever want to make an optimistic picture about his pet theme, he could do worse than to adapt the story of his own career: an outsider who makes good in Hollywood without selling his artistic soul." (#289/290, Aug. 25)

CLASSIC TAPE

"STILL, AS LOVELY as much of *The Shawshank Redemption* is, to call it a masterpiece is pushing things. In a time when 'quite good' is often a lot more than we expect, perhaps the term 'provisional masterpiece' is the correct one." (#269, April 7)

CLASSIC APE

ON *KING KONG*: "He wasn't a sneering European intellectual—in fact, he was pretty likable if you could get past the body hair and that unfortunate business with the Third Avenue El." (#305, Dec. 15)

BOTTOM SHELF

ON *IT'S PAT*: "The movie is a grisly demonstration of what happens when hubris is mistaken for common sense." (#267, March 24)

On *MALICIOUS*: "Let's call a spade a spade: Molly Ringwald as a kill-crazy femme fatale is about as scary as a pair of bunny slippers." (#299, Nov. 3)

(From reviews by Ty Burr, Bruce Fretts, and Glenn Kenny)

MOVIES, TV, BOOKS, MUSIC, MULTIMEDIA & VIDEO

almanac

THE **MOVIES**

A collection of capsule movie reviews from the pages of EW *in 1995. All reviews by* OWEN GLEIBERMAN *unless otherwise noted.*

ACE VENTURA: WHEN NATURE CALLS *(PG-13)* It's Jim Carrey's best movie yet. *When Nature Calls* finds pet detective Ventura in Africa, where he's in search of a rare white bat. As always, the verbal comedy is nonsensical and vulgar, and the physical humor is rigorously thought out and *really* vulgar. Ian McNeice plays the Englishman who accompanies Ace on his bat quest, Bob Gunton is a cackling villain, but mucus and raw vegetables might just as well receive costar billing too, for all the gleefully gross screen time Carrey gives them. There's a scene in which a mechanical rhino "gives birth" to a naked Ace that would do Buster Keaton—and Luis Buñuel—proud. **B+** (#302, Nov. 24) —*Ken Tucker*

AMATEUR *(R)* Only a fan of Hal Hartley's dissociated, Frenchified style of filmmaking—part rough action, part existentialism and cigarette smoke—is going to enjoy this fourth feature from the maker of *Trust* and *Simple Men.* Isabelle Huppert drabs down to play an unconventional ex-nun trying to divine her mission on earth. Hartley regular Martin Donovan plays a former pornographer with amnesia. Elina Lowensohn plays a girl who used to act in his films. The events that twine the three

APOLLO 13

together include the disposition of an incriminating floppy disc and pursuit by a couple of sadistic accountants, but why one event follows another is a matter of caprice. **C-** (#273, May 5) —*Lisa Schwarzbaum*

THE AMERICAN PRESIDENT *(PG-13)* President Andrew Shepherd (Michael Douglas) is a liberal-centrist baby boomer who feels the pain of everyone he meets (i.e., he's a klieg light idealization of Bill Clinton). What, the movie asks, if he were also a widower who got lonely, met a beautiful environmental lobbyist (Annette Bening), and began to court her right in the middle of his presidency? Director Rob Reiner and screenwriter Aaron Sorkin have devised a very '90s concept, a romantic comedy for the age of spin control. As long as it concentrates on such pressing issues as how, exactly, a standing president should go about ordering a dozen roses, *The American President* is pleasing fluff. Doug-

las, wearing a fast-break smile, strikes a tender rapport with Bening. But the movie's screwball charm goes down easier than its glib politics, which have been intertwined with the love story at every turn. **B-** (#301, Nov. 17) —*OG*

APOLLO 13 *(PG)* Ron Howard's uncanny docudrama about the Apollo 13 moon mission, in which an explosion forced three astronauts on a calamitous journey back to earth. The movie is so authentic in its detail that it succeeds in putting us *on* that ship. Yet Howard hasn't done enough shaping. He has made a movie of objective events—an epic of tinkering. As Jim Lovell, Tom Hanks gives a solid-guy performance encased in nobility. **B** (#281/282, June 30/July 7) —*OG*

ASSASSINS *(R)* Sylvester Stallone and Antonio Banderas as rival hitmen. The movie has a few suspenseful confrontations, but to get to them you have to wade through countless scenes of monosyllabic brooding. **C** (#296, Oct. 13) —*OG*

AN AWFULLY BIG ADVENTURE *(R)* Hugh Grant reteams with *Four Weddings and a Funeral* director Mike Newell, doing what he loves to do best: play a heel. He's fine as a theater director in 1949 Liverpool, but the story is really about a moony young thing (Georgina Cates) who gets a job as an assistant stage manager, and about the company's dashing (and, it turns out, complicated) leading man (Alan Rickman). There's a creepy allure to Rickman and it's his energy that moves this wet woolen of a story along to its surprise ending. **C** (#286, Aug. 4) —*LS*

BABE *(G)* A charmer of a family picture about a runty talking pig who learns how to do a sheepdog's job. Australian director Chris Noonan shows what talent and imagination can accomplish, even without big-name human costars. **A** (#287, Aug. 11) —*LS*

BAD BOYS *(R)* The movie is like a series of clichés exploding in your face. Martin Lawrence and Will Smith

BAD BOYS' LAWRENCE

BATMAN FOREVER

are renegade cops who joyride through Miami, talking trash and brandishing impressively large guns. **C–** (#271, April 21)   —OG

BAD COMPANY *(R)* Laurence Fishburne and Ellen Barkin are the stars of this hard-boiled egg of an espionage thriller in which people talk in a tough-assed way, do dirty deeds, have heartless sex—and none of it matters or makes any sense. **D** (#260, Feb. 3)   —LS

BAR GIRLS *(R)* A chic girl-meets-girl movie for everyone who thought the women in *Go Fish* looked too damn geeky. The eight pretty patrons at the L.A. bar in this upbeat romantic rondelet change partners easily (always wearing nice makeup), pairing off and then recombining like residents of *Melrose Place.* Keep your eyes open for a bleached-blond patron called Scorp who has one line: That's Chastity Bono, out and about. **B–** (#270, April 14)   —LS

THE BASKETBALL DIARIES *(R)* A messy adaptation of Jim Carroll's underground memoir, in which the New York author chronicled his own teenage descent into heroin addiction. As Carroll, Leonardo DiCaprio has a few great scenes, but he never seems like a true street kid. The decision to transpose Carroll's story from the '60s to the present gives the film a hazy, dissatisfying tone. **B–** (#271, April 21)   —OG

BATMAN FOREVER *(PG-13)* It's like spending two hours inside a happy asylum. The characters—heroes *and* villains—are all addicts, each swallowed up in his or her own obsession. And so is the director, Joel Schumacher, who gets high on color and movement, on the

ripe possibilities of camp villainy. As the Riddler, Jim Carrey is at his most ecstatically psychotic. By now, he's doing sarcastic takes on his own sarcasm. **B** (#280, June 23)   —OG

BEFORE SUNRISE *(R)* Riding the train to Vienna, Jesse (Ethan Hawke), a handsomely scruffy American, meets Céline (Julie Delpy), a button-cute French college student. He invites her to get off the train and explore the city with him, and that's the entire film: two wised-up young people wandering around Vienna as they flirt, joke, bicker, and confess their way to a startlingly tender romantic epiphany. **A–** (#259, Jan. 27)   —OG

BEFORE THE RAIN *(Unrated)* Macedonian writer-director Milcho Manchevski uses the geometry of circles to build this harrowing, poetic drama about the incomprehensibility—and the timelessness—of hatred, violence, and war. The three episodes link together, *Pulp Fiction*-like, to form an unexpectedly powerful whole. **A** (#266, March 17)   —LS

BEFORE SUNRISE

BELLE DE JOUR *(R)* The rerelease of Luis Buñuel's great deadpan comedy of erotic liberation. A polite young bourgeois housewife (Catherine Deneuve) plays out her sadomasochistic daydreams by going to work in a classy brothel. The film's theme is the untamability of the erotic imagination. **A** (#281/282, June 30/July 7)   —OG

BEYOND RANGOON *(R)* In John Boorman's Third World-in-crisis political drama, an American tourist,

Laura Bowman (Patricia Arquette), stumbles into the middle of a revolution: the democratic movement in Burma, where thousands of citizens rose up in protest against the country's military dictatorship. The heroine is presumably there to be the audience's representative. But since the focus is entirely on *her* naïveté, *her* struggle, *her* growth, the film effectively reduces the Burmese quagmire to a vacation from hell. It might have helped if we were remotely engaged by Laura Bowman. But Arquette gives her no special curiosity or vigor. **D+** (#289/290, Aug. 25/Sept. 1)   —OG

BILLY MADISON *(PG-13)* Adam Sandler's whiny narcissism is on full display in *Billy Madison*, a kind of dumbed-down *Kindergarten Cop* in which he plays an infantile rich kid who's forced to repeat grades 1 through 12. By the end, you feel like a drill sergeant—you want to wipe that stupid grin off Sandler's face. **D** (#263/264, Feb. 24/March 3)   —OG

BLUE IN THE FACE *(R)* The second collaboration between director Wayne Wang and novelist-screenwriter Paul Auster is set in the same cozy-seedy Brooklyn cigar store that served as the hub for their art-house hit, *Smoke.* But this time, no one's minding the store. Shot in less than seven days, *Blue in the Face* is a semi-improvisatory funk vaudeville—a rambling series of actors' riffs on the Brooklyn state of mind. Most of the actors, including Madonna, Roseanne, and RuPaul, seem stranded in a sitcom without a situation. **C** (#297, Oct. 20)   —OG

BOYS ON THE SIDE *(R)* A fake—but an effective one. Whoopi Goldberg (the mouthy lesbian), Mary-Louise Parker (the demure

hetero with AIDS), and Drew Barrymore (the pregnant cupcake who may have killed her boyfriend) play an Odd Trio on the road, bonding as only women in Herbert Ross movies know how: *meaningfully.* The acting is strong, the issues are serious, and the tears flow. The emotional re-

BRAVEHEART

frain—"There's something that goes on between women"—never leaves the screen for a minute. **B–** (#261, Feb. 10)   —LS

THE BRADY BUNCH MOVIE *(PG-13)* A sly and witty surprise. The surreal wholesomeness of the Bradys has been turned inside out, so that the film surveys its characters with the same sharp-eyed derisive glee the audience does. **A–** (#263/264, Feb. 24/March 3) —OG

BRAVEHEART *(R)* Mel Gibson plays William Wallace, the 13th-century Scottish avenger who led his countrymen in revolt against England. Gibson, who also directed, turns warfare into brutal poetic spectacle. *Braveheart*, though, doesn't always find the drama to match its images of medieval combat. Fortunately, Gibson holds the film together with his studly blue-eyed dazzle. Plus, he looks great in blood. **B–** (#276, May 26)   —OG

THE BRIDGES OF MADISON COUNTY *(PG-13)* Meryl Streep and her costar and director, Clint Eastwood, purge the Robert James Waller novella of its treacly showmanship. Set in 1965, *Bridges* tells the story of Francesca Johnson (Streep), an Italian-born farmwife who is drawn into a four-day romance with Robert Kincaid (Eastwood), a New Age Marlboro Man. What moves us is less the affair itself than the film's enraptured sympathy for all the women who've yearned, in equal measure, to be both lover and caretaker. **A** (#278, June 9) —*OG*

THE BROTHERS MCMULLEN *(R)* Edward Burns' made-on-a-shoestring story about the romantic troubles of three Irish-Catholic brothers on Long Island is pleasant but slight. Its weaknesses are due to a simplistic approach to character that will undoubtedly deepen as the bright novice filmmaker himself matures. **B-** (#288, Aug. 18) —*LS*

BURNT BY THE SUN

BULLETPROOF HEART *(R)* It's small and noir-colored, but it ain't no *Last Seduction*. Anthony LaPaglia plays a dead-hearted hitman hired by a client (Peter Boyle) to kill a broad (Mimi Rogers) who knows too much and welcomes death—but apparently causes men to melt at her feet just when they're supposed to pull the trigger. LaPaglia is great at conveying psychic emptiness, and for contrast he's paired with Matt Craven as a nervous, emotional sidekick who *aspires* to manly heartlessness. Rogers, however, is so posed in her forced sultriness that she's unbelievable as a femme fatale, slowing the whole thing down. **B** (#269, April 7) —*LS*

BURNT BY THE SUN *(R)* In one of the many moving scenes in Nikita Mikhalkov's Oscar-winning fable, Sergueï Kotov (played by Mikhalkov), a robust hero of the Revolution, takes his 6-year-old daughter (Nadia Mikhalkov) out on a rowboat. For a few minutes, we understand the Communist dream in all its utopian fervor. Set in 1936,

just as Stalin was launching the great purges, *Burnt by the Sun* is about the moment when Russian Communism passed from idealism into nightmare. **B+** (#273, May 5) —*OG*

BYE BYE, LOVE *(PG-13)* The toll divorce takes on dads and their kids is given a smooth once-over by a TV-oriented production team. Paul Reiser (the moony one), Matthew Modine (the flirt), and Randy Quaid (the angry galoot) are ex-husbands and postfeminist pops trying to get by in these complicated '90s. **B-** (#266, March 17) —*LS*

C **CANADIAN BACON** *(PG)* Playing an American sheriff who leads an invasion of Canada in this determinedly wacky comedy, John Candy (in what turned out to be his final film release) is, as usual, lovable. Directed by Michael Moore (*Roger & Me*), the film is a twist on the 1959 Peter Sellers comedy *The Mouse That Roared*: The American President makes war on Canada to boost his popularity. *Bacon*'s devilish conceit (capitalist war machine exploits socialist peaceableness) jibes with Moore's leftist politics. But something's missing: big laughs. **C+** (#295, Oct. 6) —*KT*

CANDYMAN: FAREWELL TO THE FLESH *(R)* The return of Candyman (Tony Todd), the tall, black, hook-handed slasher who looks like a depressed Eurotrash model. This cloddish sequel undermines its revenge-of-the-repressed premise with racist scare tactics: Whenever it wants to fake the audience into thinking the killer's

CONGO

around, it simply cuts to a shot of...another black man. **D** (#268, March 31) —*OG*

CARRINGTON *(R)* A tea cozy of an import with an arresting kink at its center. Emma Thompson, wearing a look of saintly rectitude, is Dora Carrington, the British painter and bohemian of the early 1900s. At the dawn of World War I, she meets Lytton Strachey (Jonathan Pryce), an eminent literary scholar 13 years her senior. Despite his awkward appearance—he's gangly and frail, with the bushy-wushy beard of a diffident rabbi—the two are drawn into a love affair that lasts for the rest of their lives. It's an affair of the spirit only, though, for Strachey is homosexual. Pryce, in a likable performance, chews on his witticisms as if they were poisoned gumdrops. But Thompson never brings Carrington's soul into focus. What the film wants to pass off as a dangerous liaison looks more like the ultimate in safe sex. **B-** (#301, Nov. 17) —*OG*

CASINO *(R)* Heady and engrossing—but only for a while. In Martin Scorsese's new blood-and-glitz underworld epic, Robert De Niro plays Sam "Ace" Rothstein, a legendary gambler who arrives in Las Vegas in the early '70s to rule the Tangiers, a posh casino-hotel that's owned by the Mob. We see him master the tricks of the trade.

CIRCLE OF FRIENDS

We see him fall for the boozy, gold-digging hustler Ginger McKenna (Sharon Stone). And we see him trapped in a lethal dance of wills with longtime pal Nicky Santoro (Joe Pesci, doing high-pitched riffs on his *GoodFellas* persona). Through it all, however, Ace remains what he always w/as: a dourly "civilized" efficiency expert. Scorsese creates an almost surgical slice of backroom intrigue. At the same time, he bombards us with so much objective information about his characters that he never quite finds their souls. **B-** (#303, Dec. 1) —*OG*

CASPER *(PG)* Casper, the boy ghost with a head like an oversize lightbulb, is supposed to be a lonely fellow, but this Steven Spielberg production is too intent on being a romper room for short attention spans to settle into an emotion like loneliness. **C** (#277, June 2) —*OG*

CIRCLE OF FRIENDS *(PG-13)* Charming in a wee, conservative way. As a small-town Irish teenager in the '50s who goes off to university, Minnie Driver has a touchingly awkward prettiness. In Dublin, she and her two comrades, all virgins, lose their innocence with a swooning trepidation that almost makes one nostalgic for a more repressed era. **B-** (#267, March 24) —*OG*

CLOCKERS *(R)* Spike Lee directed this electrifying adaptation of the inner-city novel by Richard Price. Set in Brooklyn, the movie pivots around the deceptively

146

passive figure of Strike (Mekhi Phifer), a 19-year-old crack dealer who may or may not have committed a murder. Lee creates a kaleidoscopic vision of a community mired in betrayal, psychosis, and murder. **A** (#292, Sept. 15) —*OG*

CLUELESS *(PG-13)* Cher (Alicia Silverstone), the vacuous heroine, is a Beverly Hills princess who lives in a haze of charge accounts and pop-culture references, most of which date back no further than the late '80s. There are funny bits in Amy Heckerling's high school satire, but the characters are teen-movie zombies with no personality apart from their trendoid obsessions. **C+** (#285, July 28) —*OG*

CONGO *(PG-13)* It's about a gorilla who knows sign language and a search for diamonds in the heart of Africa, but this Michael Crichton thriller looks more like a fugitive from *Mystery Science Theater 3000* than the $60 million production it is. **D-** (#279, June 16) —*LS*

COPYCAT *(R)* Sigourney Weaver is a forensic psychologist specializing in serial killers. She's attacked by a psycho (played by an uglified Harry Connick Jr.) and becomes an apartment-bound agoraphobic. But Holly Hunter, as a tough police detective, needs her help in tracking down a new multiple murderer, a copycat who commits his crimes in the manner of other famous serial killers. The plot is limp—you'll anticipate every twist—but the movie is a showcase for terrific, subtle performances by Weaver and Hunter. **B** (#299, Nov. 3) —*KT*

CRIMSON TIDE *(R)* In Tony Scott's terrific submarine thriller, Frank Ramsey (Gene Hackman), the captain of the USS *Alabama*, faces off against his young executive officer (Denzel Washington) over whether to launch a defensive nuclear strike. The two actors turn the movie into a riveting oedipal military duel. **A-** (#274, May 12) —*OG*

THE CROSSING GUARD *(R)* The second film written and directed by Sean Penn is, like his first, *The Indian Runner* (1991), a self-conscious anthem to macho despair—it's yet another tale of two men torn (and bound together) by violence. Jack Nicholson gives a powerful performance as Freddy Gale, a Los Angeles jewelry-store owner who has been living in hell ever since his 7-year-old daughter was killed by a drunken driver. To lance the boil of his rage, he becomes obsessed with murdering the man responsible, a blue-collar hulk (David Morse) who has served five years for manslaughter and emerges from prison so racked with guilt that he actually wants Freddy to kill him. *The Crossing Guard* is a work of talent, and it is also a willed exercise in purgative alienation (imagine *Death Wish* remade by Michelangelo Antonioni). What's more, so many of the film's details—late-night whiskey binges, fistfights, scenes set at a grimy strip club—echo Penn's own infamous tabloid antics that at times, he seems to be flirting with a kind of guttersnipe chic. **B-** (#302, Nov. 24) —*OG*

COPYCAT'S WEAVER

CRUMB *(R)* Terry Zwigoff's extraordinary documentary follows the underground cartoonist R. Crumb. A portrait of the artist as misanthrope, as bad-boy visionary, as joker and sex maniac, and finally as hero, this is the rare film experience that has the giddy effect of being a nightmare and a party at the same time. **A** (#272, April 28) —*OG*

THE CURE *(PG-13)* An 11-year-old boy (Joseph Mazzello) contracts AIDS from a blood transfusion, and his best friend (Brad Renfro)

concocts "cures" for his ailing buddy. The film moves us to tears about the nature of friendship; yet, curiously, it makes us not care about the deadly illness that can kill our friends. **B-** (#271, April 21) —*LS*

DANGEROUS MINDS *(R)* Slick, syrupy fraudulence, as Lou-Anne Johnson (Michelle Pfeiffer), a former Marine, takes over a high school class of taunting, rap-generation delinquents. This is the kind of smarmy inspirational-teacher fable that worships the idea of knowledge without bothering to put any on screen. **C-** (#287, Aug. 11) —*OG*

DEAD PRESIDENTS *(R)* A blazing mix of action thriller, war story, and family saga, the Hughes brothers' film follows a lower-middle-class Bronx youth (Larenz Tate) from his career as numbers runner to a stint in Vietnam to an armored-car heist. **A-** (#297, Oct. 20) —*KT*

DEATH AND THE MAIDEN *(R)* Riveting. In an unnamed South American country, Paulina Escobar (Sigourney Weaver) finds herself in close quarters—i.e., in her own living room—with the man (Ben Kingsley) she's certain raped and tortured her. Roman Polanski has turned Ariel Dorfman's play into a sadomasochistic love story that locks torturer and victim in a chillingly intimate spiritual embrace. **A-** (#260, Feb. 3) —*OG*

DESPERADO *(R)* Robert Rodriguez's propulsive rock & roll spaghetti Western. The plot has all the sophistication of a dime-store novel cover, but in *Desperado* the wittily hyperbolic gunplay *is* the story. As the mariachi with no name, Antonio Banderas is an icon of feral, strutting vengeance. The camera loves this velvet stud as much as it did the young Clint Eastwood. **B** (#289/290, Aug. 25/Sept. 1) —*OG*

DEVIL IN A BLUE DRESS *(R)* In Carl Franklin's adaptation of Walter Mosley's mystery novel, Denzel Washington

is Ezekiel "Easy" Rawlins, the amateur sleuth who steps into corruption and danger, murder and blackmail. Jennifer Beals is the title character, a slinky heap of trouble who's called

DEVIL'S WASHINGTON

Daphne Monet. Unfortunately, Franklin shows us this landscape as if we're on a bus ride through an unfamiliar part of town. **C** (#294, Sept. 29) —*LS*

DIE HARD WITH A VENGEANCE *(R)* A terrorist (Jeremy Irons) sets bombs all over Manhattan. But he's also a sick prankster who develops a mysterious obsession with Bruce Willis' John McClane. The director, John McTiernan, stages individual sequences with finesse, but they don't add up to a taut, dread-ridden whole. **C+** (#276, May 26) —*OG*

DISCLOSURE *(R)* Demi Moore and Michael Douglas star in a glibly entertaining adaptation of Michael Crichton's best-seller. The film's true subject isn't sexual harassment but the ways in which corporate paranoia and ruthlessness acquire new force in an era of advanced technology. **B+** (#253, Dec. 16, 1994) —*OG*

DOLORES CLAIBORNE *(R)* Based on Stephen King's 1992 novel, this solemnly ludicrous "psychological" thriller is like one of Hollywood's old-hag gothics—it's *Hush...Hush, Sweet Charlotte* for the age of Oprah. Kathy Bates is in full irritable cry as Dolores Claiborne, a widow who's been an outcast in her lonely Maine village ever since she was accused of killing her husband. Jennifer Jason

Leigh, as her daughter, helps unravel the mystery. **D+** (#268, March 31) —*OG*

DON JUAN DEMARCO *(PG-13)* Director Jeremy Leven's coup was to cast Johnny Depp as a young man who says he's the legendary Spanish lover, Marlon Brando as his shrink, and Faye Dunaway as the doctor's wife—and to let the whimsy rip. Pairing Depp and Brando results in a beautifully syncopated relationship. **A–** (#269, April 7) —*LS*

DROP ZONE *(R)* John Badham works big, fast, and loud in this macho action fantasy set in the daredevil society of sky divers. Wesley Snipes plays a federal marshal on the trail of a gang of parachute-proficient bad guys, including Gary Busey and Michael Jeter. The on-ground episodes tend to flop and stumble, but the aerial sequences are thrilling. **B–** (#253, Dec. 16, 1994) —*LS*

EXOTICA

DUMB AND DUMBER *(PG-13)* Rubbery handsome, with fashion-disaster bangs and the dimples of a depraved gopher, Jim Carrey turns his face into a human morph machine. *Dumb and Dumber*, which features Carrey and Jeff Daniels as nitwits traveling cross-country, is a frayed string of gags posing as a movie. But Carrey does doofdom with peerless enthusiasm—he's like a less precious Robin Williams. **B–** (#257, Jan. 13) —*OG*

THE ENGLISHMAN WHO WENT UP A HILL BUT CAME DOWN A MOUNTAIN *(PG-13)* A calculated-to-be-quirky Welsh fable with a Hugh Grant romance smuggled into the middle of it. In 1917, a pair of English cartographers (Grant and Ian McNeice)

arrive in Ffynnon Garw to measure the local landmark, a broad, grassy peak named after the village itself. If Ffynnon Garw turns out to be over 1,000 feet high, it will be labeled a mountain on all British maps; otherwise, it will be relegated to mere hill status. When the prized peak is revealed to be 984 feet high, the locals launch a campaign to heighten the top. There's something both funny and touching in the slightly batty literal-mindedness of this crusade, while at the same time, it's hard to shake the feeling that we're seeing the British Isles strip-mined for its eccentricity. Grant is already threatening to turn into a parody of himself. **B–** (#275, May 19) —*OG*

EXOTICA *(R)* The key setting is a shimmery-dark strip club, where Christina (Mia Kirshner) does table dances dressed up as a Catholic schoolgirl. The Canadian writer-director Atom Egoyan certainly knows how to exploit our attraction to sin. He lures us with jailbait naughtiness, with the passing suggestion that his hero (Bruce Greenwood) may have been involved in the murder of somebody close to him. But the odd thing about *Exotica* is that the more its intricate puzzle narrative yields its secrets, the less interesting the film becomes. In the end, the characters' "dark" compulsions are illusory. Egoyan the bad-boy voyeur turns out to be a good-boy prude. **B+** (#267, March 24) —*OG*

FAIR GAME *(R)* A thriller that's primarily about the movement of Cindy Crawford's breasts beneath a succession of ever-smaller T-shirts, this dim film finds the model/actress playing a lawyer hunted by former KGB agents. William Baldwin is a cop assigned to protect her. The movie moves briskly for its scant 90 min-

utes, and director Andrew Sipes stages a few colorful explosions, but there's nothing here you haven't seen before—other than the spectacle of Crawford making dashes to safety in tank

FARINELLI'S DIONISI

tops and high heels that are far more wobbly than any moves she's made on a fashion runway. **C** (#301, Nov. 17) —*KT*

FARINELLI *(R)* When Farinelli (Stéfano Dionisi), the most famous castrato of the 18th century, walks on stage, he may look like something out of *The Adventures of Priscilla, Queen of the Desert*, but his eerie vocal androgyny makes the countesses in the audience weep and swoon. Unfortunately, the rest of *Farinelli*—a crudely plotted pulp comic book—suggests a James Dean movie directed by Lina Wertmüller at her most threadbare hysterical. **C** (#266, March 17) —*OG*

FATHER OF THE BRIDE PART II *(PG)* Steve Martin, Diane Keaton, and Martin Short are all back for this sequel, in which Keaton's character is pregnant at the same time as her daughter (doe-eyed Kimberly Williams)—once you understand the gimmick, you can predict the jokes. *FOB Part II* starts off weak but finishes strong—wacky and weepy, silly and sweet. And oh, those adorable babies at the conclusion! It's a big, corny, old-fashioned movie, but as crowd-pleasers go, it's also an extremely shrewd one. **B–** (#305, Dec. 15) —*KT*

FEDERAL HILL *(R)* By now, homages to Martin Scorsese's *Mean Streets* are practically a genre within the independent film movement, but that shouldn't stop you from seeing Michael Corrente's powerfully engrossing first feature, which may in fact be the greatest rip-off of *Mean Streets* ever made (and yes, that is meant as high praise). Corrente artfully sketches the members of a twentysomething Italian-American rat pack, the sons of Mob lackeys in Providence, R.I. The Keitel and De Niro characters in *Mean Streets* become Nicky (Anthony De Sando), a suavely handsome drug dealer whose dreams of a life beyond Providence draw him into a love affair with a Brown University student (Libby Langdon), and Ralph (*NYPD Blue*'s Nicholas Turturro), a hot-headed master thief who—in Corrente's most inspired stroke—is both the craziest and most intelligent character in the movie. In *Federal Hill*, even the most casual and loving encounters—between father and son, buddies around a poker table, Nicky and his collegiate Madonna—are rooted in the clandestine threat of terror. **A–** (#258, Jan. 2) —*OG*

FIRST KNIGHT *(R)* In Jerry Zucker's retelling of the Camelot saga, King Arthur (Sean Connery) has become a middle-aged warlord whose fiancée, Guinevere (Julia Ormond), looks at him with affection but also with a twinge of ambiguity: Is she marrying him for true love, or because he'll protect her lands? Zucker shows his flair for lush, bounding images, and

FORGET PARIS

for wedding action to emotion. Unfortunately, Richard Gere's Lancelot is a void at the center of the movie. He's supposed to be a blank-souled narcissist ignited by love, but Gere, while great at playing blank-souled narcissists, is at a loss when he has to reveal his passion. **B-** (#283, July 14)   —*OG*

FLUKE *(PG)* Any kid who sees this disjointed, bizarro movie and expects a funsy animal story is going to need trauma therapy. Matthew Modine stars as a guy who dies in a car crash and is reincarnated as a dog—a dog who *knows* he was once a man and has the vocabulary to prove it. **D** (#278, June 9)   —*LS*

FORGET PARIS *(PG-13)* The kind of skin-crawling comedy in which clichés are used to convey "meaningful" experience. Billy Crystal, as a feisty NBA referee, and Debra Winger, as a sweetly accommodating airline official, meet cute in Paris, get hitched, see their marriage sandbagged by fashionably contempo relationship disorders—and never convince you for a moment that they're playing anything but glib concoctions. **C-** (#276, May 26)   —*OG*

FRANKIE STARLIGHT *(R)* A down-to-earth gem. An Irish immigration officer (Gabriel Byrne) takes in a stowaway (Anne Parillaud) during World War II. Her dwarf son (Alan Pentony) grows up to be an astrology-loving novelist (Corban Walker), who recounts his family's story in a warm series of flashbacks. **A-** (#304, Dec. 8)   —*Bruce Fretts*

FREE WILLY 2: THE ADVENTURE HOME *(PG)* Willy, the killer whale with the cute, man-eating teeth, is back, this time with a brother, a sister, and a mom. Jesse (Jason James Richter) is also back, this time with a noodgy half brother and a dead mom. The concept that boys and whales function best when surrounded by family is easy to digest. It's the relentlessly dire message that contemporary life

FREE WILLY 2

is mucking up nature that feels like overkill. **B-** (#286, Aug. 4)   —*LS*

FRENCH KISS *(PG-13)* Meg Ryan's every gesture is calculated for cuteness in Lawrence Kasdan's meandering comedy. Ryan plays Kate, a garrulous young woman who goes to Paris to retrieve her fiancé (Timothy Hutton) from the clutches of a French beauty. Kevin Kline is the somewhat shady Frenchman who becomes enchanted by her Ryanized tics. **C** (#273, May 5)   —*LS*

FRIDAY *(R)* Craig (Ice Cube) and Smokey (Chris Tucker) are guys who sit around getting good and messed up in this rude, raw comedy set in Los Angeles. The story is morally indefensible: Smokey blows hours away in a cloud of marijuana smoke and fast-talks his buddy into trouble—but all in all director F. Gary Gray has found an effective balance between nasty stuff and stuff that cracks the viewer up. **B** (#274, May 12)   —*LS*

FUNNY BONES *(R)* This overchewed bit of whimsy is about a young nightclub comic, Tommy Fawkes (Oliver Platt), who bombs in Las Vegas in front of his famous, overbearing comedian father (Jerry Lewis) and then travels to his childhood home of Blackpool, England—a seacoast mecca of vaudeville—to find his comic roots. Platt, a beetle-browed scene-stealer, gives a star performance, and Lewis does a smoothly funny job riffing on his own image. But the British writer-director Peter Chelsom works so hard

to be charming (and wistful and jokey and touching and visually poetic) that he ends up with a labored version of Bill Forsyth's magic realism. **C+** (#268, March 31)   —*OG*

GEORGIA *(R)* A nearly perfect movie about a nearly total screwup. Jennifer Jason Leigh plays Sadie Flood, a would-be rock star doomed to live in the shadow of her sister, Georgia (Mare Winningham), who's a *true* rock star. While Georgia has become rich and beloved, with a huge audience for her artfully sung folk-rock ballads, Sadie is perennially destitute, boozing and drugging. Leigh's performance is tremendously brave and ferocious; Winningham's is subtle and heartbreaking. **A** (#304, Dec. 8)   —*KT*

GEORGIA'S LEIGH

GET SHORTY *(R)* A cracklingly energized adaptation of Elmore Leonard's 1990 crime-caper novel. Director Barry Sonnenfeld finds a broad equivalent to Leonard's propulsive-trash style, and the movie has a wonderfully sleek hero in John Travolta, who plays Chili Palmer, the Miami loan shark–turned–would-be movie investor, with the same impervious brashness that made him such a charmer in *Pulp Fiction*. The other characters are so thin, though, that all of their encounters begin to seem weightless. **B** (#298, Oct. 27)   —*OG*

GOLDENEYE *(PG-13)* Fast cars! Exotic games of baccarat! Naughty double entendres that might have been cribbed from a 20-year-old copy of *Playboy*!

Are we having fun now or what? After three decades and 17 films, the Bond series has entered a near-terminal state of exhaustion. Like all Bond films, this one has some good bits, such as the lavishly preposterous opening sequence. Still, just about everything in *Goldeneye*, from its rote nuclear-weapon-in-space plot to the recitation of lines that sound like they're being read off of stone tablets ("Shaken, not stirred!"), has been served up with a thirdhand generic competence that's more wearying than it is exhilarating. Pierce Brosnan, for all the blitheness of his throwaway style, has a presence that's as light as balsa wood. You never really believe he's James Bond. He's just a spryly presentable British preppie—the empire's new tux. **C+** (#302, Nov. 24)   —*OG*

A GREAT DAY IN HARLEM *(Unrated)* A nostalgic, homegrown documentary (nominated for a Best Documentary Oscar) about the making of a famous photograph: Art Kane's extraordinary assembly of 57 jazz musicians—including Count Basie, Dizzy Gillespie, Mary Lou Williams, and Thelonius Monk—snapped for a 1958 issue of *Esquire*. What makes Jean Bach's hour-long movie swing are her coaxing interviews from participants (many of them now gone), the home movies shot that fine summer's day by musician Milt Hinton's wife, Mona, and the bits of great jazz heard in vintage clips. **B+** (#265, March 10)   —*LS*

HACKERS *(PG-13)* It would be nice to describe the second feature directed by Iain Softley, who made the terrific *BackBeat*, as a noble failure; in fact, it's a dismal mess. The plot, which centers on the attempts of Dade (Jonny Lee Miller), the cute new whiz on the block, to defeat an evil hacker (Matthew Lillard), has all the coherence of a scrambled disc. **D** (#294, Sept. 29)   —*OG*

HOW TO MAKE AN AMERICAN QUILT

HEAT *(R)* Neil McCauley (Robert De Niro) is a Los Angeles thief who orchestrates fantastically complicated heists. Vincent Hanna (Al Pacino) is an LAPD detective working around the clock to trap McCauley. It's no surprise to find these two characters sharing the spotlight in a movie written and directed by crime-story wizard Michael Mann. What *is* surprising is that the movie is 2 hours and 52 minutes long, and that neither character is entertaining enough to fill up the time. Mann's action scenes have an existential, you-are-there jitteriness, but when the characters are just sitting around hatching schemes, *Heat* is a dry, talky movie. Halfway through, the two actors finally get a scene together, and you can feel their joy in performing. We're not just watching McCauley and Hanna anymore; we're watching De Niro and Pacino trying to out-insinuate each other. For a few moments, *Heat* truly has some. **B-** (#306, Dec. 22)   —*OG*

HIGHER LEARNING *(R)* Set at the fictional Columbus University, John Singleton's movie starts out as a socially conscious *Academia, 90210* and soon devolves into a demagogic rabble-rouser. The usual collegiate cliques and factions are presented as rigidly as the high school caste system in any of John Hughes' teen movies. **C** (#257, Jan. 13)   —*OG*

HOME FOR THE HOLIDAYS *(PG-13)* In director Jodie Foster's bittersweet family valentine, Claudia Larson (Holly Hunter) returns to Baltimore to spend Thanksgiving at her parents' house. There, amid a handful of crackpot relatives, she is treated to a heaping portion of what the movie regards as America's real family values: dread, bickering resentment, faded dreams. Foster insists on dramatizing this emotional crazy quilt in a way that's nearly as unstable as the Larsons themselves. She produces scene after scene of rudderless banter; the actors seem lost in their busy, fractious shticks. The most fascinating character is also the most irritating: Claudia's gay brother, an infantile put-on artist played by Robert Downey Jr. with showboating obnoxiousness. **C-** (#300, Nov. 10)   —*OG*

HOUSEGUEST *(PG)* The one sharp joke buried in the Jell-O of this low-energy comedy is that white people can't tell black people apart. The comedian Sinbad—always PG, always likable, often comedically shapeless—plays Kevin, a decent-hearted wiseacre who passes himself off as the old friend of a rich, square suburbanite (Phil Hartman, doing one of his patented Republican daddies-with-a-lockjaw-smile). By the end, he has taught the whole family how to loosen up and get down. **B-** (#258, Jan. 20)   —*LS*

HOW TO MAKE AN AMERICAN QUILT *(PG-13)* A likable drama cut from the same cloth as *The Joy Luck Club.* Winona Ryder plays a Gen Xer who learns from the travails of her fore-

JADE

mothers, members of a California quilting bee. **B** (#296, Oct. 13)   —*BF*

I CAN'T SLEEP *(Unrated)* Not your usual portrait of a serial killer, this beautifully shaped film from director Claire Denis is based on a real-life 1980s Parisian crime wave in which a transvestite and his lover murdered more than 20 old women. Richard Courcet is the main killer, Alex Descas is his loner of a brother, and Katerina Golubeva is Daiga, a Lithuanian with little understanding of French who drifts through a city that appears sinister, romantic, and matter-of-fact all at once. **A-** (#291, Sept. 8)   —*LS*

I.Q.

IMMORTAL BELOVED *(R)* A robust and passionately schlocky biographical melodrama that milks Ludwig van Beethoven's deafness for its full measure of morbid romanticism. Gary Oldman's Beethoven, for all his brutish intensity, is trapped in sadness, in the experience of a sublimity he can't locate in life. The central story—about the composer's love-letter correspondent—is sketchy, but what has force here is the vision of Beethoven as a man equally driven by demons and angels. **B** (#258, Jan. 20)   —*OG*

IN THE MOUTH OF MADNESS *(R)* In John Carpenter's thriller, Sam Neill plays an insurance investigator unhinged by the novels of Sutter Cane (Jurgen Prochnow), a writer who is so diabolically hypnotic that readers of his books go insane. Look for bloody axes, disfigured zombies, and creepy visions—much of it self-indulgent and in a small way wickedly funny. **C** (#261, Feb. 10)   —*LS*

THE INCREDIBLY TRUE ADVENTURE OF TWO GIRLS IN LOVE *(R)* Incredulity is the pertinent word for Maria Maggenti's unexceptional lesbian fantasy, a movie that coasts for far too many miles on the current vogue for films about girls who love girls. Laurel Holloman plays Randy, a boyish loner (think Julie Harris in *The Member of the Wedding*) who lives in working-class disarray with her lesbian aunt (and said aunt's girlfriend and ex-girlfriend), and who's an outcast in her high school. Nicole Parker plays her classmate Evie—beautiful, cultured, affluent, popular, and black. The acting is amateurish, the dialogue is stiff, the secondary characters are caricatures, the attempts at humor are clumsy, and (for those finicky about character development, even in a lighthearted comedy), the attraction between these two isn't believable for a second. **C** (#281/282, June 30/July 7)   —*LS*

THE INDIAN IN THE CUPBOARD *(PG)* A boy (Hal Scardino) becomes chummy with magical visitors—toy figurines that, when unlocked from a wooden cupboard, turn into pocket-size people. What saves the film from an overdose of twinkles is the mix of director Frank Oz's appreciation of the non sequiturs of enchantment, Melissa Mathison's adultly funny script, and the least Hollywood-egenic cast in ages. **B** (#285, July 28) —*LS*

INTERVIEW WITH THE VAMPIRE *(R)* Beautiful but inert. Tom Cruise and Brad Pitt star in Neil Jordan's adaptation of the Anne Rice novel. When the characters aren't chomping on each other's necks (always fun to see), they're standing around in drawing rooms exchanging mournful *pensées.* **C-** (#249, Nov. 18, 1994)   —*OG*

I.Q. *(PG)* Albert Einstein (Walter Matthau) tries to spark a romance between his niece (Meg Ryan) and the mechanic (Tim Robbins) who's fallen for her. Despite many coy references to overactive minds, the film never succeeds in putting one on screen. **C** (#254, Dec. 23, 1994) —*OG*

IT TAKES TWO *(PG)* Two more reasons why TV is better than the movies: The Olsen twins are now big-screen stars. Surpris-

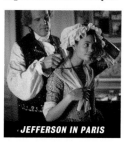

JEFFERSON IN PARIS

ingly, the 9-year-old ex–*Full House* runts made a canny choice for their debut film. In this *Prince and the Pauper/Parent Trap* hybrid, a street orphan (Mary-Kate—or is it Ashley?) and her rich doppelgänger (the other Olsen) switch places to fix up one's would-be adoptive mom (Kirstie Alley) with the other's millionaire-widower dad (Steve Guttenberg). It seems only fitting that the flavorless Guttenberg would land in this smooth tapioca concoction, but Alley deserves better. **C+** (#302, Nov. 24) —*BF*

JADE *(R)* More like a mediocre episode of *NYPD Blue* than a real feature film. David Caruso plays a DA out to solve the murder of his boss. *The Last Seduction*'s Linda Fiorentino is a supposedly irresistible combination of psychologist and hooker. Director William Friedkin can't do much with Joe Eszterhas' pervervid script; neither can Fiorentino, who's around primarily to illustrate an abstract concept: woman as predatory beast. **D** (#298, Oct. 27) —*KT*

JEFFERSON IN PARIS *(PG-13)* In this lavish Merchant Ivory film, Thomas Jefferson (Nick Nolte) emerges as a figure of passionate contradictions. He is the philosopher-saint of the American Revolution, yet he's also a cultivated aristocrat. He woos the elegant artiste Maria Cosway (Gre-

ta Scacchi), yet he begins to sleep with his 15-year-old slave, Sally Hemings (Thandie Newton). *Jefferson in Paris* brings the cocoon of prerevolutionary Paris to vivid, eccentric life. For all its historical fascination, though, the film loses the pulse of its characters. **C** (#269, April 7) —*OG*

JEFFREY *(R)* Paul Rudnick's hetero-friendly gay love story, adapted from his stage play, is about funny, neurotic Jeffrey (Steven Weber), whose vow to swear off sex out of fear of AIDS is tested by his interest in a nice, HIV-positive hunk (Michael T. Weiss). Patrick Stewart steals the show as Jeffrey's sharp-tongued decorator friend. But the clever shape of Rudnick's theater piece is flattened in director Christopher Ashley's film translation. **B** (#288, Aug. 18) —*LS*

JOHNNY MNEMONIC *(R)* Keanu Reeves plays a "mnemonic courier" with a computer chip implanted in his brain. He spends the film skulking around with his poor lobes jammed to capacity. The very notion of Keanu Reeves suffering from cerebral overload sounds like some sort of bad joke. Offhand, it would be hard to think of an actor who could use a brain implant *more*. A slack future-shock thriller, *Johnny Mnemonic* is basically *Blade Runner* with tackier sets. Most of it is set in Newark, N.J., and the big news about Newark in the 21st century is that it looks like…Newark. **C-** (#278, June 9) —*OG*

JUDGE DREDD *(R)* A big, dumb, amusingly disreputable action fantasy that barely bothers to shrug at the fact that its hero (Sylvester Stallone) is a 21st-century storm trooper. **C+** (#283, July 14) —*OG*

JUMANJI *(PG)* The title refers to a magical board game: With each roll of the dice, a different species of jungle beast comes tearing through the house. Bats fly in from the fireplace, chattering monkeys

take over the kitchen, an angry herd of rhinos and elephants and zebras races through the hallways. Simulated by the same astonishingly three-dimensional computer technology that was used to create all the dinosaurs in *Jurassic Park*, the animals in *Jumanji* are far more threatening—quicker, louder, wilder—than real jungle animals. The filmmakers re-create these safari creatures with wizardly finesse but then they can't think of anything to do with them but zap you. The plot is cardboard Spielberg, a B-movie scrap heap of spare parts lifted from *Jurassic Park* and *Gremlins* and *Back to the Future*. Robin Williams, as an adult survivor of Jumanji, spends most of the movie in his sheepish domestic-guy mode. **C+** (#305, Dec. 15) —*OG*

JURY DUTY *(PG-13)* Pauly Shore plays a slacker who hooks up with what he hopes will be the longest

JUDGE DREDD'S STALLONE

trial possible. A little Shore goes a long way, but you may find yourself laughing out of gratitude that it's not Judge Ito's courtroom you're watching. **C+** (#271, April 21) —*LS*

JUST CAUSE *(R)* Director Arne Glimcher tries like hell to spook up the screen in this thriller about a black man (Blair Underwood) on death row for the murder of a white girl. And the effort shows. As the Harvard law professor who's hired to save Underwood, Sean Connery seems exhausted. **C-** (#263/264, Feb. 24/March 3) —*LS*

KICKING AND SCREAMING *(R)* The young writer and director Noah Baumbach has a rare gift for lines that sound casual yet spin and glimmer on screen like so many verbal pinwheels. *Kicking and Screaming* charts the wayward routines of four postcollegiate slackers who shroud their aimlessness in thickets of wit, triviality, and confessional asides, most of which go by so quickly that you'll do a double take before you see how revealing they are. The actors interlock with a dexterity that, at times, rivals that of the *Seinfeld* ensemble. **B+** (#300, Nov. 10) —*OG*

KIDS *(Unrated)* Larry Clark's starkly sensational drama is about the rap-and-skateboard Manhattan kids who've honed their attitude on the knife edge of urban nihilism. But its real subject is the annihilation of empathy in American life. If *Kids* is simultaneously engrossing and detached, that's because the film is so caught up in trying to be a statement that it never develops its characters beyond their rowdy, bellicose facades. **B** (#284, July 21) —*OG*

KISS OF DEATH *(R)* In this supremely satisfying remake of the 1947 film noir. David Caruso has an implosive intensity as Jimmy Kilmartin, an ex-crook coerced back into the underworld. **A** (#271, April 21) —*OG*

LEAVING LAS VEGAS *(R)* The hero, Ben Sanderson (Nicolas Cage), drinks heavily from one morning to the next, in bars, restaurants, and casinos. Early on, he drives to Las Vegas, where he announces his plan to drink himself to death. What makes *Leaving Las Vegas* a weirdly haunting experience is that director Mike Figgis dares to view Ben's suicide by bender as a cracked form of redemption—a lost soul's gutter bid for grace. Cage gives a madly inspired performance as a man spilling over the edges of his own sanity. **A-** (#298, Oct. 27) —*OG*

LEGENDS OF THE FALL *(R)* It's supposed to be a timeless saga about a man with a Wild Soul. Instead, this fervent adaptation of Jim Harrison's macho novella is a lot of timeless hooey. Brad Pitt plays the untamed brother sandwiched between the rigid one (Aidan Quinn) and the idealist (Henry Thomas), all of whom are in love with the same woman (Julia Ormond). **C–** (#257, Jan. 13)   —*LS*

LITTLE ODESSA *(R)* The protagonist of 26-year-old James Gray's debut film is a blank-faced killer, Joshua Shapira (Tim Roth), who works as a hitman for the

LOSING ISAIAH

Russian Mob. Returning to the Little Odessa section of his native Brooklyn, he spends several days launching a shadowy assassination plot, evading the local crime boss (whom he'd betrayed in some equally shadowy way), and reconfronting his troubled family—alienated kid brother (Edward Furlong), cancer-stricken mother (Vanessa Redgrave), and abusive father (Maximilian Schell). Roth, a great actor, is reduced to a walking sneer, and the picture creeps along in a series of handsome but painfully languorous hazy-shade-of-winter tableaux. **C–** (#277, June 2)   —*OG*

A LITTLE PRINCESS *(G)* One of the great books of girlhood (by *The Secret Garden*'s Frances Hodgson Burnett), translated with a wonderful modern verve. Liesel Matthews is the beautiful, rich little girl who suffers at the hands of a spinster headmistress (Eleanor Bron, a terrific meanie) when her father goes off to World War I. The message is that all girls are princesses, and

to prove it, the costumes and sets are opulently gorgeous and the prevailing mood is magical. **A** (#276, May 26)

LITTLE WOMEN *(PG)* Gillian Armstrong's glowing adaptation of the Louisa May Alcott classic. Winona Ryder does Oscar-worthy work as Jo, the writer who dreams of a brilliant career; Trini Alvarado, Claire Danes, and Kirsten Dunst play sisters Meg, Beth, and Amy with uncommon understanding. **A** (#254, Dec. 23, 1994) —*LS*

LIVING IN OBLIVION *(R)* Tom DiCillo's gleefully clever satire celebrates the act of filmmaking as grand folly, a triumph of absurdist heroism. **A–** (#285, July 28) —*OG*

LOSING ISAIAH *(R)* The conflicting claims of biological and adoptive motherhood are given a calculated racial twist in this well-meaning but unbelievably utopian drama by screenwriter Naomi Foner and her husband, director Stephen Gyllenhaal. What, they posit, if the birth mother is a black, unmarried, reformed crackhead as pretty as Halle Berry? And what if the adoptive mother is a white, upper-middle-class, married social worker as beautifully maternal as Jessica Lange? The script is ultra-earnest, Berry is ultra-refined, but Lange is who you want to watch: She projects a compelling, womanly gravity and gives *Losing Isaiah* its dramatic focus. **B–** (#267, March 24)   —*LS*

LOVE AND HUMAN REMAINS *(R)* The characters in Denys Arcand's kink-comedy soap opera include a suavely moody gay waiter (Thomas Gibson) who prides himself on believing love doesn't exist; his roommate (Ruth Marshall), who's so fed up with men that she drifts into a lesbian affair; and a kittenish dominatrix (Mia Kirshner) who looks 14. The movie has such a daffy good time sending its characters through up-to-the-minute

erotic hoops you may not mind the fact that these people are walking lifestyle features (You and Your Gay Roommate, Why Guys Like to Brag, Is Heterosexuality Overrated?) drawn from the pages of *Cosmo.* **B** (#279, June 16)   —*OG*

MAD LOVE *(PG-13)* The gamine and wifty Drew Barrymore is Casey, the crazy new girl in town, and handsome, clear-eyed Chris O'Donnell plays Matt, the bright, responsible Seattle high school student who falls in love with her in this enjoyably soppy story directed by Antonia Bird (who made *Priest*). The two hit the road trying to outrace her demons (her parents want to have her committed, and they should—she's suicidal), but eventually Casey starts to unravel, and Barrymore demonstrates new, finely modulated depths to her acting abilities. **B** (#277, June 2)   —*LS*

THE MADNESS OF KING GEORGE *(Unrated)* Playwright Alan Bennett takes as his inspiration a time when George III, who lost the North American colonies, appears to have also lost his mind. Happily, this sharp-witted translation works even more effectively than the play. Nigel Hawthorne is dignified and affecting as

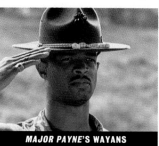

MAJOR PAYNE'S WAYANS

the miserable man who is the king but who doesn't *seem* like the king. **B+** (#258, Jan. 20)   —*LS*

MAJOR PAYNE *(PG-13)* Damon Wayans plays a sadistic simpleton of an ex-Marine who takes a job whipping a ragtag band of junior ROTC losers into shape. From the first word

he brays (in a dumb-guy voice aggravated by the addition of a couple of big gold front teeth) to the last turd reference he manages to squeeze in, Wayans has sunk to a new low. **F** (#267, March 24)   —*LS*

MALLRATS *(R)* Directed by Kevin Smith, who made a promising debut with *Clerks* (1994's weeny-budget, independent rave), *Mallrats* shows what Smith can do with a bigger budget, color film, and name actors. Well, at least one name actor: Shannen Doherty, late of *Beverly Hills, 90210* and here making a bid for hip-slacker credentials by playing a relatively small role as a girlfriend to Jason Lee, a real-life champion skateboarder making an impressively charming acting debut. Lee and Jeremy London play two lackadaisical chums hanging out at a suburban mall. As in *Clerks*, *Mallrats* is short on plot and long on dialogue. Whenever you're not chuckling, *Mallrats* leaves you wondering at the emotional emptiness of suburban youth culture, as well as at the complexity of it. **B** (#299, Nov. 3)   —*KT*

A MAN OF NO IMPORTANCE *(R)* It starts out appealingly enough. But director Suri Krishnamma's sentimental character study of Alfie (Albert Finney), a repressed bus conductor in 1963 Dublin, can't sustain the weight of its moral pretensions. Alfie is smitten in equal measure with his young bus-driving colleague (Rufus Sewell) and with Oscar Wilde; he's also terrified of (to quote Wilde's lover) "the Love that dare not speak its name." By the time Alfie comes out (big time, looking like Quentin Crisp) and his good neighbors in 1963 Dublin learn about sexual tolerance (reality check, please), the heavy life lessons have crushed the story's eggshell thinness and dissipated Finney's tender, masterful work. The cast, though, is crackerjack, including Brenda Fricker as Alfie's spinster sister, Michael Gambon

MIAMI RHAPSODY

as a conservative butcher, and Tara Fitzgerald as a young woman who is not as pure as Alfie innocently wishes her to be. **B-** (#260, Feb. 10)   —*LS*

MAN OF THE HOUSE *(PG)* Chevy Chase tries his most desperate career move yet: sincerity. As a Seattle prosecutor bent on becoming a stepfather (to *Home Improvement*'s Jonathan Taylor Thomas), Chase attempts to pass off deadpan quizzicality as *concern*. Does anyone really want to watch Chevy Chase try to be heartwarming? He had more conviction reporting the death of Franco. **D+** (#266, March 17)   —*OG*

MIAMI RHAPSODY *(PG-13)* As soon as Gwyn (Sarah Jessica Parker), the sharp-tongued heroine, delivers her opening lines, you know you're entering a suburb of Woody Allenville. The dialogue is infectiously funny, and Parker gives a terrific performance. With writer-director David Frankel, she has created an up-to-the-minute heroine, a romantic woman who earns the bittersweet luxury of refusing to define herself by love. **A-** (#259, Jan. 27)   —*OG*

MIGHTY APHRODITE *(R)* Woody Allen plays a New York sportswriter who becomes obsessed with uncovering the identity of his adopted son's biological mother. After a bit of detective work, he learns that she's a dim-bulb prostitute (Mira Sorvino) who has been laboring on the fringes of the porn industry. Allen uses the sleaze of the sex trade for a series of rudely hilarious comic shocks. And Sorvino's Linda, in her Warhol-super-

star daze, is so utterly herself that she's irresistible. **B+** (#299, Nov. 3)   —*OG*

MIGHTY MORPHIN POWER RANGERS: THE MOVIE *(PG)* A depersonalized thrill machine, yet it's exactly the film's go-go relentlessness that is likely to make kids eat it up. **B-** (#283, July 14)   —*OG*

MONEY TRAIN *(R)* A big, noisy headache of a movie, reuniting *White Men Can't Jump*ers Wesley Snipes and Woody Harrelson as New York City Transit Authority policemen. They're joined by a third cop, played by Jennifer Lopez, who instantly becomes romantically involved with both of them. Lopez gives a smashing performance, radiating braininess while making some cool martial-arts moves. Robert Blake, looking embalmed, plays a commissioner in charge of the train that carries all the money collected from the subway turnstiles. Will our heroes protect the train, or rob it? *Money Train* never gives us time to care. **D+** (#303, Dec. 1)   —*KT*

MOONLIGHT AND VALENTINO *(R)* Elizabeth Perkins plays Rebecca, who's abruptly widowed and left to the loving care of her sister (Gwyneth Paltrow), her friend (Whoopi Goldberg), and her ex-stepmother (Kathleen Turner in a haircut buzzed enough to be mistaken for Jean-Claude Van Damme's). They each help Rebecca through her grief in their own unique way (Paltrow, goofy and tentative; Goldberg, sassy and brassy; Turner, pushy and with that unplaceable annoying accent you know damn well she didn't have in *Body Heat*). The women bond ferociously—they cry,

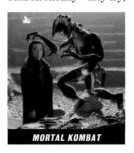

MORTAL KOMBAT

laugh, smoke cigarettes, drink white wine, and then do all that stuff over again. Written gamely, earnestly by Ellen Simon and directed tidily, preciously by David Anspaugh, the film gives sentimentality a worse name than it already has. **D+** (#296, Oct.13) —*KT*

MORTAL KOMBAT *(PG-13)* A contentedly empty-headed advertisement for the joy of joypads, filmed in a cheesily ornate *cinéma de Hong Kong* style. **C+** (#291, Sept. 8)   —*LS*

MURDER IN THE FIRST *(R)* This pressure-cooker prison melodrama is about as pleasurable as a stint in solitary. In 1938, an ignorant young prisoner at Alcatraz named Henri Young (Kevin Bacon) is tossed into "the dungeon" and then is kept there for weeks, months, years. Is it any wonder that his first act upon being released is to kill the prisoner who ratted on him? The filmmakers teach the audience a lesson in humanity none of us needs to learn. **C-** (#260, Feb. 3)   —*OG*

MURIEL'S WEDDING *(R)* Big, gawky, and freckled-pale, Muriel (Toni Collette), the heroine of this raucous Australian comedy, is a misfit caught up in daydreams as overripe as the rest of her life is empty. Virtually every scene of *Muriel's Wedding* cues us to chuckle at the superficiality of its heroine's dreams. The trouble with the movie is that there's nothing to Muriel but her false dreams: We never quite glimpse the woman they're hiding. **C-** (#267, March 24)   —*OG*

MUTE WITNESS *(R)* British director Anthony Waller's stylishly gloomy debut is half tribute to and half send-up of the suspense-thriller genre. A mute special-effects artist (Marina Sudina), working on a low-budget slasher movie in a shabby Moscow studio, thinks she has witnessed the after-hours making of a

snuff film. She and her friends get caught in an ornate plot involving the police, the KGB, a shadowy Mob figure, and a lot of fake (and real) blood, doled out with an affection for the excitement of going to the movies to get scared. **B+** (#292, Sept. 15)   —*LS*

MY FAMILY *(R)* Jimmy Smits, Edward James Olmos, and Eduardo Lopez Rojas are men who are at home with the words coming out of their mouths in Gregory Nava's drama about three generations of Mexicans and Mexican-Americans. It's one of those proud, life-affirming things you might find on public

MY FAMILY

television, but it's got the ring of *la verdad* to it, and the performances (particularly that of Smits as an angry, withdrawn son and father) are strong. **B+** (#275, May 19)   —*LS*

NELL *(PG-13)* Jodie Foster gives an audacious performance as a wild child who speaks her own language. The film milks the myth of the noble savage for all its sentimentality. **B-** (#253, Dec. 16, 1994) —*OG*

THE NET *(PG-13)* A disc belonging to terrorist hackers falls into the hands of Angela Bennett (Sandra Bullock), a shy computer-systems analyst. *The Net* is an efficient, workmanlike thriller that's held together by Bullock: When she's seated in front of a terminal, tapping into forbidden systems, her concentration is so compelling we get the ticklish sensation that we're thinking right along with her. **B** (#286, Aug. 4) —*OG*

NEW JERSEY DRIVE *(R)* Nick Gomez's explosive drama about black Newark teenagers who steal cars as casually as if they were shoplifting pencils. What makes the film a powerful experience is the way that

OPERATION DUMBO DROP

Gomez employs his volcanic, this-is-happening-*now* aesthetic to mirror the view of his characters, who see crime not as a profit-driven enterprise but as instant gratification, a blood-quickening lunge at getting what whites have. Sharron Corley and Gabriel Casseus bring the heroes' humanity movingly close to us. **A-** (#272, April 28)   —*OG*

NICK OF TIME *(R)* Johnny Depp is an accountant selected by Christopher Walken to assassinate a liberal governor played by Marsha Mason. If Depp doesn't blow away the politician, Walken will kill Depp's sweet little cherub of a daughter (Courtney Chase); he's given just 90 minutes to accomplish his task. The movie plays itself out in real time, a gimmick that's a big mistake, because it means we know early on that nothing significant is going to happen until the final seconds. Depp staggers through this bleeding-heart botch with his mouth open, his bespectacled eyes blinking with supplication. He was more of an action hero as Edward Scissorhands. **D** (#303, Dec. 1)   —*KT*

NINE MONTHS *(PG-13)* Samuel (Hugh Grant), a San Francisco yuppie, is thrown into a tizzy when his girlfriend (Julianne Moore) becomes pregnant. Director Chris Columbus' movie is cutesy and cliché-ridden, but it's carried along by Grant, whose recent embarrassment actually works in the film's favor. **B-** (#284, July 21)   —*OG*

NIXON *(R)* Oliver Stone's docudrama has an almost talismanic power, as if we were seeing a veil ripped off events we only thought we understood. Anthony Hopkins, in a towering performance, plays Nixon as an awkward, touchingly repressed figure driven by the wounded adolescent sensitivity he has carried into his adult life. Every election is personal and every opponent a rival for the public's love. As *Nixon* unspools in a hypnotic multimedia barrage, it's clear that what's driving the film is Stone's desire to see Richard Nixon not as scoundrel but as flesh, as a brilliant, warped figure whose pathology could lead America only because it meshed with an invisible pattern of corruption. Stone, zigzagging through postwar history, captures the way destruction and deceit could become the motivating soul of government. The film's irony—and tragedy—is that the Nixon we see isn't a bad man. He's a blind man who longs for the light. Stone has made a great, shattering film by bringing us closer than ever to the President that we loved—too easily—to hate. **A** (#306, Dec. 22)   —*OG*

NOBODY'S FOOL *(R)* A small, wintry story perfectly scaled to its star. Paul Newman makes acting look effortless as Sully, a broken-down 60-year-old construction worker in upstate New York. **A-** (#257, Jan. 13)   —*LS*

NOW AND THEN *(PG-13)* A distaff *Stand by Me*, as four girls in 1970 come of age to a bubblegum soundtrack. Although two actresses play each character (one Now, one Then), none have more than a single trait. **D** (#299, Nov. 3)   —*BF*

ONCE WERE WARRIORS *(R)* A tumultuous domestic drama from New Zealand. It centers on a family of urbanized Maori living under the shadow of its hard-

souled patriarch (Temuera Morrison), a man capable of wooing his wife (Rena Owen) one moment and beating her to a pulp the next. Director Lee Tamahori does his best to get a rise out of you, but his work has fire and substance. **B+** (#265, March 10)   —*OG*

OPERATION DUMBO DROP *(PG)* Danny Glover, Ray Liotta, and Denis Leary play American military men during the Vietnam War who show goodwill to friendly locals by replacing a revered elephant lost in battle, a mission that entails trucking, flying, parachuting, and surviving wacky mishaps. The whole concept, supposedly based on a true story, is weird— this is what Vietnam movies have come to?—but at least the quadruped has the grace to say nothing. **C+** (#287, Aug. 11)   —*LS*

OTHELLO *(R)* The angry young Moor is played here by Laurence Fishburne with two earrings and a lizard gaze. Kenneth Bran-

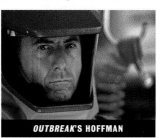

OUTBREAK'S HOFFMAN

agh is a soulless Iago, who nurtures doubt in Othello about the faithfulness of his ripe new wife, Desdemona (*Red*'s Irène Jacob, radiant as the young Ingrid Bergman but acting like an even dimmer bulb than the usual Desdemona portrayals). Fishburne is romantic but not lusty, failing to convey a pure pleasure in Desdemona that would make her imagined betrayal seem so crushing. But Fishburne's voice and bearing are suitably robust, and he knows how to throw a bloody tantrum. **B+** (#306, Dec. 22)   —*KT*

OUTBREAK *(R)* Biomedical thriller with Dustin Hoffman about a deadly virus carried into the U.S. by an

African monkey. The early sections are creepy and exciting, yet the film hurtles forward as relentlessly— and impersonally—as the disease itself. **B-** (#266, March 17)   —*OG*

PANTHER *(R)* Mario Van Peebles' hyperactive docudrama about the Black Panthers. If there's anything the movie gets right, it's the militant spectacle of young black men, armed with guns and the law, gazing with unblinking hatred at their oppressors and saying, in essence, "So, how do *you* like it?" What Van Peebles' showmanship can't conceal is *Panther*'s historical glibness and its almost total lack of dramatic depth. **C+** (#273, May 5)   —*OG*

PARTY GIRL *(R)* The star, Parker Posey, is like a sexy pony who's just had a dirty thought. She plays Mary, who flits from party to party, gliding through the champagne night on her looks, her clothes, her kitschy downtown élan. *Party Girl* moves to its own silly-surreal logic. Mary gets a job as a library clerk, becoming religiously obsessed with the Dewey decimal system. By the end, we're actually rooting for her to see the library as her salvation. Director Daisy von Scherler Mayer never lets us forget that Mary's prancing nightworld extravagance isn't just a fad she has to outgrow; it's also a playful form of feminine grace. **B+** (#280, June 23)   —*OG*

THE PEREZ FAMILY *(R)* As an ex-prostitute with a voracious love of America, of Hollywood, of life, Marisa Tomei shimmies and *cuchifritos* her way through a Cuban accent inspired by Rod Steiger in *The Specialist*. And that, amigos, is a problem in this story of Juan (Alfred Molina) and Dottie (Tomei), two unrelated Perezes who pretend to be married as they make their way through the immigration process. Director Mira Nair has taken pains to research life in Little Havana, but all that

POCAHONTAS

life-loving shimmying is hard to get past. **C-** (#275, May 19) —LS

PERSUASION *(PG)* Based on Jane Austen's posthumously published novel, this is a tricky tale of two 19th-century people who are made for each other but almost fail to get together and *get on with it.* At 27, Anne Elliott (Amanda Root) is a woman weighed down by her past: Eight years before, she fell in love with a dashing naval officer (Ciaran Hinds), but she was dissuaded from pursuing the romance by those around her. Witty and suspenseful, *Persuasion* is enthralling. **A-** (#295, Oct. 6) —KT

PICTURE BRIDE *(PG-13)* Kayo Hatta's elegant drama about Riyo (Youki Kudoh), a delicate young Japanese city girl who comes to Hawaii in 1918 to marry a sugarcane worker (Akira Takayama), based on little more than a few letters and photographs exchanged. That her husband turns out to be older and less handsome than his snapshot is Riyo's first shock; adjusting to the strange new world is her ongoing challenge. Hatta, who cowrote the screenplay based on stories from her family and those of other surviving brides, stages and lights her scenes like tranquil flower arrangements, perfectly lovely—and coolly contained. We see Riyo's emotions but are afraid to touch. **B+** (#278, June 9) —LS

POCAHONTAS *(G)* The first of the new-era Disney cartoons that feels less than animated. *Pocahontas*, a high-cheekboned update of the usual Disney princess, falls in love with the English sea captain John Smith,

a hunky oak of blond manhood. *Pocahontas* is pleasant to look at, but virtually everything in the movie is as generic as the two hygienic lovers. **C** (#279, June 16) —OG

THE POSTMAN (IL POSTINO) *(PG)* What gives this gentle film its fresh taste is the collaboration of British director Michael Radford, Frenchman Philippe Noiret, and Italian actor-comedian Massimo Troisi, who died of heart disease at 41, the day after shooting wrapped. Troisi plays Mario, a shy, mumbling man on an Italian island who finds work delivering mail to famed Chilean poet Pablo Neruda (Noiret). Curious and admiring, Mario wins Neruda over, and the two become friends. Radford aerates this story with humor and distinguishes soulfulness from pathos. **B+** (#285, July 28) —LS

POWDER *(PG-13)* The story of a teenage boy (Sean Patrick Flanery), born an albino and kept in a basement since birth, who possesses an exceptional intellect and supernatural powers. Powder's teachers (Jeff Goldblum and Mary Steenburgen) are duly impressed, but his classmates aren't: If there's one thing you don't want to be when you're a teenager, it's different. Melodramatic and overbrimming with adolescent angst, *Powder* is slow, creepy, and condescending. **C** (#300, Nov. 10) —KT

PRIEST *(R)* In Liverpool, Greg Pilkington (Linus Roache), a sternly handsome young priest, enters a

THE QUICK'S STONE

gay disco and picks up another man. The real shock of *Priest* is that the movie turns out to be anything but anti-Catholic. Instead, it suggests that Greg is actually a better priest, with a fuller experience of humanity and faith, *because* of his war with desire. **A-** (#268, March 31) —OG

THE PROPHECY *(R)* It seems to have been pasted together out of stock footage. In this occult freak show, the apostle of sitting around is an evil angel played by Christopher Walken, who sports shoe-polish hair that makes him look like Kevin Nealon's warlock uncle. **D-** (#292, Sept. 15) —OG

A PYROMANIAC'S LOVE STORY *(PG)* William Baldwin works himself into spasms of coy hysteria as Garet, a limping, love-lorn misfit who expresses his jealous heart by committing arson. John Leguizamo is a starry-eyed pastry chef who's only pretending to be a pyromaniac, and Sadie Frost, looking as plain here as she was dazzlingly Pre-Raphaelite in *Bram Stoker's Dracula*, is his object of desire. By the end, you want to slap everyone on screen and tell them to snap out of it. **D** (#279, May 12) —OG

QUEEN MARGOT *(R)* Patrice Chéreau's mesmerizing historical drama set in France in the 16th century. Isabelle Adjani, in the title role, plays the Catholic daughter of Catherine de Médicis (Virna Lisi), who is wedded to French Protestant Henry of Navarre (Daniel Auteuil) in a disastrous attempt to ease the brutal fighting between the two religious factions. Chéreau's sense of drama is so thrilling, and his choreography of characters so deft, that you won't be able to take your eyes off the opulent gore—or, for that matter, Adjani's cool, mysterious, velvety beauty. **A** (#259, Jan. 27) —LS

THE QUICK AND THE DEAD *(R)* The plot of Sam Raimi's low-camp revenge thriller is little more than an excuse

to line up one badass cowboy (or girl) opposite another and let the eyeball-to-eyeball fireworks fly. Sharon Stone, her lips glued together with sober resolve, is a mysterious loner who rides into the town of Redemption, where the locals are commencing their annual quick-draw tournament. The shoot-outs, which Raimi clearly got a kick out of staging, are stylish and fun. It's only when each one ends that you realize there's virtually nothing going on in the rest of the movie. **C** (#262, Feb. 17) —OG

READY TO WEAR (PRET-À-PORTER) *(R)* Robert Altman's contemptuous but lightweight fashion-world satire is set in Paris, during

READY TO WEAR

the week in which the world's hottest designers gather to unveil their pret-à-porter collections in a series of dazzlingly gaudy runway shows. As the huge, colorful cast swirls in front of us, we wait for a glimpse of the Altman magic. What we discover instead is that virtually every performer on screen is playing a one-joke cipher. **C-** (#254, Dec. 23, 1994) —OG

RECKLESS *(PG-13)* It starts on a promisingly bizarre note, as a weepy husband (Tony Goldwyn) tells his merry wife (Mia Farrow) that he has hired a hitman to kill her on Christmas Eve. But this nightmare-before-Christmas comedy soon devolves into a random string of oddball occurrences and impenetrable motifs. Goldwyn drinks poisoned champagne and pukes on an angel ornament; a Santa-suited Scott Glenn chokes on a champagne cork; Farrow discovers *Santa* and *Satan* are anagrams. By the time the film settles down from all this frenzied whimsy for a quietly intriguing final scene between Farrow and Stephen Dorff (as a long-lost relative), you'll wish it were all a dream. The writer-director duo of Craig Lucas and Norman Rene (*Prelude to A Kiss*) seems to have forgotten that fables should have a point. **C-** (#303, Dec. 1) —*BF*

RED *(R)* Director Krzysztof Kieslowski (*Blue*) has made his first full-blooded movie. Valentine (Irène Jacob), a Geneva fashion model, is reaching the dead end of a love affair. Jean-Louis Trintignant plays the man she turns to for comfort, a retired judge who is finishing out a lifetime of misery by spying on his neighbors. As a betrayal from his past begins to repeat itself in a karmic pattern, he gives birth to the very passion he himself was denied. This is a movie about reincarnation, yet it's as rooted in its feelings of hope, desire, and pain as Kieslowski's earlier films were blank and diffuse. **A** (#258, Jan. 20) —*OG*

RICHIE RICH *(PG)* Macaulay Culkin has become an elongated version of his *Home Alone* self. His latest vehicle, based on the popular comic book, is a kind of high-concept Capra fantasy about a poor little rich boy who defends his family empire against a villainous employee (John Larroquette). There's some amusement in

ROB ROY

the spectacle of Culkin's extravagant lifestyle, especially when he befriends some young sandlot-baseball players by treating them to motor-scooter tag games and his own private McDonald's. But just when it seems as if we're being primed for a truly outrageous slapstick comedy

showdown—*Home Alone* set in Neverland—the film devolves into a lifeless caper formula. **C** (#257, Jan. 13) —*OG*

ROB ROY *(R)* In this rousingly square romantic epic, Liam Neeson's Robert Roy MacGregor is presented as a new breed of macho domestic warrior. The film has a predictable dramatic arc, yet it has style and heart, and Neeson and Jessica Lange are superb together. **B+** (#270, April 14) —*OG*

ROOMMATES *(PG)* A relentlessly heartwarming story about a feisty ancient guy (Peter Falk) and the orphaned grandson he raises (D.B. Sweeney). Director Peter Yates bops you over the head with Very Special Moments. **C-** (#265, March 10) —*LS*

RUDYARD KIPLING'S THE JUNGLE BOOK *(PG)* A defanged live-action version colored and framed like a piece of Indian pulp art. As Mowgli, Jason Scott Lee flashes his expressive eyes as well as his martial-arts physique. **B** (#257, Jan. 13) —*LS*

SABRINA *(PG)* This remake of Billy Wilder's top-heavy soufflé of a romantic comedy has Harrison Ford and Julia Ormond taking on the roles played in 1954 by Humphrey Bogart and Audrey Hepburn. Ormond's Sabrina is a chauffeur's daughter who has spent her girlhood coveting the luxurious lives of the Larrabees, the filthy rich Long Island family that employs her father. In particular, she adores David (Greg Kinnear), the family's goofy and handsome playboy son. When he falls for her, endangering a family business merger, his older brother, Linus (Ford), takes it upon himself to woo Sabrina away. The catch is, he only *thinks* he doesn't have his heart in it. This is a Cinderella fantasy in which Cinderella has to rescue the prince, and Ford's qui-

et melancholy sneaks up on you. As a character, though, Linus no longer makes sense: He's a tough, virile wheeler-dealer who seems like a virgin. Ormond, on

SAFE

the other hand, evokes Hepburn's dazzling aristocratic delicacy, and Kinnear, a puppyish smart aleck, brings an endearing innocence to David, the short-attention-span romantic. **B-** (#305, Dec. 15) —*OG*

SAFE *(R)* Todd Haynes' movie creeps under your skin like a rash. It's about a housewife (Julianne Moore) who develops an allergic reaction to everything money can buy. Haynes tells this horror tale slowly, almost dreamily; there are moments you can feel your own lungs constricting in empathy. But at Wrenwood, a retreat for environmental-illness sufferers, his focus blurs. Is the outside world deadly, or are these canaries really cuckoos? **B+** (#281/282, June 30/July 7) —*LS*

SAFE PASSAGE *(PG-13)* Susan Sarandon portrays a woman with an estranged husband (Sam Shepard) who every now and then goes inconveniently blind, and seven sons, one of whom is a Marine in Lebanon whose base is bombed during the Gulf War. While the family waits for news of casualties, family stuff happens: Sarandon interacts with the boys; the boys do brotherly things with one another; Sarandon beams her motherly-but-sexy (or maybe it's sexy-but-motherly) eyes on everyone around her. She's fine at this work—she's always fine—and the boys (particularly Robert Sean Leonard and Nick Stahl as the oldest and youngest) are a pleasant gaggle. But Deena Goldstone's story, directed by Robert Allan Ackerman, has all of the

heft of a two-hour episode of *Party of Five*—a domestic drama loaded with the kind of emotions you see only on TV and never in your own family. **B-** (#259, Jan. 27) —*LS*

THE SANTA CLAUSE *(PG)* A weirdly cranky holiday comedy with a big fat ace up its sleeve: It stars *Home Improvement*'s Tim Allen, a big fat hit with the home-viewing audience of young malcontents, as a divorced dad tapped to inherit Santa's gig on Christmas Eve. **C** (#249, Nov. 18, 1994) —*LS*

THE SCARLET LETTER *(R)* Demi Moore, her hair hanging down in free-spirited ringlets, is Hester Prynne, who arrives on the shores of Puritan Massachusetts and falls in love with the Reverend Dimmesdale (Gary Oldman). With its dewy-eyed love story and its "action" climax pitting settlers against noble Native Americans, Roland Joffé's film is a ponderously overstuffed package. Moore brandishes her scarlet letter snootily, as if she'd been forced to wear something from last year's fashion collections. **C** (#297, Oct. 20) —*OG*

SEARCH AND DESTROY *(R)* Griffin Dunne gives an amusing performance as a scurvy, amphetamine-souled hustler, the kind of outer-boroughs-of-showbiz con artist who's so naked in his desperation that the only one he's conning is himself. In hock up to his eyeballs, Dunne, teamed with the adorably flaky Illeana Douglas, attempts to "produce" a movie based on the Nietzschean manifesto of his idol, a men's-movement guru played by Dennis Hopper (seething on cue). Directing for the first time, the New York painter David Salle pitches every encounter at toxic levels of cynicism. Just as we're primed to see Dunne get his comeuppance, John Turturro, chewing scenery by the mouthful, shows up as a hyper gangster—at which point the movie disintegrates. What began as an acrid satire dissolves into a vaudeville of "hip" actors (including Christopher Walken at his glassiest), each lost in his own private ozone. **B–** (#276, May 26)   —*OG*

THE SECRET OF ROAN INISH

(PG) John Sayles directed this sweet wisp of an Irish fairy tale about a soulful little girl (Jeni Courtney) and her mystical connection to an island off the Irish coast that was once home to her family and is now home to seals and gulls. The story is as big as a thimble and as evanescent as Tinker Bell. Only when the last seal has

STRANGE DAYS

looked squarely into the camera do you realize how unsentimental and casually magical *Inish* is. **B+** (#261, Feb. 10)   —*LS*

SENSE AND SENSIBILITY *(PG)*

Jane Austen's novel has been turned into a lushly engaging comedy of romantic mishap. In the beautiful West Country of England, two sisters, the cautious, reflective Elinor (Emma Thompson) and the younger, more recklessly emotional Marianne (Kate Winslet), both fall for suitors who mirror their own temperaments. The symbiotic dialogue between "sense" and "sensibility" no longer has the force it did in the book. But the movie, elegantly directed by Ang Lee (from a screenplay by Thompson), luminously evokes Austen's vision of the dance of the sexes. The final romantic epiphany is a stunner, at once rapturous and funny, as Thompson, choking with joy, expresses the yearning that has been building over the film's two and a quarter hours. **B+** (#305, Dec. 15)   —*OG*

SEVEN *(R)*

In a rainy, anonymous nowhere city, a serial killer slaughters people according to a fiendish

pattern: one murder for each of the seven deadly sins. Director David Fincher's canniest trick was to reveal just enough clinical carnage so that we re-create the killings in our heads. Morgan Freeman and Brad Pitt, working within a stock old cop–young cop routine, spark each other. **B** (#294, Sept. 29)   —*OG*

S.F.W. *(R)*

It's a Gen-X version of a bad counterculture youth film. A handful of twentysomething nobodies are kidnapped by terrorists, who insist that the major networks broadcast a live feed of the hostages in captivity. Upon rescue, former hostage Cliff Spab (Stephen Dorff) becomes a reluctant media star, a messianic Patty Hearst whose exclamation "So F---ing What" (get the title?) becomes the nihilist rallying cry of a generation. Yeah, right. **F** (#259, Jan. 27)   —*OG*

SHALLOW GRAVE *(R)*

Danny Boyle's glittering, deadpan, nihilistic little Scottish thriller about how three yuppie roommates (Ewan McGregor, Kerry Fox, and Christopher Eccleston) become three cold-blooded, scheming lizards following the death of a fourth tenant, a thug involved in drugs who dies of an overdose, leaving behind a suitcase stuffed with cash. At first it's shocking and weirdly thrilling to meet such unlovely people living in such a lovely flat and expending such twisted energy in the Hitchcockian service of getting rid of a stiff. But the film offers no context for the meaningless violence that takes place, and eventually the *shallow* in the title takes on a less satisfying meaning. **B–** (#265, March 10)   —*LS*

SEVEN

SHOWGIRLS *(NC-17)*

Screenwriter Joe Eszterhas and director Paul Verhoeven inflate the story of Nomi (Elizabeth Berkley), a Las Vegas stripper, into a spectacularly trashy movie of the week, a schlock *All About Eve* in fishnets. For all that, there's no denying that *Showgirls* goes over the edge into mean, tawdry exhibitionism in a way that a "salacious" TV movie never quite can. **C+** (#295, Oct. 6)   —*OG*

SMOKE *(R)*

Director Wayne Wang's delight in found comedy meets author Paul Auster's fondness for found fatalism in this loose, loungy series of vignettes set in and around an old-fashioned Brooklyn cigar store. The shop is presided over with casual dignity by Augie (Harvey Keitel, contained and understated) and frequented by blocked novelist Paul (William Hurt, Hurtishly weary). The stories are linked like smoke rings and carry about as much weight as they waft, curl, and evaporate; the ash of melancholy lingers. **B+** (#280, June 23)   —*LS*

SOMETHING TO TALK ABOUT

(R) Julia Roberts plays a Southern gal who stomps back to the family's horse farm to Find Herself after she discovers that her husband (Dennis Quaid) has been having an affair. Director Lasse Hallström's sensitivity to familial ties blunts *Thelma & Louise* writer Callie Khouri's feminist urge to run free. **C+** (#288, Aug. 18)   —*LS*

SPECIES *(R)*

A shape-shifting beastie roams Los Angeles in the form of a beautiful woman (Natasha Henstridge) searching for a mate. It's a demon-out-of-water story: *Alien* crossed with *Splash*. Unfortunately, the squishy primal horror of *Alien* has been replaced by a kind of mechanized yuckiness. **C** (#283, July 14)   —*OG*

SPEECHLESS *(PG-13)*

Michael Keaton and Geena Davis

SOMETHING TO TALK ABOUT

play competing political speechwriters who fall in love in a romantic comedy so toothless and cautiously middle-of-the-road that the two could be competing manufacturers of chewing gum. The one bright spot comes from the always likable Keaton, who shows his sharp sense of comic timing whenever he's given half a chance—even though his character evidently has no idea what he's supposed to believe in. **C+** (#254, Dec. 23, 1994)   —*LS*

THE STARS FELL ON HENRIETTA

(PG) A well-made *Hallmark Hall of Fame*-ish drama about the luck and pluck of striking oil in the Depression-era Texas dust bowl. Robert Duvall, that fine interpreter of old coots, is dang good as Mr. Cox, a dreamer with a nose for black gold; Frances Fisher and Aidan Quinn are the hardworking farm couple on whose unpromising land Cox pins his hopes. **B+** (#293, Sept. 22)   —*LS*

STRANGE DAYS *(R)*

Kathryn Bigelow's science-fiction thriller creates a darkly logical extension of our media-wired culture of vicarious sensation seekers. The hero, Lenny Nero (Ralph Fiennes), is a Los Angeles hustler who hawks virtual-reality "clips" on the black market. Beneath the movie's satire of audiovisual decadence lurks a naggingly conventional underworld thriller. **B–** (#296, Oct. 13)   —*OG*

STRAWBERRY AND CHOCOLATE

(R) In this shabby but appealing low-rent Cuban variation on *Kiss of the Spider Woman*, Diego (Jorge Perugorría), a rebellious

TANK GIRL'S PETTY

gay artist, insinuates himself into the friendly graces of David (Valdimir Cruz), a stoically prim heterosexual university student who believes, with the naïveté of a Marxist Boy Scout, in the eternal glory of the Revolution. (Meanwhile, the city of Havana is crumbling before his eyes.) Director Tomás Gutiérrez Alea has made a lopsided buddy movie in which Diego, with his cultivated flamboyance, holds the screen far more than his didactic protégé (who, we learn, is spying on him). The plot doesn't unfold with much finesse, yet the very contrast between the two men's personalities becomes a moving testament to the war that's tearing apart Cuba's soul. Perugorría gives a superb performance. His Diego has a florid, almost childlike manner that masks a valorous fury—a veritable rage for freedom. **B** (#266, Mar. 17)   —OG

STREET FIGHTER *(PG-13)* This incessantly violent, renegade-good-vs.-outrageous-evil action movie reflects the garish, militaristic, kick-and-grunt video game on which it is so calculatingly based. Jean-Claude Van Damme plays the death-defying smile-free hero; in his last big-screen role, a gaunt Raul Julia, bug-eyed with megalomania and overacting distressingly, plays the lord of darkness (or something like that) who must be destroyed. Watching them, you can't help but feel as though you were trapped all night in a video arcade with only 50 cents to blow. **D** (#257, Jan. 13)   —LS

STUART SAVES HIS FAMILY *(PG-13)* On *SNL*, Stuart Smalley (Al Franken), the

angelic recovery addict, can barely keep his composure long enough to get through one of his *Daily Affirmation* TV spots. It's a trick, though, to build a feature-length comedy around someone who is falling apart. The real problem may be that writer-star Al Franken ends up taking gentle pokes at habitual 12-steppers without really skewering their main mantra: that it's the spiritual apex of life to be "okay." **C+** (#272, April 28)   —OG

THE SUM OF US *(Unrated)* Russell Crowe, the young Australian actor who's being groomed to become the new Mel Gibson, has a Cupid's-bow smirk and the sleepy-seductive eyes of someone who has never entertained a moment of serious conflict. It's refreshing to see this take-it-easy dreamboat play a gay character—Jeff Mitchell, a plumber living at home with his widowed father, Harry (Jack Thompson), who is so accepting of his son's lifestyle that he greets the guy's latest date with a barrage of winky-poo sexual puns. Thompson's performance, which involves a lot of mugging into the camera, is so cutesy and benign it's insufferable, and the romantic relationships are borderline kitsch; the characters pursue their respective suitors as casually as they drop David Stevens' coy one-liners. **C** (#269, April 7) —OG

SWIMMING WITH SHARKS *(R)* In this exuberantly nasty Hollywood satire, Kevin Spacey takes the standard megalomaniacal executive to new levels of tyrannical bravado. Spacey's Buddy Ackerman is a famous producer of the Joel Silver blow-it-all-to-smithereens school. Nothing in his movies, however, is quite as brutal as the way he treats his eager young slave of an

SWIMMING WITH SHARKS

assistant (Frank Whaley). When Spacey goes ballistic, only to freeze the nitroglycerin in his veins a moment later, you don't want to look anywhere else. **B+** (#275, May 19)   —OG

TALES FROM THE HOOD *(R)* Rusty Cundieff's enthusiastically cheesy horror bash is essentially a black *Twilight Zone*. As soon as Clarence Williams III shows up as the hilariously dazed host (he's like the funk-zombie Vincent Price), you know the movie is in no danger of taking itself too seriously. **B** (#277, June 2)   —OG

TANK GIRL *(R)* As the baby-doll punkette heroine, Lori Petty has a deadpan effrontery; she tosses out insults like so many spitballs. Petty, though, is the only reason to go see this coy and scrappy comic-book adventure—a trash bin of sci-fi detritus. **C-** (#270, April 14)   —OG

THEREMIN: AN ELECTRONIC ODYSSEY *(PG)* Marvelously weird: a documentary about the life and career of Leon Theremin, the renegade Russian scientist who, in the 1920s, invented electronic music—more specifically, a revolutionary instrument called the theremin, which turns out to be a lot more familiar than you think. Anyone who's ever seen a '50s sci-fi movie like *The Day the Earth Stood Still* knows the sound of the theremin: that eerie, futuristic *ewww-eee-ewww* that Hollywood used time and again to evoke a mood of otherworldly anxiety. The passion of Theremin and his devotees has the purity of religion. Yet the instrument itself sounds like a violin being played by a giant mosquito. As the movie goes on, Theremin emerges as an unlikely cross between Albert Einstein and Ed Wood, a visionary of kitsch. **A** (#293, Sept. 22)   —OG

THE TIE THAT BINDS *(R)* Anyone expecting the same kind of creepy excitement

as *The Hand That Rocks the Cradle* will be simply baying at the moon—which is exactly what Daryl Hannah and Keith Carradine spend a lot of time doing as the marauding nutjobs who pass for characters in this dismal tale. Six-year-old Janie is taken away by the cops when her ma and pa—Hannah and Carradine—are interrupted during a robbery rampage. The little girl is soon adopted by Moira Kelly and Vincent Spano, a couple so loving that you *know* they'll be alive when the carnage ends. Screenwriter Wesley Strick—best known for the similarly sadistic *Cape Fear*—covers all the bases in his directing debut: ominous winds, ripped toys,

TALES FROM THE HOOD'S WILLIAMS

shadows on the wall. Add Carradine doing a war dance and Hannah striking a biblical pose, and you've got one ludicrous creeper. **D-** (#293, Sept. 22)   —LS

THREE WISHES *(PG)* A '50s single mom (Mary Elizabeth Mastrantonio) sideswipes a drifter (Patrick Swayze) with her sedan. She invites him home to mend and, with his anachronistically buff body and lone-stud air of mystery, he's destined to *change forever* the conformist, suburban-tract town in which he's landed. What tension there is arrives with a jolt when the heroine's 5-year-old develops cancer. The lad endures some mighty disturbing fever dreams before Swayze sails in with a bizarre, Spielbergian F/X flourish. **C** (#300, Nov. 10)   —Steve Daly

TO DIE FOR *(R)* In Gus Van Sant's black comedy, Nicole Kidman is Suzanne Stone, a small-town girl whose only desire is to be a famous TV personality. Suzanne has been conceived as a camp icon of celebrity psychosis, and Kidman plays her deftly. But since nothing the character does has much connection to her ambition, Van Sant simply seems to be getting off on the arbitrary viciousness of her "witchy" behavior. **B-** (#295, Oct. 6)   —*OG*

TO WONG FOO, THANKS FOR EVERYTHING, JULIE NEWMAR (*PG-13*) Patrick Swayze and Wesley Snipes are Vida Boheme and Noxeema Jackson, who share the grand prize in a New York drag contest and, along with a third partner, Chi Chi Rodriguez (John Leguizamo), take off on a cross-country road trip to Hollywood. Swayze, Snipes, and Leguizamo all evince a casual mastery of the finger-snapping, eye-rolling élan of the modern male bitch princess. But the movie reduces them to sitcom saints. **C** (#291, Sept. 8)   —*OG*

TOM AND VIV (*PG-13*) This chronicle of T.S. Eliot's famously unhappy first marriage is the kind of sodden, tasteful, here-are-a-few-nasty-warts-to-chew-on biography that raises as many dramatic questions as it answers. What is it that draws the young Tom Eliot (Willem Dafoe), a staid Oxford graduate student, together with the robustly sensual and unstable Vivienne Haigh-Wood (Miranda Richardson)? If you find "opposites attract" clichés floating through your brain, you've thought out the matter as well as the film has. Still, for all of Tom and Viv's middlebrow mustiness, Dafoe and Richardson hold the picture together. **B-** (#262, Feb. 17)   —*OG*

TOMMY BOY (*PG-13*) Just when you thought you'd erased the memory of Adam Sandler in *Billy Madison* playing a slobbo idiot who must prove he's worthy of taking over his father's business, along comes Chris Farley playing a slobbo idiot who must prove he's worthy of taking over his father's business. Yet this movie, unlike Sandler's fiasco,

TOMMY BOY

does at least have a few scuzzy laughs. **C** (#270, April 14)   —*OG*

TOTAL ECLIPSE (*R*) Imagine Arthur Rimbaud, the utopian visionary of French poetry, as a reckless 19th-century bad boy who slices through bourgeois hypocrisy by burping at the dinner table, parading nude on rooftops, and generally acting like a frat-house brat. As if to reinforce the concept, Leonardo DiCaprio comes on like a spoiled young rock star who's making his screen debut. He tosses off his lines in a blasé California monotone, as if Rimbaud were, like, this really cool guy whose tragedy was that he died a century before MTV. Lest we forget he also had Deep Thoughts, the movie has DiCaprio delivering unplayable pensées like "The only unbearable thing is that nothing is unbearable." Actually, *Total Eclipse* is pretty unbearable. **D+** (#301, Nov. 17)   —*OG*

TOY STORY (*G*) Miraculous fun. The first animated feature to be produced entirely on computer is a magically witty and humane entertainment, a hellzapoppin fairy tale about a roomful of gleaming suburban toys who come to life when humans aren't around. The hero, Woody (voiced by Tom Hanks), is a pull-string talking sheriff who's the favorite of his 6-year-old owner. But there's a new toy in town, a bulky armored space ranger named Buzz Lightyear (Tim Allen); he's so blithely egotistical he doesn't even realize he's a toy. Like Disney's earlier cartoon features, *Toy Story* invites you to gaze upon the textures of the physical world with new eyes. Only what *Bambi* and *Snow*

White did for nature, this movie does for plastic—for the synthetic gizmo culture of the modern mall brat. The heart of the film is the sequence in which Woody and Buzz end up captives of a sadistic boy named Sid, whose menagerie of schizoid playthings is like something out of a Nine Inch Nails video. Sid may be a bad kid, but in his twisted way he's the soul of *Toy Story*, the spirit of imagination gone haywire. **A** (#302, Nov. 24)   —*OG*

TWO BITS (*PG-13*) It's hard to believe that this meandering bit of Depression-era nostalgia is from the same star-director combo behind 1992's electric screen adaptation of *Glengarry Glen Ross*, Al Pacino and James Foley. *Psycho* screenwriter Joseph Stefano's memoir is supposed to be sepia-toned, but comes off more like it's yellowed with age (the film

THEREMIN

was on the shelf for a year). Looking like a cross between Giancarlo Giannini and a raisin, Pacino grumbles dime-store wisdom as a dying Italian immigrant who promises to will his 12-year-old grandson (cutesy Jerry Barone) a quarter to go to the town's new cinema palace. The kid can't wait, so he spends one long day doing odd jobs to earn the money. So many grown women hit on Barone along the way, you'll swear you're watching Madonna's "Open Your Heart" video. And when did Mary Elizabeth Mastrantonio age from playing sex bombs in *The Color of Money* and *White Sands* to bland moms in

family-value paks like this and *Three Wishes*? **C** (#303, Dec. 1)   —*BF*

UNDER SIEGE 2: DARK TERRITORY (*R*) An enjoyable Steven Seagal thriller. Essentially, it's *Die Hard IX*, and the genre's rituals—terrorist kidnappings, exploding vehicles—are, by now, as formalized as Kabuki theater. *Under Siege 2*, though, has pace, wit, and a crisp unity of action. **B** (#285, July 28)   —*OG*

THE UNDERNEATH (*R*) Director Steven Soderbergh revives the lusty, dread-driven atmosphere of the classic film noirs. Michael Chambers (Peter Gallagher), a compulsive sports gambler, returns to his hometown of Austin, Tex., and runs into his old flame (Alison Elliott), who's still very much on fire. Soderbergh assembles his story piece by piece, so that the kaleidoscopic action slowly brings into focus the nature of Michael's obsessions. And Gallagher gets deep inside this gambler's rotten, addictive core. **A-** (#274, May 12)   —*OG*

UNSTRUNG HEROES (*PG*) Set in Los Angeles in the early '60s, Diane Keaton's film is about a smart, sensitive Jewish kid, Steven Lidz (Nathan Watt), who learns that his mother (Andie MacDowell) is battling a life-threatening illness. Unable to face the pressure at home, he goes off to stay with his uncles (Michael Richards and Maury Chaykin), who share an apartment that looks like a moldering insane asylum. The two are utterly dysfunctional misfits, yet both men, we're meant to understand, have the courage of their own soulful lunacy. Unfortunately, they come off as a couple of only-in-the-movies harmless eccentrics. **C+** (#293, Sept. 22)   —*OG*

UNZIPPED (*R*) Douglas Keeve's absolutely fabulous—and wickedly funny—documentary of one fashion season in the life of designer darling Isaac Mizrahi captures the Importance of Being Isaac, but also the Hysteria of Making Fashion. **A** (#287, Aug. 11) —*LS*

THE USUAL SUSPECTS *(R)* Bryan Singer's showily complex crime drama about a pack of felons who meet in a holding cell and decide to do some business together. Their common bond is their fear of a vicious criminal named Keyser Söze, whose identity remains a mystery. When you finally catch on, you may feel elated—or soured—by the required contortions of suspended disbelief. **B** (#289/290, Aug. 25/Sept. 1) —*LS*

VAMPIRE IN BROOKLYN *(R)* Playing a bloodsucker looking for his true love, Eddie Murphy wears long, greasy tresses and a manicured goatee. He looks like a cross between Nick Ashford and Barry White, and he speaks in a vague West Indian accent that turns his every "suave" utterance into a cheesy loveman cliché. Murphy may think he's shifting gears by playing this Blaculoid prince. What he's really doing is cuing us to see how desperate he is for an image overhaul. Directed by Wes Craven, *Vampire in Brooklyn* mixes lame blood-pellet effects with lame gags. Its one lingering image is that of Eddie Murphy trying, and failing, to rise from the dead. **D** (#299, Nov. 3) —*OG*

VILLAGE OF THE DAMNED *(R)* In John Carpenter's pedestrian remake of the 1960 sci-fi chiller, a group of small-town women give birth to emotionless demon children. But when the blond, evil kids flash their glowing eyes, they really don't seem much more bizarre—or frightening—

VIRTUOSITY

than your average 10-year-old Nintendo freak. **C-** (#274, May 12) —*OG*

VIRTUOSITY *(R)* A techno-nerd nirvana of a thing, about a criminal humanoid (Russell Crowe) who escapes from virtual reality and the ex-cop (Denzel Washington) who has to neutralize the creep. This latest entry in the theater of cyber-cinema is the one that clobbers you with the biggest special effects. **D+** (#288, Aug. 18) —*LS*

A WALK IN THE CLOUDS *(PG-13)* Director Alfonso Arau translates the fairy-tale feeling of *Like Water for Chocolate* to the story of an American soldier (Keanu Reeves) returning from World War II, who poses as the husband of a beautiful, unmarried pregnant woman (Aitana Sanchez-Gijon) so that she can face her imperious vineyard-owning father (Giancarlo Giannini). Reeves' every word falls like drops of flat Diet Coke. **C+** (#288, Aug. 18) —*LS*

THE WALKING DEAD *(R)* The zombie-horror-film title is the most dramatic feature of this meandering combat melodrama, in which five Marines, all but one of them African-American, skulk through the Vietnam jungles after a devastating ambush in an attempt to hook up with a second platoon. The one performer who holds the screen is comedian Eddie Griffin, who looks like Heckle and Jeckle and snarls out his lines like a grunt Snoop Doggy Dogg. The rest of the major characters are earnestly dull, and the combat scenes look as if they were shot in the same swampy wasteland where Ed Wood filmed his octopus battles. **D+** (#265, March 10) —*OG*

WATERWORLD *(PG-13)* Kevin Costner's sci-fi Mariner spends so much time leaping in and out of the grunge-green ocean deep that you may feel like buying him a blow-dryer. *Waterworld* is a true triumph of action-adventure logistics, but it's

WHITE MAN'S BURDEN

also a brazen knockoff of *The Road Warrior.* **B** (#286, Aug. 4) —*OG*

WHILE YOU WERE SLEEPING *(PG)* An upbeat romantic comedy about a lonely woman (Sandra Bullock) who finds love with a nice guy (Bill Pullman) while pretending to be engaged to his brother (Peter Gallagher), who can't protest because he's in a coma. But if you look beneath the feel-good surface, you'll see this is a "warm-edy" cranked out by a machine. **B-** (#272, April 28) —*LS*

WHITE MAN'S BURDEN *(R)* The sort of picture you would have expected John Travolta to star in *before* his comeback. It's based on a gimmick—What if the roles of blacks and whites in American society were reversed?—that has usually worked best in science fiction or satire. Travolta plays a racially disenfranchised factory worker who loses his job after he offends the company's owner (Harry Belafonte). Having learned that the system is against him, he kidnaps the owner, and the two men spend the rest of the picture discovering—you guessed it—that they're not so different under the skin. Writer-director Desmond Nakano does little besides flip-flop clichés, and it's disquieting to watch Travolta play a shabby-lumpen schmo with badly cut reddish-brown hair. There are some actors you don't want to see robbed of their sleekness. **C-** (#303, Dec. 1) —*OG*

WIGSTOCK: THE MOVIE *(Unrated)* Lizzy Gardiner got oodles of credit for creating a few frocks for *The Adventures of Priscilla, Queen of the Desert*, but really,

dears, the drag-loving participants in the annual New York City event known as Wigstock have been looking fabulous (in a fake-hair-piled-up-to-there and eye-lashes-the-length-of-match-sticks way) for over a decade now. Using performance footage from 1993 and interviews through 1994, director Barry Shils appropriates the *Woodstock* format—the prep, the performances, the crowds, the music—to make a sweet, homemade-looking, celebratory movie that says, essentially: Dress up, dollface, you'll feel better. No political message intended. The performers appear to be well-adjusted guys who are happy to chat about what dressing up like women means to them while applying eyebrow pencil with tender concentration. Star talent includes Lypsinka, Joey Arias (who does an awesome Billie Holiday), the "Lady" Bunny (who's also the organizer of the whole extravaganza), Deee-Lite, and—who else?—RuPaul. **B** (#280, June 23) —*LS*

WILD BILL

WILD BILL *(R)* This vivid Western from writer-director Walter Hill (*The Long Riders, 48 Hrs.*) begins by galloping through the early exploits of legendary gunslinger James Butler "Wild Bill" Hickok (Jeff Bridges), an hombre so ornery he'd shoot a man just for touching his hat. Yet most of the action occurs during Hickok's final days, as the opium-smoking, glaucoma-stricken marksman reflects on his life. The movie succeeds as a character study of a man whose code of justice eventually catches up with him. Bridges' performance is a masterstroke of squinty-eyed bitterness. **B+** (#304, Dec. 8) —*BF*

Critical mas

A sampling of 50 notable films from 1995—hits, flops, independents, and critics' favorites—as graded by audiences and selected reviewers

	CINEMASCORE *Audiences across the U.S.*	ROGER EBERT *Siskel & Ebert*	GENE SISKEL *Siskel & Ebert*	JAMI BERNARD *Knight-Ridder Syndicate*	CARRIE RICKEY *Knight-Ridder Syndicate*	MIKE CLARK *USA Today*	ENTERTAINMENT WEEKLY	AVG.*
CRUMB	—	A	A	A+	A	A	A	A
TOY STORY	A	A-	B+	A+	A-	A+	A	A
APOLLO 13	A	A+	A-	A+	B+	A	B	A-
BABE	—	B	B+	A-	A	A	A	A-
THE BRIDGES OF MADISON COUNTY	A-	A-	A	A+	B-	B+	A	A-
A LITTLE PRINCESS	—	A-	A-	A+	B+	B	A	A-
THE AMERICAN PRESIDENT	A	A	A+	A	A-	B	B-	A-
NIXON	—	A	A-	B+	A-	B	A	A-
BEFORE SUNRISE	B	B	A-	A	B+	A-	A-	A-
IL POSTINO (THE POSTMAN)	—	B+	B+	A	A-	B	B+	B+
SENSE AND SENSIBILITY	—	C+	A-	A	A	B+	B+	B+
UNZIPPED	—	B	B	B+	A	B	A	B+
SMOKE	—	B+	B+	A+	A-	C	B+	B+
LEAVING LAS VEGAS	—	A+	A-	C-	A-	B	A-	B+
PERSUASION	—	B+	B	B	A	B	A-	B+
ROB ROY	B+	A	A-	B	B-	B	B+	B+
TO DIE FOR	C+	B+	A	A-	C+	A-	B-	B+
CLUELESS	B+	B+	B	A-	B+	B+	C+	B+
GET SHORTY	B+	B+	B	A-	B	B	B	B+
CLOCKERS	B	B+	A-	C	B-	B+	A	B+
BRAVEHEART	A-	B+	B-	B	B	A	B-	B
POCAHONTAS	A-	B+	A-	B	A-	B	C	B
CASINO	B-	A	C+	B	B	A-	B-	B
CRIMSON TIDE	A	A-	B	C+	B	B-	A-	B
KISS OF DEATH	B-	C	B+	B	B+	B-	A	B
THE BROTHERS MCMULLEN	—	B	B	B+	B	B	B-	B
PRIEST	—	D	A-	A-	B	A	A-	B
KIDS	—	B	A-	B+	B	C-	B	B
DEVIL IN A BLUE DRESS	A-	B	B-	A	B+	C	C	B
GOLDENEYE	A-	B-	C+	B+	B+	B	C+	B
DEAD PRESIDENTS	B+	C+	C	B	B	B	A-	B
LIVING IN OBLIVION	—	C	C	B+	B+	B-	A-	B
THE NET	B	B	C	B+	B	B-	B	B
WHILE YOU WERE SLEEPING	A	B+	B-	C+	B	C+	B-	B-
BATMAN FOREVER	A-	C+	B-	B+	C-	C+	B	B-
SOMETHING TO TALK ABOUT	A-	B	B	C-	B-	B-	C+	B-
A WALK IN THE CLOUDS	A-	A	A-	C	C	D+	C+	B-
DESPERADO	B+	C	B-	B+	C+	C	B	B-
SEVEN	B	B+	B	C-	C	C+	B	B-
OUTBREAK	A-	B+	D	B	B-	C+	B-	B-
THE BRADY BUNCH MOVIE	B+	C	D	C+	B	B	A-	B-
THE USUAL SUSPECTS	—	D	C+	B+	B	C+	B	B-
DIE HARD WITH A VENGEANCE	A-	B-	C	B	C	C	C+	C+
NINE MONTHS	A-	C-	C+	B-	B	B	C	C+
TO WONG FOO, THANKS FOR EVERYTHING...	B+	C+	B	C	B-	C-	C	C+
WATERWORLD	B	C+	D	B-	C-	B	B	C+
DANGEROUS MINDS	A-	C	C+	B	B-	D+	C-	C
ACE VENTURA: WHEN NATURE CALLS	B+	C-	D	B-	D	D+	B+	C
CONGO	B	B	B	C+	C-	C-	D-	C-
SHOWGIRLS	C	C-	C	D	D	C+	C+	C-

*Average does not include CinemaScore

Chart ■ Toppers
movies

**MOVIES RELEASED
IN 1995**
426
**MOVIES RELEASED
IN 1985**
389

....

**MOST POPULAR AC-
TOR AND ACTRESS**

**Tom Hanks and
Sandra Bullock**

....

**COMBINED TOTAL
GROSSES FOR TOP
25 ANIMATED
MOVIES**

**$391,824,939 (*Toy
Story, Pocahontas,
Casper*)**

....

**COMBINED TOTAL
GROSSES FOR
ANIMATED MOVIES
IN THE TOP 25 OF
ALL TIME**

$715,131,266

**(*The Lion King,
Aladdin, Snow White*)**

....

**MOST POPULAR
CANDY SOLD IN
MOVIE THEATERS**

Twizzlers

BATMAN FOREVER

1995 MAY NOT have been a good year for movie profits (or *Waterworld*'s Kevin Costner), but it was a banner year for Tom Hanks and Jim Carrey, who accounted for four of the top five grossers (total earnings: $322 million for Hanks'; $288.4 million for Carrey's). Though $300 million block-busters like *Forrest Gump* and *The Lion King* went missing, we saw the highest-grossing Bond flick (*Goldeneye*), a beautifully underplayed film adaptation of an overwritten novel (*The Bridges of Madison County*), and some surprise hits that far surpassed their production costs, notably Alicia Silverstone's *Clueless*, Brad Pitt's *Seven*, and Sandra Bullock's *While You Were Sleeping*. Meanwhile, the hype for screenwriter Joe Eszterhas' steamy duo *Jade* and *Showgirls* hardly paid off. If only he'd started 1995 wise to one of the most telling year-end facts: Bruce Willis' *Die Hard With a Vengeance* was the lone R-rated film to hit the $100 million mark.

TOP 25

YEAR-END GROSS

1	**BATMAN FOREVER** *Warner Bros.*, Val Kilmer, Jim Carrey	$184.0
2	**APOLLO 13** *Universal*, Tom Hanks	172.0
3	**TOY STORY** *Walt Disney*, Animated	150.0
4	**POCAHONTAS** *Walt Disney*, Animated	141.5
5	**ACE VENTURA: WHEN NATURE CALLS** *Warner Bros.*, Jim Carrey	104.4
6	**CASPER** *Universal*, Christina Ricci	100.3
7	**DIE HARD WITH A VENGEANCE** *Twentieth Century Fox*, Bruce Willis	100.0
8	**GOLDENEYE** *United Artists*, Pierce Brosnan	93.2
9	**CRIMSON TIDE** *Hollywood*, Denzel Washington, Gene Hackman	91.4
10	**WATERWORLD** *Universal*, Kevin Costner	88.2
11	**SEVEN** *New Line*, Brad Pitt, Morgan Freeman	87.0
12	**DANGEROUS MINDS** *Hollywood*, Michelle Pfeiffer	84.3
13	**WHILE YOU WERE SLEEPING** *Hollywood*, Sandra Bullock	81.1
14	**CONGO** *Paramount*, Dylan Walsh	81.0
15	**MORTAL KOMBAT** *New Line*, Christopher Lambert	70.4
16	**THE BRIDGES OF MADISON COUNTY** *Warner Bros.*, Meryl Streep, Clint Eastwood	70.1
17	**NINE MONTHS** *Twentieth Century Fox*, Hugh Grant	69.7
18	**GET SHORTY** *MGM*, John Travolta, Danny DeVito	68.8
19	**OUTBREAK** *Warner Bros.*, Dustin Hoffman, Rene Russo	67.6
20	**BRAVEHEART** *Paramount*, Mel Gibson	67.0
21	**BAD BOYS** *Columbia*, Martin Lawrence, Will Smith	65.7
22	**SPECIES** *MGM*, Natasha Henstridge, Ben Kingsley	60.0
23	**JUMANJI** *TriStar*, Robin Williams	57.5
24	**BABE** *Universal*, James Cromwell	56.8
25	**CLUELESS** *Paramount*, Alicia Silverstone	56.5

Oscar Winners

Is it just us or did 1995's Academy Awards seem a little...dated? For one, Tom Hanks' '60s and '70s time bandit *Forrest Gump* racked up the most statuettes, while Jessica Lange made Best Actress for her *Blue Sky* performance, filmed in *1991*. Not to mention the Supporting awards going to veterans Dianne Wiest and Martin Landau. The only young blood honored in a major category was Quentin Tarantino, and even *he* seemed by year's end to be toeing that line of outdatedness.

BEST PICTURE:
Forrest Gump

BEST ACTOR: Tom Hanks
(Forrest Gump)

BEST ACTRESS: Jessica
Lange (*Blue Sky*)

BEST SUPPORTING ACTRESS:
Dianne Wiest
(*Bullets Over Broadway*)

BEST SUPPORTING ACTOR:
Martin Landau (*Ed Wood*)

BEST DIRECTOR: Robert
Zemeckis (*Forrest Gump*)

OTHER AWARDS

GOLDEN GLOBE

BEST DRAMA: *Forrest Gump* ◆ **BEST ACTOR (DRAMA):** Tom Hanks (*Forrest Gump*) ◆ **BEST ACTRESS (DRAMA):** Jessica Lange (*Blue Sky*) ◆ **BEST DIRECTOR:** Robert Zemeckis (*Forrest Gump*) ◆ **BEST MUSICAL/COMEDY:** *The Lion King* ◆ **BEST ACTOR (MUSICAL/COMEDY):** Hugh Grant (*Four Weddings and a Funeral*) ◆ **BEST ACTRESS (MUSICAL/COMEDY):** Jamie Lee Curtis (*True Lies*)

N.Y. FILM CRITICS CIRCLE

BEST PICTURE: *Leaving Las Vegas* ◆ **BEST ACTOR:** Nicolas Cage (*Leaving Las Vegas*) ◆ **BEST ACTRESS:** Jennifer Jason Leigh (*Georgia*) ◆ **BEST SUPPORTING ACTOR:** Kevin Spacey (*The Usual Suspects* and his other '95 films) ◆ **BEST SUPPORTING ACTRESS:** Mira Sorvino (*Mighty Aphrodite*) ◆ **BEST DIRECTOR:** Ang Lee (*Sense and Sensibility*) ◆ **BEST DOCUMENTARY:** *Crumb*

NUMBER OF PIGS USED TO MAKE *BABE*
48 bouncing 4-month-old Large White Yorkshires

THE BUDGET OF *WATERWORLD* **($172 million)** VS. U.S. AID TO BOLIVIA **($174 million)** AND AMOUNT AMERICANS SPEND ANNUALLY ON DENTAL FLOSS **($110 million)**

STARS WHO COMMANDED $20 MILLION IN '95
Sylvester Stallone, Jim Carrey, Harrison Ford, and Tom Cruise

MOVIE TICKETS PURCHASED **1.2 billion**

BRAD PITT'S HAIR LENGTH AS OF *LEGENDS OF THE FALL*

VS.

12 MONKEYS

1995'S TOP-GROSSING PAY-PER-VIEW EVENT

The August 19 Mike Tyson–Peter McNeeley fight: $56.4 million

....

MOST POPULAR SERIES OF ALL TIME

60 Minutes

....

MOST-WATCHED EPISODE OF ALL TIME

Final episode of *M*A*S*H* (Feb. 28, 1983)

RUNNERS-UP

"Who Shot J.R." episode of *Dallas* (Nov. 21, 1980) and *Roots, Part VIII* (January 30, 1977)

....

MOST POPULAR URBAN SETTING FOR 1995–96 TV SEASON

New York: 18 series

television
Chart-Toppers

VIEWERS CARED INTENSIVELY FOR TOP SHOW *ER*

ON THURSDAYS ALL YEAR, the majority of the TV-viewing public took "Must-See TV" as a command rather than a catchy slogan and remained glued to their living room couches from 8 p.m. until the 11 o'clock news. Even newcomers like *The Single Guy* got in on the act, riding a cushy Thursday-night time slot all the way to sixth place for the year. In terms of quantity, ABC was the year-end winner, grabbing 11 slots (over NBC's 10) in the top 25, with two of its new series, *Hudson Street* and *The Naked Truth*, squeaking by in a tie for 24th place. Meantime, the beleaguered Eye network checked in with two entries on the top 25 and was still smarting from the loss of football to FOX (see entries 8 and 15).

	TOP 25	AVERAGE RATING
1	**ER** NBC, *Thursday, 10 p.m.*	19.6
2	**SEINFELD** NBC, *Thursday, 9 p.m.*	19.1
3	**CAROLINE IN THE CITY** NBC, *Thursday, 9:30 p.m.*	17.8
4	**FRIENDS** NBC, *Thursday, 8:00 p.m.*	17.6
5	**NFL MONDAY NIGHT FOOTBALL** ABC, *Monday, 9 p.m.*	17.0
6	**THE SINGLE GUY** NBC, *Thursday, 8:30 p.m.*	16.7
7	**HOME IMPROVEMENT** ABC, *Tuesday, 9 p.m.*	16.5
8	**FOX NFL SUNDAY—GAME 1** FOX, *Sunday, 1 p.m.*	14.8
9	**GRACE UNDER FIRE** ABC, *Wednesday, 9 p.m.*	14.7
10	**60 MINUTES** CBS, *Sunday, 7 p.m.*	14.0
11	**NYPD BLUE** ABC, *Tuesday, 10 p.m.*	13.7
12	**20/20** ABC, *Friday, 10 p.m.*	13.6
13	**NFL ON NBC—GAME 2** NBC, *Sunday, 4 p.m.*	13.5
14	**PRIMETIME LIVE** ABC, *Wednesday, 10 p.m.*	13.1
15	**FOX NFL SUNDAY—SINGLE** FOX, *Sunday, 1 p.m.*	12.8
16	**ROSEANNE** ABC, *Tuesday, 8 p.m.*	12.8
17	**COACH** ABC, *Tuesday, 9:30 p.m.*	12.5
18	**FRASIER** NBC, *Tuesday, 9 p.m.*	12.5
19	**MAD ABOUT YOU** NBC, *Sunday, 8 p.m.*	12.5
20	**MURPHY BROWN** CBS, *Monday, 9 p.m.*	12.4
21	**MADMAN OF THE PEOPLE** NBC, *Saturday, 9:30 p.m.*	12.1
22	**NBC MONDAY NIGHT MOVIES** NBC, *Monday, 9 p.m.*	12.0
23	**ELLEN** ABC, *Wednesday, 8 p.m.*	11.9
24	**HUDSON STREET** ABC, *Tuesday, 8:30 p.m.*	11.7
25	**NAKED TRUTH** ABC, *Wednesday, 9:30 p.m.*	11.7

emmy Winners

DESPITE EXPECTATIONS, THE 47th Emmy Awards ceremony was not *entirely* an *ER* evening. The show had its share of upsets, including *NYPD Blue*'s win over the behemoth hospital drama for Outstanding Drama Series. Not that NBC executives went home in tears. The Peacock continued its banner year by steamrolling over the other networks, capturing 28 trophies, eight of which went to their crown jewel, *ER*. The much-ridiculed CBS restored some of its dignity when both the Outstanding Lead Actor and Actress in a Drama awards went to stars on their payroll. And while ABC took home the coveted Drama award, 1995's No. 1 rated network left with only five Emmys, two of which were in technical categories.

AVERAGE NUMBER OF *FRIENDS* VIEWERS
25.9 million

VS. THE POPULATION OF PERU
24 million

NUMBER OF PETS ON THE TOP 25 TV SERIES
One cat (*Caroline in the City*), 10 fish and 24 pigeons (*NYPD Blue*), two dogs (*Frasier* and *Mad About You*), and one monkey (*Friends*). Total: 38

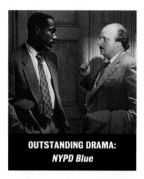

OUTSTANDING DRAMA: *NYPD Blue*

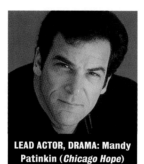

LEAD ACTOR, DRAMA: Mandy Patinkin (*Chicago Hope*)

LEAD ACTRESS, DRAMA: Kathy Baker (*Picket Fences*)

OUTSTANDING COMEDY: *Frasier*

LEAD ACTOR, COMEDY: Kelsey Grammer (*Frasier*)

LEAD ACTRESS, COMEDY: Candice Bergen (*Murphy Brown*)

HIGHEST-PAID TV PERSONALITY
Oprah Winfrey ($74 million)

RUNNERS-UP
Roseanne ($19 million), David Letterman ($14 million), Jay Leno ($11–14 million)

OTHER AWARDS

GOLDEN GLOBE

BEST DRAMA SERIES: *The X-Files* ◆ **BEST ACTOR (DRAMA):** Dennis Franz (*NYPD Blue*) ◆ **BEST ACTRESS (DRAMA):** Claire Danes (*My So-Called Life*) ◆ **BEST MUSICAL/COMEDY SERIES:** *Frasier, Mad About You* (tie) ◆ **BEST ACTOR (MUSICAL/COMEDY):** Tim Allen (*Home Improvement*) ◆ **BEST ACTRESS (MUSICAL/COMEDY):** Helen Hunt (*Mad About You*)

DAYTIME EMMYS

BEST DRAMA SERIES: *General Hospital* ◆ **BEST ACTOR:** Justin Deas (*Guiding Light*) ◆ **BEST ACTRESS:** Erika Slezak (*One Life to Live*) ◆ **BEST SUPPORTING ACTOR:** Jerry verDorn (*Guiding Light*) ◆ **BEST SUPPORTING ACTRESS:** Rena Sofer (*General Hospital*) ◆ **BEST TALK SHOW:** *The Oprah Winfrey Show* ◆ **BEST TALK-SHOW HOST:** Oprah Winfrey ◆ **BEST GAME SHOW:** *Jeopardy!*

books

Chart-Toppers

SOURCE: PUBLISHERS WEEKLY

IF YOU DIDN'T read it, hear about it, or decide to live your life based on it, you were either in another country or dead. Robert James Waller's *The Bridges of Madison County*, at a meager 171 pages, continued to topple its weightier contenders in capturing readers' hearts. Why? This steamy little story about the passionate love between housewife Francesca Johnson and photographer Robert Kincaid set pulses racing, sparked a movie, and sired schmaltzy spin-offs (like the blank-page diary *The Bridges of Madison County Memory Book*). Look for a connection between Waller's book and the No. 1 nonfiction best-seller and you see wannabe Francescas wondering why their real-life Roberts seem to be from another planet.

TOP 5 FICTION

WEEKS ON CHART

1 **THE BRIDGES OF MADISON COUNTY**
Robert James Waller, *Warner* 157

2 **THE CELESTINE PROPHECY** James Redfield, *Warner* 93

3 **POLITICALLY CORRECT BEDTIME STORIES**
James Finn Farner, *Macmillan* 59

4 **BEACH MUSIC** Pat Conroy, *Doubleday/Talese* 24

5 **DEBT OF HONOR** Tom Clancy, *Putnam*.................................23

TOP 5 NONFICTION

1 **MEN ARE FROM MARS, WOMEN ARE FROM VENUS**
John Gray, Ph.D., *HarperCollins*...140

2 **MIDNIGHT IN THE GARDEN OF GOOD AND EVIL**
John Berendt, *Random House* 78

3 **THE BOOK OF VIRTUES** William J. Bennett, *Simon & Schuster* 55

4 **SISTERS** Carol Saline and Sharon Wohlmuth, *Running Press*.............44

5 **THE HOT ZONE** Richard Preston, *Random House* 39

TOP 5 TRADE PAPERBACKS

1 **THE 7 HABITS OF HIGHLY EFFECTIVE PEOPLE**
Stephen R. Covey, *Fireside* 254

2 **WHAT TO EXPECT WHEN YOU'RE EXPECTING**
A. Eisenberg, H. Murkoff, and S. Hathaway, *Workman*.................126

3 **THE SHIPPING NEWS** E. Annie Proulx, *Touchstone* 59

4 **REVIVING OPHELIA** Mary Pipher, *Ballantine*........................36

5 **THE STONE DIARIES** Carol Shields, *Penguin* 33

TOP 5 MASS-MARKET PAPERBACKS

1 **EMBRACED BY THE LIGHT** Betty J. Eadie, *Bantam* 36

2 **CONGO** Michael Crichton, *Ballantine* 32

3 **INTERVIEW WITH THE VAMPIRE** Anne Rice, *Ballantine* 28

4 **SMILLA'S SENSE OF SNOW** Peter Hoeg, *Dell* 23

5 **THE ALIENIST** Caleb Carr, *Bantam*.................................23

Chart-Toppers

music

FACTS, FIGURES & FACES

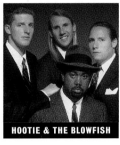

HOOTIE & THE BLOWFISH

THE BIGGEST SURPRISE on 1995's pop charts was an unassuming South Carolina outfit whose debut, at 11 million served, has become one of the best-selling albums of all time. Never mind that *Cracked Rear View* came out in 1994: February '95 saw *View* crack the top 10 for the first time, and it's '95 that will go down as the Year of the Blowfish. Not everyone who scored this year was a Johnny-come-lately like Hootie; but like *View*, almost every album that rated in the annual tally was released in '94—from the graying ol' Eagles with their lucrative reunion junket to new-jack punks Green Day's debut, which at 92 weeks and counting holds one of the year's longevity records.

TOP 15 ALBUMS*

WEEKS ON CHART

1 **HOOTIE & THE BLOWFISH** *Cracked Rear View*, Atlantic 70
2 **GARTH BROOKS** *The Hits*, Capitol Nashville 48
3 **BOYZ II MEN** *II*, Motown 63
4 **EAGLES** *Hell Freezes Over*, Geffen...53
5 **TLC** *CrazySexyCool*, LaFace 52
6 **PEARL JAM** *Vitalogy*, Epic 48
7 **GREEN DAY** *Dookie*, Reprise 92
8 **LIVE** *Throwing Copper*, Radioactive 81
9 **KENNY G** *Miracles: The Holiday Album*, Arista 14
10 **THE LION KING** *Soundtrack*, Walt Disney 76
11 **OFFSPRING** *Smash*, Epitaph 78
12 **THE CRANBERRIES** *No Need to Argue*, Island 58
13 **NIRVANA** *MTV Unplugged in New York*, DGC..54
14 **ALANIS MORISSETTE** *Jagged Little Pill*, Maverick/Reprise 22
15 **SHERYL CROW** *Tuesday Night Music Club*, A&M 89

TOP 12 SINGLES†

1 **"GANGSTA'S PARADISE"** *Coolio Featuring L.V.*, MCA Soundtracks 15
2 **"WATERFALLS"** *TLC*, LaFace 25
3 **"CREEP"** *TLC*, LaFace 32
4 **"KISS FROM A ROSE"** *Seal*, ZTT/Sire 23
5 **"ON BENDED KNEE"** *Boyz II Men*, Motown 27
6 **"ANOTHER NIGHT"** *Real McCoy*, Arista...45
7 **"FANTASY"** *Mariah Carey*, Columbia 9
8 **"TAKE A BOW"** *Madonna*, Maverick/Sire 30
9 **"DON'T TAKE IT PERSONAL (JUST ONE OF DEM DAYS)"**
  Monica, Rowdy..29
10 **"THIS IS HOW WE DO IT"** *Montell Jordan*, PMP/RAL 29
11 **"I KNOW"** *Dionne Farris*, Columbia 38
12 **"WATER RUNS DRY"** *Boyz II Men*, Motown...28

**TOP-GROSSING
TOURS OF 1995**
The Rolling Stones
The Eagles
R.E.M.
Elton John
Grateful Dead

**BEST-SELLING
ALBUM OF ALL TIME**
Michael Jackson's
Thriller (24 million)

**BEST-SELLING
SINGLE OF ALL TIME**
Bing Crosby's
"White Christmas"

**1995'S MOST
STAR-SPANGLED
PERFORMANCES**
At the Super Bowl:
KATHIE LEE GIFFORD
At the World Series:
DARIUS RUCKER OF
HOOTIE & THE BLOWFISH
CHRISSIE HYNDE
TRISHA YEARWOOD
THE REMBRANDTS
JOE WALSH
JON SECADA

media

Chart-Toppers

MYST WAS NOT TO BE MISSED

THE NEW AGEY *Myst* dominated CD-ROM sales charts throughout most of the year with its dreamy landscapes and ambient music, spawning clones and talk of a sequel and a possible film version. Many gamers, however, seemed more interested in violence, quenching their thirst for blood with a deluge of titles ranging from gory (*Mortal Kombat 3*) to gorier (*Doom II*). On other battlefronts, government pundits pondered whether they should (or could) regulate sexually explicit materials transmitted over the Internet. And Bill Gates' Microsoft empire launched its new PC operating system, Windows 95, with a media blitz that included the Rolling Stones' tune "Start Me Up." While recent sales figures have slackened notably, the kickoff did help propel the software to the top of the year's CD-ROM sales chart.

TOP 25 CD-ROM SALES

		NO. OF UNITS SOLD*
1	**MICROSOFT WINDOWS 95** *Microsoft*	1,200,000
2	**MYST** *Brøderbund*	810,000
3	**DARK FORCES** *LucasArts*	550,000
4	**DOOM II** *GT Interactive*	430,000
5	**THE PRINT SHOP DELUXE CD ENSEMBLE** *Brøderbund*	400,000
6	**MICROSOFT PLUS!** *Microsoft*	350,000
7	**MICROSOFT ENCARTA** *Microsoft*	300,000
8	**QUICKEN DELUXE** *Intuit*	280,000
9	**DISNEY'S ANIMATED STORYBOOK: THE LION KING** *Disney*	275,000
10	**NASCAR RACING** *Virgin*	260,000
11	**ULTIMATE DOOM: THY FLESH CONSUMED** *GT Interactive*	250,000
12	**7TH GUEST** *Virgin*	230,000
13	**COREL GALLERY** *Corel*	215,000
14	**MICROSOFT FLIGHT SIMULATOR 5.1** *Microsoft*	210,000
15	**MECHWARRIOR 2** *Activision*	200,000
16	**ALADDIN ACTIVITY CENTER** *Disney*	200,000
17	**DESCENT** *Interplay*	195,000
18	**STAR WARS REBEL ASSAULT** *LucasArts*	190,000
19	**SIM CITY 2000 COLLECTION** *Maxis*	185,000
20	**D!ZONE COLLECTOR'S EDITION** *WizardWorks*	185,000
21	**QUICKEN** *Intuit*	170,000
22	**FULL THROTTLE** *LucasArts*	170,000
23	**STAR TREK: TNG A FINAL UNITY** *Spectrum HoloByte*	168,000
24	**ONE STOP CD-SHOP VOL. 1** *SoftKey*	157,000
25	**STREET ATLAS USA** *DeLorme*	155,000

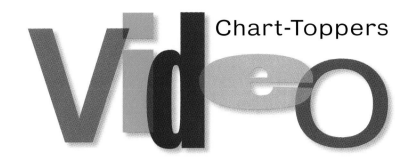

Chart-Toppers

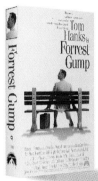

STUPID IS AS STUPID does, and it's obvious that the makers of *Forrest Gump*, winner of six Academy Awards, weren't fools in any market. Priced affordably enough for *Gump* groupies to buy—which enough of them did to push it to the No. 2 spot on the sales chart—the cross-generational feel-good movie of the decade topped the rentals chart as well. And when renters finally tired of the simpleton from the South, played by runaway sensation Tom Hanks, they turned to breathe new life into movies that had died at the box office. The critically acclaimed prison tale *The Shawshank Redemption*, which paired Tim Robbins and Morgan Freeman, sprang itself to the No. 3 spot, while the more critically challenged comedies *Little Giants* and *Renaissance Man* also fared well and reached the No. 13 and No. 15 slots, respectively, in rentals.

TOP 15 TAPE RENTALS

		NO. OF RENTALS PER STORE
1	**FORREST GUMP** Tom Hanks, *Paramount*	525
2	**TRUE LIES** Arnold Schwarzenegger, *FoxVideo*	478
3	**THE SHAWSHANK REDEMPTION** Tim Robbins, *Columbia TriStar*	421
4	**THE MASK** Jim Carrey, *New Line*	409
5	**LEGENDS OF THE FALL** Brad Pitt, *Columbia TriStar*	374
6	**THE SPECIALIST** Sylvester Stallone, *Warner*	353
7	**THE RIVER WILD** Meryl Streep, *MCA/Universal*	339
8	**THE LITTLE RASCALS** Bug Hall, *MCA/Universal*	328
9	**OUTBREAK** Dustin Hoffman, *Warner*	320
10	**DISCLOSURE** Demi Moore, *Warner*	313
11	**CLEAR AND PRESENT DANGER** Harrison Ford, *Paramount*	306
12	**TIMECOP** Jean-Claude Van Damme, *MCA/Universal*	298
13	**LITTLE GIANTS** Rick Moranis, *Warner*	292
14	**INTERVIEW WITH THE VAMPIRE** Tom Cruise, *Warner*	274
15	**RENAISSANCE MAN** Danny DeVito, *Touchstone*	274

TOP 10 TAPE SALES

		NO. OF TAPES SOLD PER STORE
1	**THE LION KING** Animated, *Walt Disney*, $26.99	1,172
2	**FORREST GUMP** Tom Hanks, *Paramount*, $22.95	760
3	**CINDERELLA** Animated, *Walt Disney*, $26.99	654
4	**BATMAN FOREVER** Val Kilmer, *Warner*, $19.96	490
5	**THE MASK** Jim Carrey, *New Line*, $19.98	470
6	**THE SANTA CLAUSE** Tim Allen, *Walt Disney*, $19.99	460
7	**CASPER** Christina Ricci, *MCA/Universal*, $22.98	250
8	**ANGELS IN THE OUTFIELD** Danny Glover, *Walt Disney*, $19.99	220
9	**THE CROW** Brandon Lee, *Miramax*, $19.99	210
10	**APOLLO 13** Tom Hanks, *MCA/Universal*, $22.98	207

JERRY GARCIA

(b. 1942) EVEN WHEN HE was young, even during those freewheelin' Haight-Ashbury days when his hair was black and his heart was healthy, Jerry Garcia had the voice of an old man. High, creaky, and supremely gentle, his tenor didn't seem to suit the leader of a pack of slovenly San Francisco outlaws like the Grateful Dead. Garcia's voice sounded more like it belonged to some trippy Appalachian codger—an echo of his early days jamming with bluegrass bands like the Sleepy Hollow Hog Stompers.

Eventually, it made sense. Garcia wasn't just the singer and nine-fingered guitarist in the Dead; he was the counterculture's bearded, beaming grandpappy—its old man. When his 53-year-old heart gave out on Aug. 9 at a California rehab center called Serenity Knolls, a nation unraveled—a rambling republic of Deadheads who had looked upon Garcia as the psychedelic Santa Claus to their eternal Christmas. He had Saint Nick's girth—years of junk food, smoking, and drugs didn't keep his ticker in tip-top shape—as well as his generosity of spirit. "It was easy for him to inspire people to go out and do things," says his widow, Deborah Koons Garcia. *The wrong things*, countered conservatives. But Garcia never wanted to be a counterculture chieftain. He preferred simply to play the songs, delivered in a voice that quavered with the joy and ache of the ages. *—Jeff Gordinier*

GINGER ROGERS

(b. 1911) IN MORE THAN 70 films from 1930 to 1965, Ginger Rogers handled every genre thrown at her with pluck and underrated skill. She fought for serious roles and won a Best Actress Oscar for 1940's *Kitty Foyle*. By 1941, she was the highest-paid woman in America.

And yet you can watch one of her films and never get a sense of her. *Swing Time* and *Monkey Business* are supreme works, but are they Ginger Rogers movies the way *Camille* is a Greta Garbo film? Unlike Garbo, Rogers never had a cult beyond that which clustered around Fred Astaire. Her sass, her romantic yearning, even her dancing was deceptively ordinary; she could give hope to a hatcheck girl, but deeper mystery there was none.

Which is why she succeeded when she did. The face of American movies in the '30s is the face of Rogers, singing "We're in the Money" in pig latin in *Gold Diggers of 1933*, spitting fire at Katharine Hepburn in *Stage Door*, gliding across liquid parquet with Astaire in film after ethereal film. She was necessary not only to bring warmth to Fred's chilly perfectionism, but as Hollywood's paramount working girl—proof that behind all that soft soap is elbow grease, cheerfully applied. —*Ty Burr*

DEAN MARTIN

(b. 1917) IN AN INDUSTRY of self-publicists, Dean Martin was unknowable. Jeanne, his wife for 23 years (they divorced in 1972), once sighed, "There's either nothing under there or too much." Nick Tosches' 1992 biography, *Dino*, calls him a *menefreghista*, Italian for "one who simply does not give a f---."

Born Dino Paul Crocetti, Martin grew up in Steubenville, Ohio, worshiping at the altar of Bing Crosby. He made a go at a singing career until, in 1946, he met comedian Jerry Lewis. Sixteen Martin-and-Lewis films later, Martin, tired of his partner's egotism, made the break in 1956. He joined up with Sinatra's Rat Pack and began carving out an image as a lovable lush. In 1964 "Everybody Loves Somebody" knocked the Beatles out of the No. 1 spot, and Martin starred in Billy Wilder's *Kiss Me, Stupid*—a comedy whose playboy nihilism looks to be the closest Martin ever came to a personal statement.

The Dean Martin Show, a variety hour, debuted on NBC the next year and ran for nine seasons. But in the '70s and '80s, Martin sloped off into halfhearted singing engagements and celebrity roasts that played like Last Suppers for the borscht belt. After son Dino Jr., 35, died in an '87 plane crash, he seemed to vanish into himself. Yet the tragic vision doesn't square, says Tosches: "He had no interest in his own life. He was completely content in his solitude." —*TB*

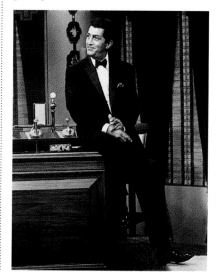

SELENA

(b. 1971) ON MARCH 31, at a motel near her home in Corpus Christi, Tex., Selena Quintanilla-Pérez confronted Yolanda Saldívar, the founder of her fan club. The singer's family had accused Saldívar of embezzlement; Saldívar felt betrayed by Selena's father. Suddenly, Saldívar fired a .38-caliber pistol into Selena's back, killing her. In the ironic way of American culture, Selena finally became a national figure—her posthumous album, *Dreaming of You*, hit No. 1 on the pop charts, a biopic and books are in the works—and it was a legacy of which she would have been proud. —*David Browne*

LANA TURNER

(b. 1920) EIGHT marriages, three stillbirths, two abortions, one murder, a suicide attempt, a religious awakening, and uncounted romances. That was Lana Turner's life, but it could have been one of her 54 films. She specialized in tramps moved by inarticulate lust (*The Postman Always Rings Twice*) or tormented, couture-swaddled heroines (*The Bad and the Beautiful*). Her last major role was on CBS' *Falcon Crest*, a fitting retirement home for a grande dame of unconscious carnality. —*TB*

HOWARD COSELL

(b. 1918) "ARROGANT, POMPOUS, obnoxious, vain, cruel, persecuting, distasteful, verbose, a show-off—I've been called all of these," Howard Cosell once wrote. "Of course, I am." With his patented nasal-drippy tone and stilted staccato, the ABC radio/TV commentator known for "telling it like it is" revolutionized sports broadcasting while coanchoring *Monday Night Football*, hosting *SportsBeat*, calling boxing bouts, and never pulling his punches. —*Dan Snierson*

EAZY–E

(b. 1964) HE RAN WITH gangs. Dealt drugs. Owned Uzis. But it was a different peril that felled rapper Eric Wright, a.k.a. Eazy-E, at age 31: AIDS. In 1989, N.W.A (Niggaz With Attitude)—the crew he formed with Dr. Dre and Ice Cube—released the triple-platinum *Straight Outta Compton*, and its anthem "F--- tha Police" branded Eazy an outlaw hero. He was also a godfather of the gangsta genre. As Eazy noted, "Everyone in America started paying attention to the boyz in the 'hood." —*DS*

ELIZABETH MONTGOMERY

(b. 1933) SHE LEFT US bewitched, bothered, bewildered, and bereaved when Elizabeth Montgomery succumbed to cancer on May 18, but death couldn't break the spell cast by Samantha Stephens, *Bewitched*'s suburban sorceress with the wiggling nose. She also won Emmy nominations playing a rape victim, a pioneer woman, even Lizzie Borden, but her most fitting epitaph is Nick at Nite's: There was no nicer witch than you. —*Chris Willman*

WOLFMAN JACK

(b. 1938) UNSUITABLY BORN as Robert Smith, he dubbed himself Wolfman Jack in the wee hours of the early '60s, howled and hooted from a high-power radio station in Mexico, and shook America with the lascivious rumble of rock & roll. The ultimate late-night deejay turned himself into a barking madman with lupine hair, and, like the moon, his fame waxed and waned. He died of a heart attack at 57. *—JG*

SHANNON HOON

(b. 1967) SHORTLY AFTER Kurt Cobain's 1994 suicide, Blind Melon frontman Shannon Hoon appeared on *Late Show With David Letterman* with a question mark drawn on his forehead. On Oct. 21, a drug overdose ended the riddle far sooner than even the ironist Hoon could have anticipated. Friends said the 28-year-old had been happily doting on his 4-month-old daughter, Nico Blue—"I need to start caring for myself if I'm going to be the proper father," he confided after one rehab stint. No question. *—CW*

EVA GABOR

(b. 1921) SHE WAS BELOVED as *Green Acres'* agriculturally challenged socialite, Lisa Douglas—but that TV fame was eclipsed by her real-life role as the youngest of the glitzy, Budapest-born Gabor sisters. Eva was the first to come to America, where she, Zsa Zsa, and Magda found fame singing in Vegas and leading tumultuous love lives. "Marriage is too interesting an experi-ment to be tried only once or twice," cooed the five-times-wed Eva, who appeared in 17 films (*Gigi*) and founded a company that is the world's largest wig manufacturer. *—DS*

LOUIS MALLE

(b. 1932) TO CINEMAPHILES, Louis Malle, who died of lymphoma at 63, was a master chronicler of the human condition. The French director (and husband of Candice Bergen) could go from ocean depths (codirecting Jacques Cousteau's 1956 documentary *The Silent World*) to city streets (*Pretty Baby, Atlantic City*), and empathize with a peasant (*Lacombe, Lucien*) or an intellectual (*My Dinner With André*). In 1994's *Vanya on 42nd Street*, he was still compassionately at ease. *—Glenn Kenny*

DAVID BEGELMAN

(b. 1922) HE REPRESENTED the two extremes of a movie exec's existence: spending and despair. As president of Columbia Pictures, David Begelman oversaw such films as *Close Encounters of the Third Kind, Taxi Driver*, and *Shampoo*. Then he embezzled $40,000 he had no need for from his own studio. The 1977 scandal, chronicled in David McClintick's *Indecent Exposure*, brought him down. He then ran two small production companies; one filed for bankruptcy—despair closed in. He booked a room at L.A.'s Century Plaza Hotel and shot himself. He was 73. *—TB*

FRIZ FRELENG

(b. 1906) WHEN THE END came, there wasn't one falling anvil or exploding TNT stick to mark it. Cartoon director Isadore "Friz" Freleng juggled such 'toon slapstick elements at Warner Bros. for some 30 years, putting his stamp on the likes of Tweety Bird and Bugs Bunny and making the Pink Panther a star in film credit sequences and on TV. His fans will never have to say, "That's all, folks." *—Steve Daly*

DONALD PLEASENCE
b. 1919
Actor (*The Great Escape, You Only Live Twice*)

CHARLIE RICH
b. 1932
Country singer ("The Most Beautiful Girl")

ROXIE ROKER
b. 1929
Actress (Helen Willis on *The Jeffersons*)

BOB ROSS
b. 1942
Host of PBS' *The Joy of Painting*

TERRY SOUTHERN
b. 1924
Screenwriter (*Dr. Strangelove, Easy Rider*)

BOB STINSON
b. 1959
Original guitarist of the Replacements

WOODY STRODE
b. 1914
Actor (*Spartacus, The Man Who Shot Liberty Valance*)

KRISSY TAYLOR
b. 1978
Model

RANDY WALKER
b. 1968
Rap musician known as Stretch, of Live Squad

MARY WICKES
b. 1916
Actress (*White Christmas, Sister Act*)

FRONT COVER Banderas, Kidman: Stephanie Pfriender; Eisner: Stone/Sygma; *Friends*: Thurnher/Outline; Garcia: Jeff Kravitz; Hanks: Greenfield/Sygma; leg: Frank Micelotta; *Pocahontas*: Walt Disney Co.; Rucker: Malluk/Retna; Stipe: Anton Corbijn; Duchovny/Anderson: Edward Gajdel; Selena: John Dyer; Simpson: Butow/Pool/Sipa **2-3:** Paul Corio **7:** Steven Freeman **10-11:** (l-r) Adams/Sygma; Chris Little **34-35:** (clockwise from top right) Gasper Tringale (2); Paul Corio; n/c; Murray/Sygma; Robert/Sygma; Viavant/Sipa; Glynis Sweeny; Canapress

THE YEAR IN ENTERTAINMENT

36-37: TIMELINE (clockwise from top right) DMI; Ferguson/Galella; Globe; Glynis Sweeny; Corminas/Sygma **POL ATTACKS** (top row, l-r) Haston; Johnson/Gamma-Liaison; Markowitz/Sygma; Caruso; Berman/Sipa; Kraft/Sygma; Trippett/Sipa; Johnson/Gamma-Liaison (bottom row, l-r): Ferguson/Globe; Sobol/Sipa; Weissman/Globe; Kraft/Sygma; Adams/Sygma; Steven Freeman; n/c; Baldwin **38-39:** (counterclockwise from top left) Glynis Sweeny; n/c (4); Carol Rosegg; Paul Corio; Watson; Daniel Hulshizer **40-41:** (clockwise from top right) Strong/Sipa; Paschal/Celebrity Photo; Coupon/Onyx; Paul Corio; Maass/Sipa; Winter/Celebrity Photo; Jenkinson/Onyx; Fineman/Sygma; Wheeler/Retna **42-43:** (clockwise from top right) Hanover; ABC; Close; *Calvin and Hobbes* © 1995 Watterson. Reprinted with permission of Universal Press Syndicate. All rights reserved; CBS; n/c; Eisen; Michal Daniel; Sygma **44-45:** Aniston: Eccles; Beckford: Pace/Retna; Campbell: Maria Chandoha Valentino; Clooney, Thurman: Marissa Roth; Gershon, Love/

DeCadenet: Berliner/Gamma-Liaison; Karan dress, tube, Sui shorts: Major/LFI; Klein ads: Stone/Sygma; Lee: Larry Laszlo; Leopard head, Schiffer projection: Berman/Sipa; Madonna in Gucci: Davila/Retna; Madonna's nails: Somoza/Outline; mannequins, wig heads: Freeman/Retna; O'Donnell: Nelson; pants: Santiago; Pitt: Fisher/LFI; Stewart: Granitz/Retna; tattoo: Frank Micelotta; Tyler: Sipa; Winfrey: Paschal/Celebrity Photo **48-49:** Autograph request, Gibson/La Salle, Louis-Dreyfus, Rice, Spelling: Marissa Roth; Banderas/Griffith: Shen/Celebrity Photo; Brown, Dylan/Springsteen, Freeman, Jackson, Tarantino, Tilly: Mazur/LFI; Cage/Arquette, Grant/Newell, Kidman, Thompson, dancers, Stone: Larry Laszlo; Carrey/Holly: Winter/Celebrity Photo; Delpy, snow sculpture: Henny Garfunkel; Depp/Moss: Talesnick/Retna; DeVito/Perlman: Ortega/Celebrity Photo; Etheridge, Fonda/Field, Travolta: Berliner/Gamma-Liaison; Locklear/Zuniga: Jeff Kravitz

ENTERTAINERS OF THE YEAR

53: Thurnher/Outline **55:** Dan Winters **56-57:** (l-r) Busacca/Retna; Visages/San **58-59:** (l-r) Hanauer/Onyx; Schiffman/Onyx **60-61:** (l-r) Stephanie Pfriender; Strick/Onyx **62-63:** (l-r) Sirota/Outline; Theo Westenberger **64-65:** O'Neill/Outline; George Lange **66-67:** (clockwise from left) Sandra Johnson; Claiborne/Onyx; Cooper/*Select*; Jay Blakesberg **68-69:** (clockwise from top left) Emma Bass (2); George Lange; Pam Francis; Townley; Blake Little; Larry Laszlo

THE BEST OF EW

72-73: Stephanie Pfriender (3) **74-75:** (l-r) Foreman; Weinstein **76-77:** Scott Menchin **78-79:** (clockwise from

top right) Sebastian; Regan, D'Amico; Ferguson/Globe; n/c; Smale/Outline; St. Louis/Retna; Ortega/Celebrity Photo; Furmanovsky/Globe **80-81:** (l-r) Sygma; Lange/Outline **82-83:** Davis/Shooting Star; Wyatt Gallery **84-85:** (l-r) Staniforth; Hanauer/Onyx **86-87:** (l-r) Lynda Barry; Hanoch Piven; Owen Smith; Christian Clayton **88-89:** (l-r) Henry Grossman; Otte/Outline **91:** Holz/Onyx **92-93:** Stephen Kroninger **95:** Lange/Outline **96-97:** (l-r) Glass; Davis/Shooting Star **99:** Anton Corbijn **100-101:** (l-r) Anton Corbijn; Blakesberg/Retna **102-103:** (l-r) Tucker/Outline; Parry/CPI **104-107:** Typography: Dynamic Duo **105:** photos (clockwise from top left) Cadette; Matthew; Sorel; Watson; Wetcher; Fitzgerald; Adler; Fellman **107:** photos: (clockwise from top left) Batzdorff; n/c; Close; Hyun; Staniforth; Baer **108-109:** (l-r) Kaluzny/Gamma-Liaison; Rendon/LGI **113:** Baldwin **114-115:** (l-r) Walt Disney Co.; Regan; Marks; Foreman **116-117:** (clockwise from top left) Michael Dougan; Chen; Eric Palma; Collins; Sygma; Megret/Sipa; Chen; Slenzak/H.A. Roberts **119:** Andrew Eccles **120-121:** (l-r) Chris; H.B.; Watson; Fitzgerald; Mifsud; Tom; Adler

THE YEAR IN REVIEWS

122-123: (clockwise from top left) Maloney; Batzdorff; Wayno; Gifford/Gamma-Liaison; Camerique/H.A. Roberts; Null; Feld; Chip Waas **125:** Ettlinger/Outline **126-127:** (clockwise from top right) Maiman/Sygma; McHugh/Photo Researchers; J.D. King; P. Aresu **129:** Clinch/Outline **130-131:** (clockwise from top left) Clinch/Outline; Mortensen/Outline; Owen/Visages; Low/Shooting Star; Ockenfels 3/Outline; Greenberg/Onyx **132-133:** (clockwise from top left) Otte/Outline; Drew Friedman; Wagner/Retna; Barrett/Globe; Aroch/Retna; Michael Dougan **135:** Gary Panter **136-137:** (clockwise from top right) Brylan/Gamma-Liaison; Wayno; Warner/Sygma; n/c **139:** Hurrell/MPTVPA **140-141:** (clockwise from top left) Photofest/Jagarts; n/c;

Photofest; Brandenstein; n/c; Vinet **142-43:** (clockwise from top left) Steven Freeman; Loss; Chip Waas; S.B. Whitehead; Everett Collection; Photofest

ALMANAC

144-145: (l-r) Batzdorff; Farmer; Nelson; Brandenstein; Cooper **146-147:** (l-r) n/c; Morton; Appleby; Moseley; Zahedi **148-149:** (l-r) Eisen; n/c; McBroom; Baldwin; Rudolphe **150-151:** (l-r) Feingold; Vaughan; Photofest; Borrel; Blanshard **152-153:** (l-r) Foreman; Bailey; Weinstein; n/c; Torres **154-155:** (l-r) Bramley; Sorel; Walt Disney Co.; Close; Georges **156-157:** (l-r) Collins; n/c; Wallace; Sorel; n/c **158-159:** (l-r) Tenner; n/c; Scott; Helcermanas-Benge; n/c **160:** (l-r) Birmelin; Marshak; Emerson **162:** (counterclockwise from top) Michael Bartalos; Nelson; Kenneth Willardt; Rudolph; Batzdorff **163: OSCARS** (clockwise from top left) Caruso; King/Gamma-Liaison; Granitz/Retna (2); Barr/Gamma-Liaison; Granitz/Retna **STRIP** (top to bottom) H.A. Roberts; Photofest; Caruso **164:** (top to bottom) Michael Bartalos; Jeffery Newbury; Hart/S.I. Picture Collection; CBS; Everett Collection **165: EMMYS** (clockwise from top left) Baer; Robert/Sygma; Granitz/Retna; Smeal/Galella; King/Gamma-Liaison; Null; **STRIP** (top to bottom) Criton/Sygma; Ortega/Celebrity Photo **166-167:** (counterclockwise from top left) Michael Bartalos; Renault/Globe; Weiner/Retna; Iacono/S.I.; Hogan/All Action/Retna; Michael Bartalos; Darryl Estrine; Steven Freeman; **168:** (top to bottom) Michael Bartalos; n/c; Eccles; Frank Micelotta; **169:** (top to bottom) Michael Bartalos; Paramount; (l-r) Kobal Collection; n/c; (bottom) n/c **170-171:** (l-r) Wolman/Retna; Kobal Collection; Gray/MPTVPA **172-173:** (l-r) Archive Photos/American Stock; Sygma/Sunset Blvd.; Eichner/Retna **INSIDE BACK COVER** David Cowles **BACK COVER** Bullock: Stephanie Pfriender; Clooney: Strick/Onyx; Coolio: George Lange; Garcia: Otte/Outline; Hanks: David Cowles